Teaching with Technology Package

Teaching with Technology Package

Edited by

Dr.A.MARIYAMMAL

Assistant professor

Sakthi institute of Teacher Education
and research Dindigul, Tamil Nadu

RANDOM PUBLICATIONS

NEW DELHI (INDIA)

Teaching with Technology Package

ISBN 978-93-5111-749-0

Published in 2015 in India by

RANDOM PUBLICATIONS

4376-A/4B, Gali Murari Lal, Ansari Road
New Delhi-110 002
Phone : +9111-43580356, 011-43142548, 011-23289044
e-mail : sales@randompublications.com
info@randompublications.com
randomexports@gmail.com

Reprinted 2023

Type Setting by : Shah Computer Graphics, Delhi-110094
Printed at: Replika Press Pvt. Ltd.

Contents

3

4

5

19

20

21

22

23

24

25

28 **269**

29

30

1

Implications of Multimedia in Teaching Economics with Special Reference to Higher Secondary Students

Introduction

The computer has revolutionized the whole society overwhelmingly inclusive of all human activities especially those of education. The computer is changing the total educational system namely, content, methodology, learner participation learning process, teacher roles, curricular implication etc. "The computers are very powerful instructional media that enhance quality of instruction". By programming the subject of study in computers, teaching and learning become full of contexts and situations. The student can take his own time to learn the contents because they are individualized instructional situation. The performance of the student in instruction as well as in test will automatically record in the computer. The present study aims to find out the implications of multimedia in teaching economics with special reference to higher secondary education in Chennai. A samples of 155 samples selected randomly were studied. A questionnaire method of survey was used to find out the implications of multimedia in teaching economics. The data were collected by using questionnaire as an instrument. Primary data were collected by conducting direct structured interview using questionnaire. All the respondents were asked the same questions in the same fashion and they were informed the purpose of study. t-test, ANOVA and Correlation analysis were applied to test the hypotheses. The findings and observations are the result and outcome of the interpretations made during the study of analysis.

In 1965, Lorence settler and Danieal Davis developed most complicated teaching process in which computer was used for presenting instruction in place of teacher. They divided the teaching process of the computer in two parts.

1. Pre-tutorial phase

2. Tutorial phase.

In the first phase, computer assisted instruction is given to the pupils to achieve the specific objectives on the basis of his entry behaviour. In the second phase instructing material is presented accordingly. The pupil is evaluated. After presenting the instruction, computer also controls it. It also provides reinforcement to the pupils.

In the modern age, the use of computers in the field of education, made in the following areas.

3. All the researches do all analytical tasks with the help of computers in the research work.

4. Computers are also used in educational guidance and counseling.

5. Remedial teaching of the pupils is also done by the computers.

6. Computers help in sought for preparing the results of the examinations.

Learning with aid of computer through computer, aided instruction, computer simulation etc. It is a self learning strategy in teaching learning process. Students learnt their subjects at their own pace.

Internet is world wide computer network that contains a large collection of information which could be made available to you on your computer. The person having internet connection can retrieve any information on individual interest. Purves, A.C.[6] (1998) says that, the internet is the abbreviation of inter network system. The internet is the name for a vast, world wide system consisting of people, information and computers. It is also described as a network of networks because these are more than one lakh readily accessible through the Internet. Internet is the largest and most complete learning tool for a group of people with varied educational background and interests. Teachers, students, businessmen and other educators can share ideas instantly across vast distances. For scientific and research community, internet is an essential and indispensable tool. Through Internet scientist can gain and enjoy instant access to the world's most advanced research facilities and discuss their research problems with others, working in the same field.

Review of Literature

Coyne, Margaret Ann, Ed.D., (2006), in their paper "Emerging literacy Assisted parents to scaffold the emerging literacy skill of their pre-school-aged children through the used of electronic storybooks", reported that, that importance of parents reading to their young child is well supported by research (Health, 1986). However, Edwards (1989) found that parents whose own literacy skills are emerging have difficulty supporting the emerging literacy skills of their young children through storybook reading.

The development of a new paradigm, Universal Design for Learning (UDL) (Meyer & Rose, 1998 and 2002) provides a framework for the use of computer technology to support learning. Drawing on Vygotsky's (1978; 1986) socio constructive theory of learning and the latest advances in the neurosciences, UDL investigates how technology can support diverse learners. This study examined whether UDL –based technology might help parents who are themselves emerging readers support their children's literacy development.

When parents use of targeted storybook reading behaviours increased if their children's pre-intervention scores on language measures were below age-level, the children's scores on post-intervention measures improved to age-level or above. In addition, the children's scores on measures of story retelling and print knowledge improved.

BEABVIS C., Deakin University, Literacy and the new technologies in the middle years. (2006) This paper explores young people's textual engagements with electronic and other forms of popular culture, and the changing nature of literacy in the context of COM modification, mass marketing and the new technologies. Building on school based studies exploring computer games in the classroom and the Poke on phenomenon, it examines ways in which popular texts are read, and narrative and generic elements incorporated into the curriculum and into students' spoken and written texts. Drawing on Green's model of cultural, critical and opal dimensions of (technological) literacy, it examines issues of literacy and culture, identity and critique for teachers and students in the middle years, and their implications for constructions of literacy and curriculum.

BERRY L. and CHAPMAN E, University of Sydney Effects of Background Information and Audiovisual Presentation Modes on Students' Attention Styles and Enjoyment in Listening to Unfamiliar Music.(2006) Research has indicated that students typically do not enjoy or engage with unfamiliar pieces of music. This is discouraging and puzzling to music educators who whish to introduce their students to a diverse range of musical genres. This study explored the effects of two factors on students' initial reactions to an unfamiliar Shakuhachi piece. Using a 2 by 2 crossed-factor design, 438 students in grades 9-11 were assigned at random to listen to the piece in either audio-only or audiovisual form, and with or without verbal background information.

Results indicated that while the provision of information significantly ($p<0.05$) increased students' enjoyment of the music and their interest in hearing more of the same kind of music, it had no effect on their listening attention styles (e.g., focusing on the melody or idiomatic details of the piece). Conversely, use of the audiovisual presentation mode significantly impacted on one aspect of students' attention styles (focus on idiomatic details) and perceived familiarity with the piece, but had only a marginally significant effect on their enjoyment or interest. Implications of these results for the introduction of unfamiliar music to high school students will be discussed.

BLACKMORE J., JOHNSON R., WARREN W., (2006) States that the potential of new learning technologies for transforming teaching and learning, and indeed the organization of schooling. Much has also been written about teacher responses to new learning technologies-how they resist, ignore, or innovate. A number of recent reports indicate a gap between policy, practice and the capacity of organizations to provide the conditions and resources sin schools to creatively use new learning technologies. Few of these discourses draw upon theories of educational change, in particular those which relate to the dissonance between attitudes and feelings about radical change, and how it impacts on teacher work identity with respect to learning technologies. Much of the literature has focused upon the technical aspects, the hardware and software, but not the 'warm ware', so critical to sound pedagogical practice. This paper draws from the Learning in New Environments Research Group action research project, a pilot study in a large metropolitan secondary college, which is exploring the social implications of new learning technologies for changing relations between students, between teachers and students, between teachers and between family and school. The paper draws from the first round of data collection from the teachers in an on going action research project in a region with a high level of socio-economics and cultural diversity.

It draws on concepts of Lieberman's notion of learning networks and Wenger's notion of communities of practice, as well as past research on the reception of gender equity reform in educational organizations, which focuses upon emotional aspects of professional work identity and organizational change.

Joseph Kacharayll (2006) – "Suitability of colleges for Web Bases Learning" reported that Web based learning environment is expensive to establish, government and private managements should take necessary steps to provide adequate infrastructure facilities in colleges for web based learning. A proper utilization of available human resources would help improve web based learning. In order to overcome technical limitation, training has to be given to both teachers and learners to create flexible and uninterrupted learning environment. The training of material designers should be especially focused upon. Most of the colleges have not properly utilized the available web resources in their teaching learning strategies. There is only nominal technical support and assistance from technical staff and from government and private managements at the institutional level for web based learning. The author collected sample for the survey of 152 college lecturers was obtained through random sampling.

Objectives

1. To find the effect on learning competency of the students by using Multi media for teaching economics
2. To find the active participation of the teachers in using multi media for teaching economics.
3. To find how the teaching of economics has been efficiently improved using the multi media.
4. To find the importance of computers and internet in teaching economics.

Methodology

The investigator, for the present study adopts the survey method of research. It is a procedure in which data is systematically collected from a population through some from of direct solicitation such as face to face interview, questionnaire or schedule. The survey is extensive and cross sectional dealing with the relatively large number of cases of a particular time and yielding statistics that are abstracted from particular cases. It is the method of investigation which attempts to describe and interpret what exists at present in the form of conditions, practices, process, trends, effects, attitudes, and beliefs. Using this method the investigator had gathered informations measure the Effect of Multi Media Aids in teaching economics for Higher Secondary Students in Chennai.

Sample

For the present study 155 Higher Secondary Students in Chennai.

Data Collection

Primary data, required for the present research work were collected by conducting direct interviews using questionnaire. All the respondents were given sufficient information about the study. These respondents were provided with the same questionnaires. They were also informed that they have to answer in the same fashion.

Statistical Tools for Analysis

The following tools statistical tools were used for the analysis of data. t-test, one way ANOVA and correlation analysis is used for the present study.

Analysis and Interpretation

Table 1

Six wise distribution of "t" value between the boys and girls of the higher secondary economics students using multimedia resources in their schools

Dimensions	Boys N = 55		Girls N = 100		Calculated value of "t"	Level of significance at 5% level
	Mean	S.D	Mean	S.D		
Working knowledge of computers	79.42	8.17	80.42	8.68	0.71	NS
Knowledge about internet	78.15	9.51	76.88	9.80	0.91	NS
Knowledge using A.V. Aids	79.76	7.48	76.26	10.79	2.37	S
Preparation of computer based study materials	76.40	7.97	74.77	11.04	1.06	NS
Assignment and project	81.75	6.31	78.35	10.18	2.56	S
Interaction with others through web	395.47	28.53	386.5	42.77	1.56	NS

(At 5% level of significance, the table value of "t" is 1.96)

It is refereed from the above table that there is a significant difference between boys and of Higher Secondary Students of economics group in their, Knowledge in using A.V. Aids and Assignment and project but there is no significant difference between Male and Female Higher Secondary students of economics group in their Working knowledge of computers, knowledge about internet, Preparation of computer based study materials, interaction with others through web.

Table - 2

Area wise distribution of "t" value between the urban and rural higher secondary economics students using multimedia resources in their schools

Dimensions	Boys N = 55		Girls N = 100		Calculated value of "t"	Level of significance at 5% level
	Mean	S.D	Mean	S.D		
Working knowledge of computers	79.42	8.17	80.42	8.68	0.71	NS
Knowledge about internet	78.15	9.51	76.88	9.80	0.91	NS
Knowledge using A.V. Aids	79.76	7.48	76.26	10.79	2.37	S
Preparation of computer based study materials	76.40	7.97	74.77	11.04	1.06	NS
Assignment and project	81.75	6.31	78.35	10.18	2.56	S
Interaction with others through web	395.47	28.53	386.5	42.77	1.56	NS

(At 5% level of significance, the table value of "t" is 1.96)

It is referred from the above table that there is no significant difference between urban and rural Higher Secondary Students of economics group in their, Knowledge in using A.V. Aids, Assignment and project, Working knowledge of computers, Knowledge about internet, Preparation of computer based study materials, Interaction with other through web.

Table - 3

"F" value among the boys and girls of Higher Secondary economics Group Students in Using Multimedia resources

Dimensions	df= 2,152			Calculated "f" Value	Remarks at 5% Level
	Source of variation	Sum of squares	M.S.V		
Working knowledge of computers	Between With in	118.75 11110.63	59.38 73.10	0.81	NS
Knowledge about internet	Between With in	7.94 14650.81	3.97 96.39	0.04	NS
Knowledge in using A.V. Aids	Between With in	23.44 15123.38	11.72 99.50	0.12	NS
Preparation of computer study materials	Between With in	155.56 15619.63	77.78 102.76	0.76	NS
Assignment and project	Between With in	164.39 12793.88	82.19 84.17	0.98	NS
Interaction with others through web	Between With in	216.00 23034.00	108.00 1515.39	0.07	NS

(For 2,152 df. At 5% level of significance, the table value of "f" is 3.06)

It is inferred from the above table that there is no significance difference among the boys and girls of Higher Secondary economics group students in using Multimedia resources in the Higher Secondary schools of Chennai.

Table - 4

"F" value among the Rural and Urban Higher Secondary Students of economics Group in Using Multimedia source in Chennai

Dimensions	df= 2,152			Calculated "f" Value	Remarks at 5% Level
	Source of variation	Sum of squares	M.S.V		
Working knowledge of computers	Between With in	39.50 11189.88	19.75 73.62	0.27	NS
Knowledge about internet	Between With in	394.39 14264.50	197.16 93.85	2.10	NS
Knowledge in using A.V. Aids	Between With in	130.31 15016.50	65.16 98.79	0.66	NS
Preparation of computer study materials	Between With in	444.44 153330.75	222.22 100.86	2.20	NS

Assignment and project	Between With in	364.69 12593.56	182.32 82.85	2.20	NS
Interaction with others through web	Between With in	5628.00 224924.00	2814.00 11479.76	1.90	NS

(for 2,152 df.at 5% level of significance, the table value of "f" is 3.06)

It is inferred from the above table that there is no significance difference among the Rural and Urban Higher Secondary students of economics group in using Multi media resource in the Higher Secondary Schools of Chennai.

Table - 5

"F" value among the Higher Secondary Students of economics Group in Using Multimedia source in Government and Private Higher Secondary Schools in Chennai

Dimensions	df= 2,152			Calculated "f" Value	Remarks at 5% Level
	Source of variation	Sum of squares	M.S.V		
Working knowledge of computers	Between With in	39.50 11189.88	19.75 73.62	0.27	NS
Knowledge about internet	Between With in	394.39 14264.50	197.16 93.85	2.10	NS
Knowledge in using A.V. Aids	Between With in	130.31 15016.50	65.16 98.79	0.66	NS
Preparation of computer study materials	Between With in	444.44 153330.75	222.22 100.86	2.20	NS
Assignment and project	Between With in	364.69 12593.56	182.32 82.85	2.20	NS
Interaction with others through web	Between With in	5628.00 224924.00	2814.00 11479.76	1.90	NS

(For 2,152 df. at 5% level of significance, the table value of " is 3.06)

It is inferred form the above table that there is no significance difference among the Government and Private Higher Secondary students of economics group in using Multi media resource in the Higher Secondary School of Chennai

Table - 6

The Correlation value between the Male and Female Higher Secondary Students in using multimedia resources in the Higher Secondary Schools of Chennai

Category	?X	?X^2	?Y	?Y^2	?XY	Calculated	Remarks
Boys	683	8595	545	5495	6775	.68	NS
Girls	1199	14757	970	9584	11740	.425	S
Total	1882	23354	1515	15079	18515	.325	S

(Table value of Correlation Co-efficient at 5% level of Significance is 0.161)

It is inferred from the above table that there is no significant relationship between the rural and high secondary economics group boys in using multimedia resources and there is a significant relationship between rural and urban high secondary economics group girls in using multimedia resources.

Findings

There a significant difference among the higher secondary commence group students of boys and girls, higher secondary commence students of government and private schools, higher secondary commence group students of rural and urban schools, in their interest to wards learning commence through multimedia resources in Chennai.

There is significant difference among the higher secondary economics group students in their levels of using multimedia shows moderate knowledge except interaction with others through web and no significant difference in low of using multimedia except interaction with other through web and no significant difference in higher level knowledge of using multimedia.

There is no significant difference among the higher secondary economics group boys in their level of using multimedia shows moderate knowledge and higher level of using multimedia and there is a significant difference low of using multimedia at the area of assignment and project, interaction with others though web.

There is no significant difference among the secondary economics group girls in all the levels of using multimedia resources. There is no significant difference among the higher secondary economics group students of government school in their level of using multimedia shows moderate knowledge and there is a significant difference in low level of interaction with others though web and shows significant difference in higher level of in knowledge about internet, knowledge in using A.V.aids and in the preparation of computer based study materials.

There is no significant difference among the higher secondary economics group students of private school in their level of using multimedia shows moderate knowledge and higher level knowledge of using multimedia and there is a significant difference in low level of using multimedia at the area of working of computer and in interaction with others though web.

There is no significant difference among the higher secondary economics group of rural school in their level of using multimedia shows moderate knowledge and there is a significant difference in low level of preparation of computer in high level of using multimedia at the is a significant difference in high level of using multimedia at the area of working knowledge of computer and in interaction with others with through web.

There is no significant difference between boys and girls or higher secondary students of economics group in their, knowledge in using A.V aids and assignments and project but there is no significant differences between male and female higher secondary of economics group in their working knowledge of computers, knowledge about internet, preparation of computer based study materials with others thought web.

There is no significant difference between urban and rural higher secondary of economics in their, knowledge in using A.V aids, assignment and project, working knowledge of computer knowledge about internet preparation of computer based study martial interaction with others web.

There is no significant difference among the Male and female higher secondary schools of economics group in using multimedia resource in the Higher secondary schools of Chennai.

There is no significance difference among the Rural and urban higher secondary students of economics group in using Multi media resource in the higher secondary of Chennai.

There is n no significant difference among the Government and private Higher Secondary students of economics group in using Multi media resource in the higher schools of Chennai.

There is no significant relationship between the Rural and urban high secondary group boys in using multimedia resources and there is a significant relationship between Rural and Urban high secondary economics group girls in using multimedia resources.

1. The research overwhelmingly demonstrates that usages of multimedia will definitely improve the quality of teaching economics in higher secondary classes.
2. The research found that the students are actively involved in learning part if the multimedia is introduced in classroom teaching.
3. The research shows the students are highly motivate towards the subject by using multimedia teaching aids and they are attracted more and improve their understanding and memory power in various economics topics like advertising, banking, etc. While using multimedia resources.
4. It is concluded that there is a positive effect of using multimedia aids in the economics achievement of the students in economics in Chennai.

Conclusion

The present study aims to find out the implications of multimedia in teaching economics with special reference to higher secondary. The researcher framed objectives and hypotheses on the basis of the above context. The research was carried out in 155 samples based randomly. A questionnaire constructed by R was used to collect the relevant data. After collecting the data they were analyzed using statistical tools such as t-test, ANOVA and Correlation analysis. The result concluded that students have average implications of multimedia in teaching at Higher Secondary level.

Reference

1. Beavis C. (2006), popular culture, textual practice and identify and identify: literacy and the new technologies, in the midde years
2. Berry l. And Chapman e, (2006); Effect of Background Information and Audiovisual Presentation Modes on Students' Attention style and enjoyment listening to Unfamiliar Music.
3. Best, (1982); J., Johnson R., Warren W. (2006), A hand book of Education Technology.
4. Blackmork j., Johnson R., Warren W. (2006), A handbook of Education Technology.
5. Bruce B.C (2004); Diversity and critical social engagement: How changing technologies enable new modes of literacy in changing circumstances. IN D.E. Alvermann (E.d), Adolescents and illiteracies in a digital world (pp. 1-18). New York: Peter Lang publication.
6. Chisamore, chris (2006), Multimedia and Education today.
7. Coyne, Margaret Ann (2006), Emerging Literacy: Assisting Parents to scaffold the emerging literacy skills of their pre school aged children through the use of electronic story books.
8. Joseph Kacharayll (2006); Educational Technology Year Book, 1998.
9. Lanksherar, C and Knoble, M (2003); New literacies: changing Knowledge And classroom learning. Philadelphia: Open university press.
10. Lewis, C and Finders, M. (2004); implied adolescents and implied teachers; A generation gap for new times. D.E Alvermann (Ed.), Adolescents and literacies in adugital world (pp.101-113).New York: peter Lang publishing.

2

The Blended Teacher: Teachers' Role in Blended Learning

Technology is a fact of present day's human life. Computers, televisions, videos, telephones, radio, and telecommunication networks exert an incalculable influence on how we live, work and play – an influence likely to expand as hardware and software more powerful, more affordable and pervasive. New technologies are already essential tools for human endeavours and for students, the ability to use technology has come to be recognised as indispensible skill. However students and educators are grappling with a host of challenges and presented with a kaleidoscope of remarkable new learning opportunities. From unprecedented budget pressures and over-burdened teachers to the need for more effective, more personalized learning to accommodate each student's individual learning style, schools are facing complex issues. The opportunities are enormous as well. Many new concepts like blended learning, flipped classrooms etc. have crept into the field of teaching and learning. Whether it is tapping the vast stores of digital information now available or using new technology tools to learn, teachers and students alike have the opportunity to move the learning experience forward in new ways. Nevertheless teachers are at the centre of effective use of instructional technologies and it is a teacher who oversees the daily activities of the classroom. Indeed, teaching has been called many things: an art, a science, a calling, a way of life. Through the history, teachers have taken up the tools at hand to help them teach – whether making on clay with a stylus, or writing on a blackboard with a chalk. As new technologies have emerged teachers have used them to extend the range of what they could teach, illustrate ideas in different ways, bring new materials to students, and motivate learners. Hence this paper tries to analyse the role of teachers in blended learning.

Blended learning is a major emerging issue in education fields, and many education programs provide students with online learning. While we all understand the benefits of traditional brick-and-mortar classrooms, the benefits of the online learning piece tend to be more debatable. Given its organic development over time, myths abound about what it is and how it works. Misconceptions like online learning is "teacher-less," that courses are easy, that students spend all their time in front of computers, and that they work in isolation and thus don't get the benefits of collaboration and socialization are in vogue. In reality quality blended learning programs are able to address these issues.

In general terms, Blended Learning combines online delivery of educational content with the best features of classroom interaction and live instruction to personalise learning, allow thoughtful reflection, and differentiate instruction from student to student across a diverse group of learners. For some teachers, blended learning is describing what they have been doing successfully for years: that is, using a range of resources and activities to provide individualised, student-centred learning experiences for their students. The real difference today is the unparalleled access to the internet with its rich sources of information and services and more importantly, the connectivity it offers students and teachers, particularly the ability to create online communities and support networks. In addition, there is a growing use of mobile technologies such as flip cameras, voice recorders, mobile phones and GPS devices extending learning beyond the classroom walls. For other teachers, blended learning represents a challenge. They are not comfortable with nor do they fully understand the technologies and media that their students use every day, or the potential that these can offer their learners. To assist teachers in implementing blended learning activities, this paper reinforces the concept that blended learning comes in many guises and isn't a "one-size-fits-all" educational solution.

Definitions of blended learning range from the very broad where practically any learning experience that integrates some use of ICTs qualifies, to others that focus on specific percentages of online curriculum and face-to-face instruction.

"The concept of blended learning is rooted in the idea that learning is not just a one-time event—learning is a continuous process. Blending provides various benefits over using any single learning delivery medium alone." Singh (2003)

"Blended learning should be viewed as a pedagogical approach that combines the effectiveness and socialisation opportunities of the classroom with the technologically enhanced active learning possibilities of the online environment, rather than a ratio of delivery modalities." Dziuban, Hartman and Moskal (2004).

Generally the term 'blended learning' is adopted as the principal means of addressing the use of Information and Communication Technologies (ICTs) to enhance teaching learning activities. "Blended learning is realised in teaching and learning environments where there is an effective integration of different modes of delivery, models of teaching and styles of learning as a result of adopting a strategic and systematic approach to the use of technology combined with the best features of face to face interaction." (Krause, 2007)

Online and blended learning offer flexibility, opportunity and convenience, and because of these positives, as well as the simple fact that the public is demanding it, use is on the rise. Clearly, the benefits are affordability, accessibility and convenience for students and educators alike. Not only do online and blended learning models allow learning to take place outside of classroom walls and schedules, they make the opportunity of school a more realistic endeavour for those students whose family lifestyles and needs tend to impede the ability to adhere to a more rigid school day.

Why blend?

Blended learning is about effectively integrating ICTs into course design to enhance the teaching and learning experiences for students and teachers by enabling them to engage in ways that would not normally be available or effective in their usual environment, whether it is primarily face-to-face or distance mode. In many cases the act of "blending" achieves better student experiences and outcomes, and more efficient teaching and course management practices. It can involve a mix of delivery modes, teaching approaches and learning styles.

Advances in technology provide new opportunities for teachers to design and deliver their courses in ways that support and enhance the teachers' role, the students' individual cognitive experiences, as well as the social environment; three key elements in successful learning and teaching. Blended learning technologies can:

1. Broaden the spaces and opportunities available for learning;
2. Support course management activities (e.g., communication, assessment submission, marking and feedback);
3. Support the provision of information and resources to students;
4. Engage and motivate students through interactivity and collaboration.

So it is not just about using technology because it is available; blended learning is about finding better ways of supporting students in achieving the learning objectives and providing them with the best possible learning and teaching experiences, as well as supporting teachers in their role (including the management and administration of courses). Of course, the integration of blended learning in courses will naturally vary according to such factors as: discipline, year level, student characteristics and needs, course or program learning objectives, as well as the academic's approach to teaching, and confidence and experience in using technology.

Teachers' Role in Blended Learning:

One of the greatest challenges facing teachers today is meeting the changing expectations of students. Subjects must be offered which allow flexibility in terms of learning opportunities. Students are becoming more diverse in terms of socio-political backgrounds and as a result they bring competing personal needs and demands to their learning environments. Accommodating these needs is a necessity for teachers today. Blended learning strategies provide flexibility in terms of learning design for both the teachers and the student.

The growth of blended learning and its potential for the transformation of teaching and learning are enormous. The literature reveals that it has the potential to provide flexible, collaborative, student-centred, multimedia-rich, authentic, quality learning experiences (Miller & King, 2003; Palloff & Pratt, 2001). However, the research also clearly indicates that this potential cannot be realized without a fundamental shift in not only the institution and the learner, but also the pedagogy and the teacher (Miller & King, 2003). Such a shift requires, in turn, new models for preparing teachers who embrace innovation and change (Childs, 2004; Crichton & LaBonte, 2003; Kemshal-Bell, 2001).

This fundamental shift in pedagogical methodology and the re-conceptualization of teaching that Brennan (2003) calls for require "teachers and trainers who are both confident and comfortable with this new way of working" (Brennan et al., 2001, p. 51). However, preparing for blended teaching represents a massive shift in theory and practice for many of these teachers. It appears that the time has come for a new model that introduces teachers, at a formative point in their teaching careers and later throughout their career, to the emerging body of knowledge of effective blended pedagogical practices. One of the most frequent questions that appear at this point is "What is the role of teachers in blended learning?"

In the blended learning approach, a student's day typically includes a combination of online learning and small group instruction time with teachers. This learning model shifts the classroom teacher's focus away from more traditional curricular and administrative tasks in the direction of working with data and providing more individualized support to students. Because the focus in this model has shifted from planning lessons and delivering content to being a facilitator of student learning, the classroom teacher's role can expand in challenging and stimulating ways.

Rather than following the traditional roles of sharing content and grading papers, classroom teachers in the blended learning model must:

Be willing to learn

In a blended learning program, the teacher should be prepared to: Use data as an integral part of the planning process for each individual student, groups of students and the whole class. Use benchmark tests and other assessments to direct instruction at different levels (individual, group, class).

To help teachers learn their new roles and to understand blended learning, many blended learning programs require that the teachers take a training themselves as part of the required professional development. Having an experienced blended learning mentor as a guide and participating in training on the data management system also is important. With proper professional development, a "traditional" teacher can develop the data-analysis skills needed to get the most out of the blended learning model.

Be open to new teaching strategies

The blended learning teacher should:

Have a wide breadth of content knowledge in order to teach multiple subjects. Differentiate instruction based upon student needs (as determined by the data).Focus on academic intervention and enrichment

While blended learning instructors still need to be able to maximize learning time and manage a classroom effectively, they have more individual time with students and can give them the attention and support they need.

Be leaders

To help guide students in a blended learning environment, teachers should:

Model learning and show students how to *find* information and answers (or ask the right questions). Be able to manage project-based learning activities. Have strategies in place to keep students on-task, engaged and motivated.

The blended learning instructor helps students move beyond simply "regurgitating" rote responses to learning to apply content to new situations. Just as the teacher must interpret and analyze information, students need to learn to reason, integrate information and demonstrate knowledge through application.

So, what might blended learning mean to teachers? Continued growth as they modify their existing strategies to lead students to become independent learners themselves? Technology can also give teachers crucial information to understand individual needs of students to support and strengthen their learning. When teachers use good technology effectively, it provides them the power to become even greater experts in the content areas they teach.

Sir Francis Bacon said, many years ago, "Knowledge is power." So why not gain more power in the classroom by building the teacher's expertise in the use of technology?

Designing Blended Learning

Designing for blended learning requires a systematic approach, starting with:

1. **Planning** for integrating blended learning into the course, followed by;
2. **Designing** and **developing** the blended learning elements;
3. **Implementing** the blended learning design;
4. **Reviewing** (evaluating) the effectiveness of the blended learning design, and finally;
5. Planning for the next delivery of the course then involves **improving** the blended learning experience for both teachers and students.

What Blended Learning Activities should be planned?

Through a blended learning program, educators can move beyond the "one teacher, one textbook model" of education in a host of ways, including:

1. Allowing students to move at their own pace and excel
2. Providing "just-in-time" intervention
3. Grouping students more effectively
4. Providing real world experiences
5. Helping students construct meaning rather than just memorizing (and forgetting) facts
6. Creating learning opportunities across grade levels, subjects, departments and between teachers and students.
7. Teaching problem-solving in multidisciplinary units.
8. Encouraging 21st century collaboration through video conferencing with authors, speakers and other students from around the world.
9. Increasing productivity – both for themselves and students.

The level of learning that students' achieve is often dependent on the type of activities and assessment tasks, and whether they are aligned with the set objectives or desired learning outcomes. One useful framework for considering learning objectives and suitable activities is Bloom's Taxonomy. Bloom's taxonomy has been recently revised to suit a blended learning environment (Churches, 2008). This revision includes suggestions for tasks that can be used to support particular objectives. For example:

*arning Typs*Levels of Learning	Types of Blended Learning Activities
Creating Designing, constructing, planning, producing, inventing	Programming, filming, animating, video/ blogging, mixing/re-mixing, web publishing, webcasting, directing or producing – used to create a film, presentation, story, program, projects, media product, graphic art, vodcast, advertisement, model.
Evaluating Checking, hypothesising, critiquing, experimenting, judging, testing	Debate or panel (using webcasting, web conferencing, online chat or discussion), investigating (online tools) and reporting (blog, wiki, presentation),persuasive speech

	(webcast, web document, mind map-presentation mode), commenting/ moderating/reviewing/posting (discussion forums, blogs, wiki, chat room, twitter) as well as collaborating and networking.
Analysing Comparing, organising, deconstructing, interrogating, structuring	Surveying/polling, using databases, relationship mind maps, online SWOT analysis, reporting (online charts, graphing, presentation or web publishing),mashing, meta-tagging.
Applying Implementing, carrying out, using, executing, editing	Simulation games or tasks, editing or developing shared documents (wiki, video and sound tools), interviews (e.g., making podcast), presentation ordemonstration tasks (using web conferencing or online presentation tools), illustration (using online graphic, creative tools).
Understanding Interpreting, summarising, paraphrasing, classifying, explaining, comparing	Building mind maps, blog journaling, wiki (simple page construction), categorising and tagging, advanced internet (Boolean) searches, tagging with comments or annotations, discussion forums, show and tell (with audio, video webcasting).
Remembering Recognising, listing, describing, identifying, retrieving, naming, locating	Simple mind maps, flash cards, online quizzes, basic internet searches (fact finding, defining), social bookmarking, Q & A discussion forums, chat,presentations.

Source: Adapted from Churches, 2008;

retrieved http://www.scribd.com/doc/8000050/Blooms-Digital-Taxonomy-v212

With blended learning still early in its development, there's no teacher preparation. All teachers are equally new to this concept. Though teachers of today are creating best practices and developing techniques for teaching, it's both very rewarding and very difficult work. Preparing them to face this challenge is a marathon task. It takes both discipline and agility to monitor teacher preparation both pre-service and in-service in preparing teachers for blended classrooms.

Conclusions

We live in a world that is constantly changing; it can change so quickly that some of the technologies referred to here may have evolved long back. However, the underpinning principles of good curriculum design rarely change, even with the integration of technology. The following principles highlight key aspects of the process of designing technology-enhanced learning (adapted from JISC, 2009a);

1. Where technology is used, it should extend the potential for learning, and not be used simply for its own sake.
2. Quality learning occurs when there is coherence and alignment between the technology, course environment, learning objectives, teaching and learning activities, and assessment demands of a course.
3. Effective practice in blended learning requires selecting the most appropriate tools for the purpose; that is, the learning to be achieved.
4. The adoption of blended learning should ideally exploit the capacity of technology to promote active and participative learning in both face-to-face and online contexts.
5. When unfamiliar technologies are integrated into learning designs, the rationale and benefits need to be clearly communicated to students.
6. Even advanced users of technology look to their teachers for guidance on how to use technology in learning; so ensure there is appropriate support for students in using the technology for learning.
7. Ongoing review and evaluation, drawing on a range of perspectives, helps to ensure quality learning experiences for both teachers and students.

References

1. Advisory Committee for Online Learning. (2001). The e-learning e-volution in colleges and universities: a pan Canadian challenge. Retrieved September 15, 2004 from Industry Canada Web Site: http://mig-gam.ic.gc.casitesacol-ccael/em/report/index.html

   Blackboard. (n.d.). Retrieved September 6, 04, from http://www.blackboard.com/

2. Brennan, R. (2003). One Size Doesn't Fit All (ISBN 1 4096 157 9). Retrieved August 12, 04 from http://www.ncver.edu.au
3. Brennan, R., McFadden, M., & Law, E. (2001). All That Glitters is not Gold. Australia: National Center for Vocational Education Research.
4. Crichton, S., & Childs, E. (2005). Clipping and Coding Audio Files: A Research Method to Enable Participant Voice.
5. Crichton, S., & Childs, E. A. (2003). Teachers as Online Educators: Requirements for Distributed Learning and Teacher Preparation. Educational Technology, 44(4), 25-30.
6. Crichton, S., & Kinash, S. (2003). Virtual Ethnography: Interactive Interviewing Online as Method. Canadian Journal of Learning and Technology, 29(2), Retrieved November 19, 04, from http://www.cjlt.ca/content/vol29.2/cjlt29-2_art-5.html
7. Crichton, S., & LaBonte, R. (2003). Innovative Practice for Innovators: Walking the Talk. Education Technology and Society, 6(1) . Retrieved October 15,04 from:http://ifets.ieee.org/periodical/vol_1_2003/crichton.html
8. Dziuban C., Hartman J. and Moskal P. (2004)"Blended Learning" *EDUCAUSE*, vol 2004, issue 7 http://net.educause.edu/ir/library/pdf/ERB0407.pdf
9. Good, M. On the Way to Online Pedagogy. In John Stephenson (Ed.), Teaching & Learning Online (pp. 166-174). London: Kogan Page.
10. Goodyear, P., Salmon, G., Spector, J. M., Steeples, C., & Tickner, S. (2001). Competencies for Online Teaching: A Special Report. Educational Technology Research and Development, 49(1), 65-72.
11. Singh H. (2003) Building Effective Blended Learning Programs. *Educational Technology*, Volume 43, Number 6, Pages 51-54. http://asianvu.com/bookstoread/framework/blended-learning.pdf

3

Role of Blended Learning in Education

Introduction

Since the advent of online learning and the fact that it has not been the panacea that everyone thought it would have been, schools and companies have increasingly turned to a more moderate blend of the technological methods and strategies with the traditional ones in an attempt to optimise the benefits of both. In this unit, you will examine the concept of blended learning, and discuss the benefits and limitations of using blending learning approaches. Blended learning is defined as "combining online delivery of educational content with the best features of classroom interaction and live instruction to personalize learning ,allow thoughtful reflection and differentiate instruction from student-to-student across a diverse group of learners". In simple words, blended learning combines teaching methods from both face–to –face and online learning.

Blended Learning

Blended Learning refers to a combination of online and face-to-face methods in response to learners' needs and for the achievement of instructional objectives. This means that multiple approaches, methods and resources to teaching or to educational processes are combined and utilized by the teacher who now expects the students to learn not only from assigned web pages and communication tools (e.g. email, discussion board and chat rooms) but also from face to face lectures, tutorials, person to person discussions and seminars. Examples include combining technology-based materials and traditional print materials, group and individual study, structured pace study and self-paced study, conference calls, tutorial and coaching. It may also include CD-ROM courses, video, simulations and integrated learning systems. Overall, the best mix of resources is used to provide an optimum learning experience for all the students.

Growing Need

From unprecedented budget pressures and over-burdened teachers to the need for more effective, more personalized learning to accommodate each student's individual learning style, schools are facing complex issues. The opportunities are enormous as well, whether it is tapping the vast stores of digital information now available or teachers and using new technology tools to learn, teachers and students alike have the opportunity to move the learning experience forward in new ways. Blending learning, which typically extends classroom instruction online, is giving schools new approaches and strategy for taking advantage of the exciting new learning opportunities that are now available.

Implementation methods

Blended learning comes in a wide range of implementation models. This chart below summarizes the continuum of models used in schools throughout the country, giving educators working picture of the many ways in which online learning blends with and supports traditional instruction.

Benefits

1. The ability for schools to maintain their central role in managing a student's educational process and personalizing instruction.

2. Providing curriculum developers and learners and teachers the flexibility to address standards and maintain curriculum fidelity while integrating digital content and learning experiences that better engage these day's learners.
3. Giving teachers valuable experiences using technology effectively in their professional development courses, preparing them to use blended models creatively and strategically as this approach becomes more and more prevalent in the classroom.

Proof of efficiency

Blended learning performs as well or better than face-to-face instruction. According to a 2009 report from the U.S,Department of Education, "In recent experimental and quasi-experimental studies contrasting blends of online and face-to-face instruction with conventional face-to-face classes, blended instruction has been more effective, providing a rationale for the effort required in design and implement blended approaches.

The study's main findings are noteworthy:

1. Student's who took all or part of their class online performed better, on average, than those taking the same course through traditional face-to-face instruction than did purely online instruction.
2. Instruction combining online and face-to-face elements had a larger advantage relative to purely face-to-face instruction than did purely online instruction.
3. The effectiveness of online learning approaches appears quite broad across different content and learner types.
4. Online learning can be enhanced by giving learners control of their interactions with media and prompting learning reflection.

Advantages of Blended Learning

1. The organization offering the course can create his/her own content.

2. The global reach of the blended approach to education and training continues to be one of its greatest advantages. Uses concerning distance are eliminated.
3. The speed with which you can reach thousands of people is unmatched by traditional methods as they can all be reach simultaneously without the restrictions of time and space.
4. Not all content can be properly delivered online. The challenges of using a purely online modality are eliminated when a blended approach is used.
5. By making use of traditional approaches where they work best and applying the technology related methods only where they are most appropriate for the achievement of the instructional goals, organizations can avoid the exponential increase in costs that can accompany a complete switch to online methods only. It also allows students to avoid costs that are incurred through travel, accommodations and other expenses that are tied to 'time and place studies'.
6. Blended learning allows learners the flexibility with their time to do their lessons anytime and anyplace until a meeting with the lecturer becomes compulsory.
7. It can make it easier to deal with educational administration and communication with all students. Virtual office hours make tutors far more accessible than in a strictly face-to-face scenario.
8. Students get their learning needs and styles catered to whether they prefer online or face-to-face because it offers both in a single course.
9. For sessions held online, the communication between teacher and student is open and everyone can benefit from it because everyone can view the responses sent by the teacher.
10. Some lecturers experience an improvement in the quality of students' writing and discussion.

Disadvantages of Blended Learning

1. Before a blended learning scenario can be considered ready for use, the lecturer has to do long, detailed and extensive work. Preparation for startup is very time consuming.

2. There can be limited contact between lecturer and students and so some of the dynamism that comes with face-to-face interaction can be lost.
3. Based on what students are used to, they often prefer the paper versions of the materials than to see them online so the face-to-face sessions in the blended programmes usually have a comparatively more successful "feel" for the students.
4. The materials developed by the lecturers cannot simply be the same set that they had developed for handouts. They have to be reformatted so that they guide the students through a process of independent study when they are not in a face-to-face session. This additional task required of the lecturers is yet to be appreciated for what it is worth.
5. Students sometimes feel that they are given more work to do when distance modalities are used.

Conclusion

Blended learning allows businesses and schools alike to make maximum use of the technologies and other resources that they have available to them. This means that it allows both businesses and schools to take a look at all the technologies and tools that they have and see how it can best be used to bring the greatest benefit to employee/students and the organization even as they spend as little as they possibly can and still maintain effectiveness. So, Blended learning is clearly a rapidly growing instructional practice. It should be adopted to get expected results.

References

1. Seidl, M. (2005). Blended Learning With Model: Didactical and Technical Aspects of Blended Learning Scenario with Model.
2. Abate, Lisa. (2004) "Blended Learning in the Elementary Classroom." *techLearning.* Retrieved Oct. 12, 2005
3. Albany institute of history and art virtual field trips. (n.d.). Retrieved Oct. 06, 2005,

4. Alonso, Fernando; Genoveva Lopez Daniel Manrique; Jose M. Vines.(2005)An instructional model for web-based e-learning education with a blended learning process approach. "British Journal of Educational Technology." Vol. 36, No. 219.

5. Alvarez, S. (2005). Blended learning solutions. In B. Hoffman (Ed.), *Encyclopedia of Educational Technology.* Retrieved October 10, 2005, a memory collection. (n.d.). Retrieved Oct. 03, 2005.

6. American Society for Training and Development (2005). "Learning Curcutis Glossary of Terms." Retrieved on October 12, 2005.

7. Beal, Candy, & Mason, Cheryl. (1999) Virtual Fieldtripping. "Meridian: A Middle School Computer Technologies Journal, volume 2" (Issue 1). Retrieved October 9, 2005.

8. Barking Spider. (n.d.). Retrieved October 2, 2005.

9. Belanger, Yvonne. *Laptop computers in the K-12 classroom* Retrieved October 10, 2005.

10. Bersin & Associates. (May 2003). *Blended Learning: What Works?*

11. Bersin, Josh. (2004). "The Blended Learning Book: Best Practices, Proven Methodologies, and lessons Learned. Retrieved October 2, 2005.

12. "Blended Leanring". (2005). Retrieved on October 12, 2005.

4

Cloud Computing in Higher Education

Introduction

In the current financial crisis, educational institutions and universities are facing difficulties in providing necessary support for educational, research and development activities. Cloud computing is the alternative to address the issues there by improving agility and obtain savings. Cloud computing is an emerging area which can be used for sharing the resources with the help of web technology like Software as a Service (SaaS), Platform as a Service (PaaS) and Infrastructure as a Service (IaaS). Practically Cloud Computing is extension of Grid computing with independency and smarter tools and technological gradients. Healthy Cloud Computing helps in sharing of software, hardware, application and other packages with the help of internet tools and wireless media. Cloud computing can be a welcomed optioned in the universities and educational institutes for higher studies. And also the educational institutes, universities and industries are playing vital role in transforming the society and entire world economy. Various researches are carried out to update the present IT infrastructure especially in the area of education.

Cloud computing provides shared resources, software and information through Internet as a PAYGO (Pay-as-you-go) basis. Cloud Computing is a kind of virtualization; thus also known as Virtualization Technology. Cloud Computing and its benefits attracts several other field. Education Systems also interacts with Educational applications for Cloud Computing. Cloud Computing provides several benefits in Educational Systems such as creation of Virtual teaching learning environment, making interacting and speedy smart class room, it also minimizes the time of knowledge collection model preparation and delivery. Cloud Computing and its benefits are used around the world and especially in the Western countries. Due to poverty and underdevelopment; Asian and African and other undeveloped countries are still unable to offer such benefits to teachers, student, administrator, instructor and other stakeholders related to education systems. The challenges and issues are one of the important concerns for strong and healthy educational systems powered by cloud computing and virtualization technique.

Higher Education

Higher education was acknowledged in time as one of the pillars of society development. Through the partnerships between universities, government and industry, researchers and students have proven their contribution to the transformation of society and the entire world economy. The tendency observed during the last few years within the higher education level is the universities' transition to research universities and ongoing update of the IT (Information Technology) infrastructure as foundation for educational activities and Science research.

With the evolution of technology, the number of services which migrate from traditional form to the online form grows as well. For these specific services, an adequate providing form must be found in the online environment, using the proper technologies, guaranteeing the access of large number of users, fast and secure services. Due to this aspect, at the moment universities are confronting with a dramatic increase of costs in higher education, more than the inflation rate and a decrease of universities' budgets, which leads to the pressure of finding some alternative means of reaching their purpose i.e. the education of students and accomplishing the research.

Cloud Computing (CC)

Cloud Computing is a new technology which is an improvement of distributed computing, parallel computing and grid computing. The basic principle of cloud computing is making tasks distributed among large number of computers but not in local computers or remote servers. This is a dynamic model, based on pay-per-use (subscription) or scalable system in which configuration of resources (hardware, platform/services) can be graded to suit the needs of the users for optimum utilization of resources. In simple words, it is a subscription- based or pay-per-use real time service over the internet.

The following **National Institute of Standards and Technology (NIST)** definitions are used for deployment models:

Private cloud The cloud infrastructure is operated solely for an organization. It may be managed by the organization or a third party and may exist on premise or off premise.

Community cloud The cloud infrastructure is shared by several organizations and supports a specific community that has shared concerns (e.g., mission, security requirements, policy, and compliance considerations). It may be managed by the organizations or a third party and may exist on premise or off premise.

Public cloud The cloud infrastructure is made available to the general public or a large industry group and is owned by an organization selling cloud services.

Hybrid cloud The cloud infrastructure is a composition of two or more clouds (private, community, or public) that remain unique entities but are bound together by standardized or proprietary technology that enables data and application portability (e.g., cloud bursting for load balancing between clouds).

Characteristics of Cloud Computing

There are many distinguishing features of cloud computing but some important features are.

(a) Versatility

(b) Cost-effectiveness (pay-per-use)

(c) Virtualization

(d) Security

(e) Sustainability

(f) Scalability

(g) User-friendly

(h) Resource Optimisation

(i) Infrastructure and service-level agreements (SLAs)

Types of Cloud Computing

The following is a list of the three main types of services that can be offered by the cloud:

1. Software as a Service (SaaS): The applications, such as e-mail, people use every day.
2. Platform as a Service (PaaS): The operating environment in which applications run.
3. Infrastructure as a Service (IaaS): The on-demand data centers.

Outsourcing some capabilities to the cloud makes the most of what's on-site by freeing time, budget, and people. For example, with SaaS, you can add services, like e-mail, affordably. With PaaS, you can deliver services broadly without having to manage the infrastructure. With IaaS, you get pay-as-you-go data center capacity for adding CPUs, storage, networking, or Web hosting. Take, for example, a typical university with an IT infrastructure that caters for the needs of students, teaching staff and management, research staff and software developers (e.g., Web developers).

Demand for IT services in this environment is directed to the IT Services Department whose job is to:

- provide students and staff with software (e.g., email accounts, operating systems, productivity applications, malware detectors and cleaners, etc.) and hardware (e.g., PCs, Servers, etc.);

- provide researchers and postgraduate students with the required special software and hardware to run experiments that are likely to involve a great deal of processing and computation;
- provide Web developers with the development tools needed to write and host Web applications.

Many aspects of this arrangement can be migrated to the cloud. For example, students, administrative staff and lecturers can be made to use the services of providers of SaaS and IaaS clouds. These services will be ideally accessed through thin clients. Any software launched by these groups of people resides on the servers of the SaaS cloud provider and is accessed online.

A growing number of academic institutions are turning to SaaS for their desktop applications. For example, Madras University uses an e-mail solution hosted in the cloud. Students now have the free collaboration tools they want, people on campus have the tools they need to work together, and administrators are finding it easier and more cost-effective to manage.

SaaS for education: Microsoft Live@edu

Microsoft Live@edu is a program that provides students, staff, faculty, and alumni long-term, primary e-mail addresses and other applications that they can use to collaborate and communicate online—all at no cost to education institutions. Students will be using Microsoft products similar to those used in many workplaces that help to prepare them for jobs after college.

Cloud computing initiatives

There are good number of cloud computing initiatives undertaken by Amazon, Google, Microsoft and others offering various types of cloud computing services for the organizations, businesses, and individuals. IBM Cloud Academy, IEEE Cloud Computing initiatives are offered some services in Education.

IBM Cloud Academy

IBM (International Business Machines) launched the IBM Cloud Academy (2009), a global forum for educators, researchers and information technology (IT) personnel from the education industry to pursue cloud computing initiatives, develop skills and share best practices for reducing operating costs while improving quality and access to education.

IEEE Cloud Computing

The IEEE (Institute of Electrical and Electronics Engineers) Cloud Computing Initiative represents the first, broad-based collaborative endeavor for cloud computing to be offered by a global technical professional organization. Six interdependent activity tracks are included in the IEEE Cloud Computing Initiative: the Web portal; conferences; continuing education courses; publications; standards development; and a test bed to be used in the development of cloud standards and applications as well as for education and research.

Amazon Web Services (AWS)

Amazon is perceived as one of the major players in the business, offering a wide range of prominent cloud computing services such as elastic compute cloud (EC2), simple storage service (S3), simple DB and simple queuing service (SQS). It provides a reliable, scalable, low-cost infrastructure platform in the cloud that powers hundreds of thousands of businesses in countries around the world. Some of the solutions offered by Amazon through cloud computing include application hosting, web hosting, backup and storage, enterprise IT, content delivery, and database.

Google Apps

Google Apps cloud services, a multi-tenant, and internet-scale infrastructure, offers faster access to innovation, superior reliability, and security, and maximum economies of scale as compared to on-premises, hosted and software plus services technologies8. Google Apps is available free for individuals and organizations (limited up to 10 user accounts), educational institutions and US non-profitable organizations and for a price to businesses and organizations.

Microsoft Windows Azure

Microsoft is also investing heavily in this new computing service delivery model and has introduced Azure, as its cloud offering. Azure has three components: Windows Azure (which provides developers with on-demand compute and storage to host, scale, and manage Internet or cloud applications), SQL Azure (which extends the capabilities of Microsoft SQL Server into the cloud as a Web-based distributed relational database) and Azure .Net Services (which include a set of Microsoft-hosted, highly scalable, developer-oriented services that provide key building blocks required by many cloud-based and cloud-aware applications).

Education and the Cloud Computing

Colleges and universities are always on the lookout to upgrade their software and IT hardware in order to attract students and keep pace with the rapid developments in digital technologies. Cloud computing could provide those institutions with the means to achieve those ambitions at prices they can afford. Furthermore, shifting responsibility to external providers for managing some aspects of their software and hardware infrastructures could also result in cost savings with relation to labor, as fewer IT services staff will be needed than before. Cloud Computing is gaining popularity in educational systems, especially in online education and corporate education; E-Learning is gaining popularity through web 2.0 platform of Cloud Computing ; Still in India, higher educational institutes are not moving towards healthy Cloud Computing solutions; Governmental grants, non availability of software and packages related to educational field are important issues.

1. The online and e-learning systems may gain rapidly with the help of Cloud Computing; the aspects such as online question paper distribution, paper collection, full text book and module delivery is possible with Cloud Computing.
2. Social Computing such as Social 2.0 powered web technologies is also a kind of Cloud Computing; which allows sharing of educational data, text, notes and recorded video without extra support. The challenges of such systems are mainly people

awareness, student awareness, teachers and faculty towards sharing and creation of group of learner. Many teachers and students may not aware about IT and Social Networking usages.

3. Creation of smart class room, online and continuing education university education has come to the door step of learner. Here Cloud Computing is used in several cases.
4. More importantly, Cloud Computing based education systems saves cost by centralized IT Infrastructure, rapid transfer, elasticity, flexibility and other benefits in education
5. Cloud computing also promotes some new educational mode such as-corporate learning, industry integrated learning programme; where students get knowledge and classes from online media in his/her office or corporate house. It is helpful for the working students. But for that a mutual understanding between education service provider and corporate agency is essential. The main reason behind this is, space for projection, tools and technological and electricity support and so on.

Advantages of Cloud Computing

1. There is no need to own all infrastructure facilities as cloud computing takes care of it.
2. With the help of Broadband and healthy connection anywhere and anytime services are possible;
3. It provides large amounts of processing power comparable to supercomputer level.
4. It provides an effective and creative service delivery model;
5. Cloud Computing model does not support any long term commitments.
6. Capital expenditure is minimized

A convenient tool to engage in the scholarship of teaching and learning.

Cloud Computing Based Education: Challenges and Issues

Many challenges of clod computing for higher education relate to its relative newness and the underdevelopment of the marketplace for cloud services. For higher education, decisions to adopt cloud computing will be influenced by more than technical and cost considerations.

Information is the lifeblood of higher education, and decisions on how to manage that information can have far-reaching political, social, and economic considerations. Adoption of cloud computing presents many of the same risks and challenges as deciding to use a more traditional outsourcing arrangement. The increased possibility that the service provider or its resources may reside outside of a government's legal or territorial jurisdiction, however, can make some of these concerns more acute. At present, as many universities are trying to update their IT infrastructure and data, but they are facing few challenges which can be solved by cloud computing. The challenges are as follows:

1. **Cost**: choose the subscription or PAYGO plan.
2. **Flexibility**: cloud computing allows to dynamically scale the investment in infrastructures as demand fluctuate.
3. **Accessibility**: making the data and services available publicly without losing the sensitive information
4. **Security**: making data secure.

Conclusion

Cloud computing is a new baby in the computer systems technology emerged owing to the developments in internet and associated technologies. It is in the evolving stage, requires some amount of careful considerations before organizations think about hosting some of their services. E-Learning or online education is need of hour. Today several modes of education have originated with the help of IT and computing. It provides several opportunities; Cloud Computing plays an important role for overall IT infrastructure development. Regular education may also benefit from Cloud Computing. The small room, mobile based education is the wonderful gift of IT and especially Cloud Computing. Universities, Engineering colleges, and other higher educational institutes should go for Cloud Computing and virtualization. Proper funding and planning are essential for healthy Cloud Computing packages. Proper and adequate training programme on Cloud Computing need to be introduced.

Reference

1. Aladwani, Adel M,(2002) "An integrated performance model of information systems projects", *Journal of Management Information Systems,* 19(1).
2. AbdulKalam, APJ (2003) "IT Strategy in Defense Environment", DESIDOC *Bulletin of Information Technology,* 20(1 & 2): 7-12.
3. Bates, M (1990) "where should the person stop and the information search interface start?' *Information Processing & Management,* 26(5): 575–591.
4. Belkin, N. J., & Robertson, S.E. (1976) "Information science and the phenomena of information." *Journal of the American Society for Information Science,* 27(4):197–204.
5. Denning, P. J., & et al. (1989) Computing as a discipline. *Communication of the ACM,* 32(1),23.
6. Dhawan, Neelam (2011) Cloud computing can counter illiteracy. *Times of India,*
7. Fox, A. (2009) Cloud computing in education. *Berkeley iNews,* https://inews. Berkeley.edu/articles/Spring2009/cloud-computing
8. Hayes, B. (2008) Cloud computing. *Communications of ACM,* 51(7): 9-11.
9. Scale, Mark-Shane E (2009) Cloud computing and collaboration. *Library Hi Tech News,* 26(9): 10-13.
10. Wikipedia. Cloud computing. http://en.wikipedia.org/ wiki/ Cloud computing.

5

Designing Learing Environment of Tomorrow for Effective Academic Excellence

Introduction

Education plays a very significant role in developing an individual to his full potential by bringing out his latent talents and nurturing them. The forces of environment begin to influence the growth and development of the individual right from the womb of the mother. A proper and adequate environment is very much necessary for a fruitful learning of the child. In recent years, we have witnessed rapid social and cultural changes, phenomenal advances in communication and information technologies, as well as the introduction of the Internet within schools. These factors have contributed to shape the teaching and operating cultures of schools and created shifts in our expectations of the physical learning environment. They have affected teachers, educators and researchers the world over. These miniature revolutions have given rise to an urgent need for a new generation of facilities to cater for 21st century teaching and learning needs. Good learning environment is one in which staff, students and, parents build safe and peaceful environment where people feel accepted and respected and where learning is the main focus. Therefore a positive learning environment where all students feel comfortable, wanted, valued, accepted, and secure must be created. The use of innovative methods in educational institutions has the potential not only to improve education, but also to empower people, strengthen governance and galvanize the effort to achieve the human development goal for the country. The present paper deals with the effective, appropriate and interactive use of computer – related technologies for designing learning environment of tomorrow which induce and pave ways for academic excellence.

Education plays a very significant role in developing an individual to his full potential by bringing out his latent talents and nurturing them. Education shapes a person. According to Dewey 'Education is a continuous process of experiencing and of revising or non-revising experiences. It is the development of all those capacities in the individual, which enables him to control his environment and fulfill his possibilities'. The forces of environment begin to influence the growth and development of the individual right from the womb of the mother. A proper and adequate environment is very much necessary for a fruitful learning of the child. Especially the school and home should provide the necessary stimulus for learning experience. In recent years, we have witnessed rapid social and cultural changes, phenomenal advances in communication and information technologies, as well as the introduction of the Internet within schools. These factors have contributed to shape the teaching and operating cultures of schools and created shifts in our expectations of the physical learning environment. They have affected teachers, educators and researchers the world over. These miniature revolutions have given rise to an urgent need for a new generation of facilities to cater for 21st century teaching and learning needs. Good learning environment is one in which staff, students and, parents build safe and peaceful environment where people feel accepted and respected and where learning is the main focus. Therefore a learning environment, where all students feel comfortable, wanted, valued, accepted, and secure, must be created. A positive school climate affects everyone associated with the school, be it the students, staff, parents, and the community. Improved school climate is a goal to pursue. Educators need to constant up work towards improving their school climate, culture, and conditions to that students learning is improved. The world could be synchronized with the development of science and technology. Education is the means for all these developments. Education is the essence of every civilization. The use of innovative methods in educational institutions has the potential not only to improve education, but also to empower people, strengthen governance and galvanize the effort to achieve the human development goal for the country.

Conceptual Framework

Learning takes place effectively only when proper and congenial environment is provided for children. Positive learning environment exists when all students feel comfortable, wanted, valued, accepted, and secure in an environment where they trust. Many of the modern learning environments being built today promote and support a range of pedagogies including delivering, applying, creating, communicating and decision-making. Modern learning environments support strengths-based teaching and can offer students and teachers flexibility, openness and access to resources. Providing teachers with an open, flexible learning environment can lead to the development of a robust, continuously improving community of practice.

Learning environment should support multiple perspective or interpretations of reality, knowledge construction, and experience based activities. In the age of globalization the modern computer – related technologies help in changing the learning environment rapidly and make the pedagogy more and more interactive. With the use of computer technology, classroom learning process tends to accelerate day by day. Computer technologies increase the level of teaching and motivate students to provide information in an interesting and innovative way by making teaching more and more effective. The appropriate and effective use of technology facilitates to gain information in depth. The present paper deals with the effective, appropriate and interactive use of computer – related technologies for designing learning environment of tomorrow which induce and pave ways for academic excellence.

Computer – assisted learning provides a huge amount of information to the learners in a short period of time. Learners are reinforced in a powerful way through the medium of discussion in classroom. It helps in stimulating the students to learn through the use of multimedia, provides students different varieties of information, provides more powerful ICT tools for problem solving and learning and allows the students to work at their pace. Every learner should not only be a computer literate but also develop competencies in the effective usage of computers and all the technologies that are related to learning, Age –old method of chalk and talk in classroom should be dead and gone.

Changing the learning process

In the late '90s' many in the education field and government, as well as in the media and public, recognized a 'digital divide' in which some school districts and classrooms were "wired" and had up-to-date computer technology, while others did not, Accordingly, there were efforts undertaken by government, business and educators to wire classrooms and make computer technology available to a greater number of students and teachers. While many teachers and students are engaging in innovative forms of research and novel projects, there are still many traditional teachers who resist learning new computer skills and do not want to bring computer- based technologies into their classrooms.

Teachers have to develop the ability to demonstrate how these technologies can be used for academic purposes and convey the educational advantages of computers and the Internet to their students. This means acquiring and teaching new literacy involving teachers and students in innovative types of research projects, and interacting in novel ways as everyone learns to use new technology and media.

Indeed, to meet the challenges of an always- evolving high-tech society, teachers today need to develop multiple forms of computer and information literacy to help improve education. This means using technology in the classroom to illustrate lesson topics; teaching students how to use the Internet and information technology to research topics; and using technology to enhance education outside the classroom, ideally in the ways that involve students in the learning process.

Teachers might share large learning spaces, rather than traditional classrooms, with children at different levels, learning different things. Classroom design developments include flexible teaching spaces that can be expanded or reduced in size depending on what's being taught and what technology requirements are needed. Some modern options include hexagonal shapes with a shared common centre area, and outdoor areas and decking off each learning space. Sliding glass walls can be used to open up or close down spaces providing both flexibility and an open, bright environment. Specialist equipment within a school can be shared by all, and with the wider community. This could be a fully-fitted industrial kitchen, or a modern science laboratory lined with wall-to-wall glass that allows other students to walk past and observe what's going on. Whole walls can be whiteboard, or white-boards can be movable. Teachers can opt to change the way the class is facing, or break children up into groups.

The key principles of Learning Environment of Tomorrow Flexibility

Creating flexible spaces that accommodate a wide range of current and future teaching and learning styles is the key. While we cannot anticipate all of the future needs for educational facilities we can know with certainty that they will change. Teaching spaces that can be adapted and support the educational agility of teachers and students will be an environment that can deliver outstanding educational outcomes. We should not get stuck with replicating 'business as usual' solutions when we could have spaces that support innovation and creative learning.

The Learning Community

The modern learning environment can gain significant benefits from being designed for the community it serves. While funding is a one-size-fits-all model, the project team can actually deliver a project that reflects and supports the wider school community. And when a school is designed as a learning community it is a powerful way to engage with students, staff and parents.

Classroom / Learning Studio

A classroom can offer so much more when combined with other spaces such as small seminar or breakout rooms, group learning areas or even external learning decks can offer the opportunity for a wide variety of learning styles. Adjacencies and visibility are so important in making this work well.

Group Learning Areas

Group learning spaces can take over from the corridor for circulation but also create wonderful opportunities for teaching and learning at different scales – from small groups or combined classes. They can also be a powerful physical manifestation of the learning community described above, and surrounded by visible learning studios and small seminar / breakout rooms they support the flexible, agile leaning of the future.

Outdoor Learning Environment

Often the external spaces for the school are an afterthought and yet they represent a fantastic opportunity to create great learning spaces. The key is visibility. The power of passive surveillance through being able to remotely supervise a space through good visibility can transform behaviours and learning outcomes. Careful thought by designers can unlock the potential of the neglected areas in your school grounds, bringing them back into the overall learning environment. School buildings should support and inspire the wonderful learning opportunities that can happen in and around them.

Learning environment of tomorrow must encompass a holistic approach that relates the pedagogy of learning to the physical and virtual spaces in which learning occurs. Each of the following characteristics can pose to design a learning environment of tomorrow:

1. a dynamic transformative learning centre that provides a welcoming, vibrant and culturally inclusive environment
2. a place of awe and enchantment, exploration and curiosity
3. a large, flexible learning space based on fluid design principles
4. a space that includes print, e-resources, and multi-media, and provides access to a range of ICT hardware and software fully supported by robust ICT infrastructure

Functional elements within a learning environment of tomorrow

1. Enable learning to be demonstrated by students participating, reading, watching, publishing, creating, researching, and performing in groups or individually.
2. Have flexible spaces that can be adapted for individual, small or large group use with acoustic considerations. This will allow students to work individually, to reflect, as well as collaborate on projects, and discuss and share ideas.
3. Have interiors designed using modular, flexible, multi-use furniture. Power points will be installed everywhere and offer charging for mobile learning devices.

For augmenting and strengthening the use of innovative strategies in the classrooms of India, we need to work on the following areas:

1. Curricular reforms
2. Faculty development
3. Academic leadership
4. Renewal of Higher Quality standards
5. E-skill development
6. Adopting the under privileged or Rural villages
7. Professional competence.

Conclusion

Academic excellence is one of the most important goals of education. It can be defined as excellence in all disciplines. It encompasses student ability and performance. The effective growth and development, the desirable learning experiences, attitudes and values to be developed in the child depends upon the main factor learning environment. The study demands the designing of learning environment of tomorrow. Further the educational resources and infrastructure needs to be updated in rural schools so that the academic excellence can be uplifted in such schools.

References

1. Dillenbourg, Pierre. "Virtual learning environments" (PDF). EUN Conference 2000: Learning in the new millennium: Building new education strategies for schools
2. Dinesh Kumar, Amit Singh. Computer technology as an interactive teaching system a new trend in education, Edutrack, January 2013, Vol.12, No: 5.
3. G. Kearsley and B. Shneiderman, 'Engagement theory: A framework for technology-based teaching and learning', Educational Technology, 38, 5 (September-October 1998), pp. 20-23. accessed as http://home.sprynet.com/~gkearsley/engage.htm on 21 February 2000
4. G.Madhavi, N. Ramnath Kishan. Development of positive learning environment, Edutrack, November 2012, Vol.9, No: 3.
5. Jagannath.K, Dange, Praveen.R. Online learning a new way of education, Edutrack, July 2009, Vol.8, No: 11.
6. M. J. Stiles, 'Developing Tacit and Codified Knowledge and Subject Culture within a Virtual Learning Environment', IJEEE, 37, No1 (January 2000) pp 13-25
7. Moult, R. R. (2005), Learning to listen: Using ICT to capture pupils' perceptions and help the teacher to respond (PDF), p. 19.
8. Pea & K. Sheingold (Eds.), Mirrors of minds: Patterns of experience in educational computing (pp. 147-177). Norwood, NJ: Ablex Publishing

9. Pea, R. D., & Kurland, D. M. (1987). On the cognitive effects of learning computer programming. In R. D.
10. Puneet,Rahi.Innovations in teaching learning, Edutrack, July 2012, Vol.11, No: 11.
11. Seale, J (2009), A Research Briefing by the Technology Enhanced Learning Phase of the Teaching and Learning Research Programme (PDF).
12. Weller, M. (2007), Virtual Learning Environments: Using, choosing and developing your VLE, London: Routledge.
13. *Modern Learning Environments*, by Mark Osborne (PDF, 3.1mb)
14. www.events.core-ed.org/modern-learning-environments

6

Web Based Learning Services

Introduction

This is the age of technology. Its influence is being reflected in all productive endeavours, whether it be an industry or an agricultural project. Education too, it being a developmental endeavour aiming at raising the level of productivity of a nation, has been very much influenced by the message of technology – this message being maximizing the output in both quality and quantity. Teaching is an art. The aim of teacher education is to acquire the knowledge and competency required to master that art. The shift of education from the 'Gurukula' system to the 'Learner – centered' approach has necessitated the acquisition of several competencies for successfully meeting the functions of instruction. The developments in the field of science and technology and the emergence of a number of significant theories of instruction have made scientific study of the instructional process essential. Students getting instructional facilities through online services are called **e-tutoring**. Students should have their own computer and an internet connection to get avail this service. Those who wish to avail the facility of e-tutoring should register themselves with the agency which provides this service, by paying the requisite fees. With quick advances in dispersed multimedia technology, the concept of real-time interactive distance learning has established more consideration than ever before. While conventional classroom activities are distinguished by their intrinsic geographical limitation, the initiation of distant e-learning applications has facilitated students to listen classes anywhere with an online computer. With existing commercial products of media applications, two chief categories are gladly valid for remote e-learning. In order to sustain the achievement of a specific educational objective, a learning service provider is provided. This is attained by producing a learning environment consisting of communication infrastructure, educational material, meeting places, educators, etc.

An emerging topic in software engineering is referred to as the component-based development 9 (CBD). The advantage of CBD technology discussed in (6) is its underlying software component model, which defines components and their composition mechanisms. In this work, the author survey and analyze current component models and classify them into a taxonomy based on commonly accepted desiderata for CBD. In spite of the materialization of the new creation of Web based learning systems, customary learning mode, where teachers and students are face to face with each other in an unchanged classroom persists to have its unequaled advantages. Not like many Web-based learning systems embracing an a synchronized way, the teacher brings out learning content statically on the Internet and students acquire static learning materials at diverse times, genuine classroom learning tracks a synchronized learning process, where students in and out of classroom pay attention to the reside instruction while the teacher gives the lectures. In the majority cases, synchronized learning capture participants' thought and attention much more efficiently than a synchronized one. As a result, real-time interactive classroom with tele-education experience is of requisite consequence in distance learning.

There are numerous issues arise in the design of a remote e-learning system. The bandwidth conditions are low, inefficient real time interactive data. But, classroom-based e-learning systems help both the teacher and students in the learning process and have achieved successful results. Even all web based learning services are provided interactive learning services more efficient, the main drawback is that if more number of service requests queued up, then is difficult to sustain and respond all those services for the students. To make an online tutoring scheme more efficient, middleware interactive components are built. Middleware is a software layer that locates between the network and the application to provide reusable solutions to regularly met problems like interoperability, security, heterogeneity. The main contribution of the present work is to build a component software framework which is described is section 2 briefly based on web services and learning object chosen by the students in an appropriate environment.

LSCM for online tutoring scheme through web services

The proposed learning software component model is designed to build a framework for online tutoring scheme which run under web services. It renders the communication services to applications like messaging, chatting etc,. The proposed LSCM architecture consists of two main strategies. The first strategy is to build a component model framework based on web related communication services. The second strategy is to provide the communication services through the LSC framework to the students participated in online tutoring schemes.

In the learning software component building strategy, the learning communication services are analyzed based on students' environment. The learning software component framework is built with learning services and each component is built with the learning objects chosen by the students. Each component contains as appropriate service based on respective students' level functionality. The second strategy is to process of communication services through the component invocation based on LO at the student required levels. Before delivering the service of the component to the students, the authorization of students are interpreted based on their skills. So, only the authorized and demanded communication services are delivered to respective environment application student.

Using learning software components of services, the framework is built which has several types of communication services like messaging, chatting etc. Based on interactive component based middleware service architecture, the components are built with the services and it efficiently achieved the interoperability service on providing a learning service to the students. The proposed component based middleware service architecture consumes less time for building the components and less storage services.

Learning Software Component Building phase

The LSCM is built based on the learning services provided by the online tutoring scheme. Based on communication services like messaging, chatting and the component are built with an appropriate service and LSC model. The process of LSCM is:

Step 1: Input: Different types of web services

Step 2 : Analyze the type of services

Step 2.1 : Communication services: Messaging, chatting

Step 3 : Based on students' request to service

Step 3.1 : Invoke the services

Step 4 : Based on services

Step 4.1: Build structural components

Step 4.2 : Construct the set of components

Step 4.3 : Invoke the services for different set of components

Step 4.4 : Each components may have different set of services

Step 5 : Output : Build the components efficiently

The process of building the component framework based on communication services is described in steps. The applications may have several services to interact with the other services. Based upon the communication services, the component based middleware service architecture with corresponding components based communication services.

Steps to provide communication service through LSCM framework

The procedures below described the process of providing communication service through LSCM framework.

Step 1 : Based on learning object (LO)

Step 1.1 : Invoke the software component architecture from LSCM

Step 2 : Before delivering the service

Step 2.1 : Identify the authorization of the student, based on their skills

Step 3 : Deliver the demanded service component to the student

Based on communication service component, the component function is evaluated to show the coordinate value of the message event. Render the services to students' applications need. After rendering the services, only the authorized students can demand the services are applicable to the student environment.

Experimental Evaluation

The learning software component model (LSCM) is implemented by using the Java platform. The experiments were run on an Intel P-IV machine with 2 GB memory and 3 GHz dual processor CPU. The performing evaluation tests aimed at comparing the online tutoring scheme with challenging interactions through web services. LSCM framework is depended on interception. At set up it built the components based on communication services rendered. The service used with component building architecture to raise the online tutoring scheme more efficient. A LSCM framework carries two types of operations generic (building components based on LO, service rendering...). Operations can be assigned to different services and components in the infrastructure.

The performance of LSCM is evaluated by the following metrics:

1. Delivery report rate
2. Maintenance of tutoring sessions
3. Reliability

Results and Discussion

In this work, we have seen how a component can be designed for communication service composition to capture the common design patterns for online tutoring scheme written in mainstream languages such as Java. We run independent tests with growing number of applications, and number of students' service requests responded by each trainers is 30-35% requests per client. Many users are participated in the experimentation to validate LSCM. Comparison result of LSCM with an existing online tutoring through web services based on delivery report rate, measured in terms of milliseconds. When number of students' service requests applications increases, the delivery report rate based on communication services is high in the proposed LSCM contrast to an existing online tutoring scheme through web services. The performance graph of the proposed LSCM in component building phase is shown in the figure. The variance in the delivery report rate would be 12-20% high in the proposed LSCM. The maintenance of tutoring sessions even when number of user increases. Since the services are built as components framework, the maintenance of tutoring sessions was easy. When number of students' service requests applications increases, the maintenance of tutoring sessions is also being high in the proposed LSCM contrast to an existing online tutoring scheme through web services. The performance graph of the proposed LSCM in component building phase is shown in the figure. The variance in the maintenance would be 15-20% high in the proposed LSCM. The reliability of the proposed LSCM with an existing online tutoring scheme through web services. Various numbers of applications are used in the experimentation to improve the reliability of LSCM. Comparison result of LSCM with an existing online tutoring scheme through web services shows that the proposed LSCM perform better the reliability of the proposed LSCM also is improved.

Finally, it is observed that the proposed LSCM framework is efficiently built based on learning object and the web communication services are also rendered to users' based on their environment. The reliability and performance rate also be improved in the proposed LSCM framework.

Conclusion

The progression of proposed LSCM for online tutoring has showed us that the growth of a suitable culture for online tutoring is rapidly high. According to the users' need, the learning services are offered to the students by building the component for communication services efficiently. The middleware interactive service components are developed from building the service components efficiently. A desirable feature of the proposed LSCM framework is high maintenance of tutoring session based on communication services. LSCM with service rendering approach allows trainers to interact with the students based on learning object aspects and communication services. The experimental results showed that the improved performance of delivery time, maintenance rate and reliability.

References

1. Yue suo, Naoki Miyata, Hiroki Morikawa, Toru Ishida, and Yuanchun Shi, "Open smart classroom: Extensible and scalable Learning System in Smart Space Using Web Service Technology", IEEE transactions on knowledge and data engineering , Vol.21, no.6, June 2009
2. N. Friesen, A. Roberts, and S.Fisher, "Cancore: Metadata for learning objects". Canadian Journal of Learning and Technology, 28(3):43-53, 2002.
3. Ke Zhou, Gui-Rong Xue, "Learning with positive and Unlabeled Examples using Topic-sensitive PLSA", IEEE Transactions on knowledge and data engineering, vol.22, no.1 January 2010.
4. Alrifai, M., Dolog, p., Balke, W.T.Nejdl,W.L3S Res. Center, Leibniz University of Hannover, Hannover, Germany, "Distributed management of concurrent web service transactions ", IEEE Transactions on services computing vol.2, December 2009.
5. Qianxiang Wang Jin Shao Fang Deng Yonggang Liu Min Li Jun Han Hong Mei Sch. Of Electron Eng & Comput. Sci., peking Univ., Beijing, China, "An online monitoring Approach

for web service requirements" IEEE transactions on services computing vol.2, Dec 2009.

6. Kung-Kiu Lau and Zheng Wang, "Software component models" IEEE transactions on software engineering, vol.33, no.10 oct 2007.

7. M. sintek and S. Decker, " Triple – a query, inference, and transformation language for the semantic Web Conference (ISWC 2002), saridinia, Italia, June 2002.

8. L. Stojanovic, S. Staab, and R.Studer, "E-learning based on the semantic web". In proceedings of the world conference on the WWW and Internet WebNet 2001, Orlando, Florida, USA, 2001.

9. H. Allert, C. Richter and W. Nejdl, "Learning objects and the semantic web explicitly modeling instructional theories and paradigms". In proceedings of e-learn 2002: World conference on e-learning in corporate, Government, Healthcare & Higher education (formerly the webnet conference), Montreal, Canada, Oct. 2002.

10. A Maedche and S. Staab, "Services on the move – towards p2p – enabled semantic web services". In proceedings of the tenth international conference on information technology and travel & tourism, Enter 2003, Helsinki, Jan. 2003.

11. Fryer, W and John Couch, "Delivering measurable achievement", NECC presentation Retrieved April 24, 2006, from http://webpages.acs.ttu.edu/wfryer/necc2003/couch.html

12. Addison Wesley, the tutor center. Retrieved September 20, 2005 from http://www.aw-bc.com/tutorcenter/index.html

13. Christ, F.L, "Achieving student retention, satisfaction and success through online pedagogy". A presentation at TechEd, California state University, Long Beach, February 2002.

14. ebXML, Business process specification scheme http://www.ebxml.org/specs/ebBPSS.pdf

15. Doherty. B and Atkinson, M, " A pilot study of online tutoring using smarthinking". PowerPoint presentation. Retrieved June 15, 2004 from http://www.smartthinking.com

16. Mr. M. Balakrishnan and Dr. K. Duraiswamy, "Learning Software Component Model for online Tutoring", published in International Journal of Computational Intelligence and Informatics, Vol.1 : No.2, July – September 2011.

7

Teacher Education

Introduction

Educational systems around the world are under increasing pressure to use new information and communication technologies (ICTs) to teach students the knowledge and skills they need in the 21st century. It should be accepted that teachers are vital players in any initiative aimed at improving teaching and learning processes. Moreover, ICYs at schools will have little impact if teachers are not actively involved in all phases of their integration to the curriculum (Hepp et. al 2004) Therefore the role of teacher at this point is vital. It is known that teachers do not have time to thoroughly evaluate the educational strengths and weaknesses of a considerable portion of the existing curriculum materials, software and texts before they are used.

In the new phase of the knowledge revaluation the source of knowledge has shifted from one source to a different source. In other words, we can say that there is a decentralization of the knowledge source is a need facilitate on ICTs for teacher both at the pre service level and in service level. ICT comprise a complex and heterogeneous set of good application and services used to produce, process, distribute and transform information. ICT embody a full range of old and new technologies such as e-mail and internet services, telephones, fax, scanner, printer, photocopiers, radio, television and mobile.

Information and communication technologies (ICTs) are a major factor in shaping the new global economy and producing rapid changes in society. Within the decade, the new ICT tools have fundamentally changed the way people communicate and do business. Thay produced significant transformation in industry, agriculture, medicine, business, engineering and other fields. They also have how learning takes place and the roles of students and teachers in the learning process. It is clear that ICTs can provide powerful tools to help learners access vast knowledge resources, collaborate with others, consult with experts, share knowledge. And solve complex problems using cognitive tools. ICTs also provide learners with text, images, graphics, and video. Therefore question arises automatically –How can we promote the use of ICT in teacher education? Teaching is becoming one of the most challenging professions in our society where knowledge is expanding rapidly and much of it is available to students as well as teachers at the same time (Perraton, Robinson and Creed, 2001). As new concepts of learning have evolved, teachers are expected to facilitate learning and make it meaningful to individual learners rather than just to provide knowledge and skills. Recent developments of innovative technologies have provided new possibilities to teaching profession but at the same time have placed more demands on teachers to learn how to use these technologies in their teaching. (Robinson and Latchem, 2003).

ICT in teacher education

1. The first and foremost thing that needs done is to develop a positive towards the processes and products of ICT. For this purpose, attempt should be earnestly initiated to develop a culture that value ICT. The students should be made to appreciate the fruits of ICT.
2. Use of ACTIONS model i.e.

Access; Cost; Teaching requirements; Interaction; Organization; Novelty; Speed.

3. Access; The fact that educators need access to current technologies, software, and networks. However, this access must be consistent across all the environments that are part of the preparation of teachers. Access should be adequate and consistent throughout the educational experience of students in the process of becoming teachers. Access must be in classrooms as well as lab settings, and provisions must be made for special populations. Creative partnerships are often required to make this happen. Additionally, there needs to be access to technology appropriate to the subject areas being studied, such as word processing programs and Internet access in in English, or computer labs and microscopes for science labs. Otherwise, opportunities to use technology tools for teaching students or communication tools mentoring or staying connected with parents will be limited.
4. Support Policies: - Policies can either support or hinder the implementation of technology. As decision – makers develop new policies; they must consider how the policies affect acquisition of and access to technology. Some major barriers to the use of technology relate to faculty expectations about incentives and rewards structures. The expectation for the use of technology must cut across all subject areas and techer preparation contexts so that faculty and teacher candidates are assure that their work will be valued. A key element is access to computer network (Lawson Comber, 2000) We can see that our different Learning Management Systems work as a catalyst for working with more ICT in the course. And in learning environments in our colleges where computers are rare, digital networks are not complete and other important technical equipment (e.g. digital cameras and projectors) are missing, we also find less development of ICT used for learning in the courses. The institutions need to have well-reasoned information technology strategies, including issues.
5. Shared Vision-From the administration to the grounds personnel, there is an understanding of commitment to, and

sense of advocacy for the implementation of a technology. When the implementation of a technology initiative is problematic, a major reason often cited is a breakdown in the common understanding of the institution's goals among those who hold the decision–making power. These situation can occur over something as simple as unlocking the door to a lab, or as complex as modifying existing operational budgets to provide allocations for technology funding. Facilitating the integration of technology may require a change in policy or rules, and the decision–makers have to be willing to look at the situation, and ensure communication among all parties. The cooperative environment necessary for creating a shared vision is also needed to sustain that vision.

6. Increasing the investment in new hardware, software, network access and educational content for higher education institutions.

7. Develop ICT infrastructure within the higher education institutions and provide in –house training through e-learning systems.

8. Providing incentives for those instructors that use ICT in their daily training.

9. Developing strategies that support online education and make sure that the employees are loyal to the teachers and students to carry out the teaching-learning tasks using the mechanism of ICT. For this purpose, an institution can venture to create an effective on-line learning course proving as a substitute for the live classroom instruction or use its bewsite as a tool for providing appropriate support to the traditional classroom and school activities. For this, some points should be considered.

10. It must fit to the age, level, clearly defined instructional objectives and local needs.

11. Provision for an interactive element in the website which enable students to interact with their teachers. Options for self-puzzles or simulations should be included in the websites.

12. Make provision for the due enrichment of the website from time to time as per need.
13. Utilize the institution website as a communication tool to connect with other institutions of the region or country for the exchange of information and enhancing learning experiences.
14. Use the services for making contacts to the parents and society. It will surely provide a proper platform for seeking involvement of parents and the society for the enhancement of e-learning facilities.

ICT pedagogy approach

This approach emphasizes on integrating ICT skills in respective subjects, drawing on the principle of constructivism, pre-service teachers design lessons and activities that centre on the use of ICT tools that will foster the attainment of learning outcomes. This approach is useful to the extent that the skills enhance ICT literacy skills and the pedagogy allows student to further develop and maintain these skills in the context of designing classroom-based resources. Students who have undergone this type of training have reported significant changes in their understandings associated with effective implementation strategies, as well as their self-efficacy as to their ICT competencies.

Subject- specified approach: Here ICT is embedded into one's own subject area. By this method teachers not only expose students to new and innovative ways of learning, but also provide them with a practical understanding of what learning and teaching with ICT looks and feels like. In this way, ICT is not an 'add on', but an integral tool that is accessed by teachers and students across a wide range of the curricula.

Practice-driven approach: Here the emphasis is on providing exposure to use of ICT in practical aspects of teacher-training also. Emphasizing on developing lessons, assignments etc. using ICT and implementing these in their practical work experience at various levels, the students are provided with an opportunity to assess the facilities available at workplace and effectively use their own skills to manipulate these facilities. Based on the concept that the pre-service teacher is a learner, manager, designer and researcher, he is expected to research their practicum school's ICT facilities, design ICT activities with their tutor-teacher, manage those activities in the classroom, and evaluate their effectiveness in terms of student learning ideally, an integrated approach is to be followed for developing ICT skills in teaching. Whatever may be the approach followed in the institutions to develop knowledge about ICT, it has its own limitations and coupled with other reasons, they are not making student-teachers fully confident of using ICT in their day-to-day classrooms and other situations. In the opinion of authors, all the four approaches are required to develop awareness of expert level skills in student-teachers.

ICT Training Inputs for Teachers Education

For the successful implementation of ICT, teacher trainees, teachers and teacher- educators need to be trained in the following dimensions. The commercially available training programs are designed to provide exposure only to system software, some of the application software and the basics of internet.

1. **Awareness phase**: The input should be to make the teachers aware of the importance and possibilities of ICT-the current trends and future projections.
2. **Learning theories and technology integration**: Traditional and modern view of learning, shift from teaching to learning, constructivism, role of ICT in lifelong learning.
3. **Basic hardware skills** : Hands on experiences in operating a) the PC and laptops-switching on, shutting down, and networking, b) storage devices- using floppy drive, CD ROM drive, flash drive, and burning CD-ROM , c) output devices-using printers and speakers, d) input devices using keyboard (Including shortcuts), mouse, modem, scanners, web cam, digital camera, camcorders, date loggers and d) display devices- data projectors, and interactive white boards.
4. **Understanding system software**: Features of desktop, starting an application, resizing windows, organizing files

(Creating, editing, saving and renaming), switching between programs, copying etc.

5. **Using application/productivity software**: Word processing, spreadsheet, database, presentation, publishing, creation of Portable Document Format (PDF) files, test generation, data logging, image processing etc.
6. **Using multimedia:** Exposure to multimedia CD ROMs in different subject, installing programs, evaluating CD ROMs, approaches to using CD ROMs, creating multimedia presentations.
7. **Using internet: e-mail, communities, forums, blogging , wiki**: subscription to mailing lists, e-mail and internet projects, web searching strategies (navigating, searching, selecting, and saving information) videoconferencing, designing web pages, freeware and shareware, evaluating website resources, virtual fieldtrips, learning opportunities using the web, and netiquette.
8. **Pedagogical application of ICT tools**: Specific use of application software in different subject, appropriate ICT tools and pedagogy, unit plan integrating ICT tools, approaches to managing ICT-based learning groups, assessment of learning, electronic portfolio and assess men rubrics, creating teacher and student support materials, supporting students with special needs.
9. **Introduction to open source software**: Concept, types, advantages, working on open sources application software.
10. **Social, legal, ethical and health issues**: Advantages and limitations of computer use, privacy violations, copyright infringement, plagiarism, computer security (hacking, virus, misuse, abuseand staying safe) healthy use (seating, light, sound, radiation, exercise)
11. **ICT for professional and personal productivity:** ICT for administration, record keeping, reporting and transfer of information, attendance, research, careers in computers and professional development opportunities.

As an advanced training website development, installation and use of server based applications, training in course management system, e learning course content development using various authoring tools; audio/video/image editing, animation etc. can be introduced. In addition othehand son experiences every training program could include an ICT awareness /familiarity quiz, exhibitions of ICT books and multimedia CD ROMs by commercial agencies, poster session on success stories, case study presentations and analysis, ICT based demonstration lesson in the schools (whole class, small group, internet based, etc) exhibitions and presentations by commercial agencies on emerging technologies

Impact of ICT on Teacher-Education

1. It acts as the gateway to world of information and enables teachers to be Updated.
2. For professional development and awareness of innovative trends ininstructional methodologies, evaluation mechanism etc.
3. For effective implementation of certain student - centric methodologies such as project -based learning which puts the students in the role of active researches and technology becomes the appropriate tool.
4. It is an effective tool for information acquiring - thus students are encouraged to look for information from multiple sources and they are now more informed then before.
5. It has enabled better and swifter communication, presentation of ideas is more effective and relevant.
6. The dissemination of ideas to a larger mass now seems possible due to technology.
7. Student-teachers are transformed into self learners.
8. ICT creates awareness of recent methodologies and thus teacher educators feel empowered.

ICT pedagogy approach

This approach emphasizes on integrating ICT skills in respective subjects, drawing on the principle of constructivism, pre-service teachers design lessons and activities that centre on the use of ICT tools that will foster the attainment of learning outcomes. This approach is useful to the extent that the skills enhance ICT literacy skills and the pedagogy allows student to further develop and maintain these skills in the context of designing classroom-based resources. Students who have undergone this type of training have reported significant changes in their understandings associated with effective implementation strategies, as well as their self-efficacy as to their ICT competencies.

Subject- specified approach: Here ICT is embedded into one's own subject area. By this method teachers not only expose students to new and innovative ways of learning, but also provide them with a practical understanding of what learning and teaching with ICT looks and feels like. In this way, ICT is not an 'add on', but an integral tool that is accessed by teachers and students across a wide range of the curricula.

Practice-driven approach: Here the emphasis is on providing exposure to use of ICT in practical aspects of teacher-training also. Emphasizing on developing lessons, assignments etc. using ICT and implementing these in their practical work experience at various levels, the students are provided with an opportunity to assess the facilities available at workplace and effectively use their own skills to manipulate these facilities. Based on the concept that the pre-service teacher is a learner, manager, designer and researcher, he is expected to research their practicum school's ICT facilities, design ICT activities with their tutor-teacher, manage those activities in the classroom, and evaluate their effectiveness in terms of student learning ideally, an integrated approach is to be followed for developing ICT skills in teaching. Whatever may be the approach followed in the institutions to develop knowledge about ICT, it has its own limitations and coupled with other reasons, they are not making student-teachers fully confident of using ICT in their day-to-day classrooms and other situations. In the opinion of authors, all the four approaches are required to develop awareness of expert level skills in student-teachers.

ICT Training Inputs for Teachers Education

For the successful implementation of ICT, teacher trainees, teachers and teacher- educators need to be trained in the following dimensions. The commercially available training programs are designed to provide exposure only to system software, some of the application software and the basics of internet.

1. **Awareness phase**: The input should be to make the teachers aware of the importance and possibilities of ICT-the current trends and future projections.
2. **Learning theories and technology integration**: Traditional and modern view of learning, shift from teaching to learning, constructivism, role of ICT in lifelong learning.
3. **Basic hardware skills** : Hands on experiences in operating a) the PC and laptops-switching on, shutting down, and networking, b) storage devices- using floppy drive, CD ROM drive, flash drive, and burning CD-ROM, c) output devices-using printers and speakers, d) input devices-using keyboard (Including shortcuts), mouse, modem, scanners, web cam, digital camera, camcorders, date loggers and d) display devices- data projectors, and interactive white boards.
4. **Understanding system software**: Features of desktop, starting an application, resizing windows, organizing files (Creating, editing, saving and renaming), switching between programs, copying etc.
5. **Using application/productivity software**: Word processing, spreadsheet, database, presentation, publishing, creation of Portable Document Format (PDF) files, test generation, data logging, image processing etc.
6. **Using multimedia:** Exposure to multimedia CD ROMs in different subject, installing programs, evaluating CD ROMs, approaches to using CD ROMs, creating multimedia presentations.
7. **Using internet: e-mail, communities, forums, blogging, wiki**: subscription to mailing lists, e-mail and internet projects,

web searching strategies (navigating, searching, selecting, and saving information) videoconferencing, designing web pages, freeware and shareware, evaluating website resources, virtual fieldtrips, learning opportunities using the web, and netiquette.

8. **Pedagogical application of ICT tools**: Specific use of application software in different subject, appropriate ICT tools and pedagogy, unit plan integrating ICT tools, approaches to managing ICT-based learning groups, assessment of learning, electronic portfolio and assessment rubrics, creating teacher and student support materials, supporting students with special needs.
9. **Introduction to open source software**: Concept, types, advantages, working on open sources application software.
10. **Social, legal, ethical and health issues**: Advantages and limitations of computer use, privacy violations, copyright infringement, plagiarism, computer security (hacking, virus, misuse, abuse and staying safe) healthy use (seating, light, sound, radiation, exercise)
11. **ICT for professional and personal productivity:** ICT for administration, record keeping, reporting and transfer of information, attendance, research, careers in computers and professional development opportunities.

As an advanced training website development, installation and use of server based applications, training in course management system, e learning course content development using various authoring tools; audio/video /image editing, animation etc. can be introduced. In addition to the hands on experiences every training program could include an ICT awareness /familiarity quiz, exhibitions of ICT books and multimedia CD ROMs by commercial agencies, poster session on success stories, case study presentations and analysis, ICT based demonstration lesson in the schools (whole class, small group, internet based, etc) exhibitions and presentations by commercial agencies on emerging technologies

Impact of ICT on Teacher-Education

1. It acts as the gateway to world of information and enables teachers to be updated.
2. For professional development and awareness of innovative trends in instructional methodologies, evaluation mechanism etc.
3. For effective implementation of certain student - centric methodologies such as project -based learning which puts the students in the role of active researches and technology becomes the appropriate tool.
4. It is an effective tool for information acquiring - thus students are encouraged to look for information from multiple sources and they are now more informed then before.
5. It has enabled better and swifter communication, presentation of ideas is more effective and relevant.
6. The dissemination of ideas to a larger mass now seems possible due to technology.
7. Student-teachers are transformed into self learners.
8. ICT creates awareness of recent methodologies and thus teacher educators feel empowered.

ICT pedagogy approach

This approach emphasizes on integrating ICT skills in respective subjects, drawing on the principle of constructivism, pre-service teachers design lessons and activities that centre on the use of ICT tools that will foster the attainment of learning outcomes. This approach is useful to the extent that the skills enhance ICT literacy skills and the pedagogy allows student to further develop and maintain these skills in the context of designing classroom-based resources. Students who have undergone this type of training have reported significant changes in their understandings associated with effective implementation strategies, as well as their self-efficacy as to their ICT competencies.

Subject-specified approach: Here ICT is embedded into one's own subject area. By this method teachers not only expose students to new and innovative ways of learning, but also provide them with a practical understanding of what learning and teaching with ICT looks and feels like. In this way, ICT is not an 'add on', but an integral tool that is accessed by teachers and students across a wide range of the curricula.

Practice-driven approach: Here the emphasis is on providing exposure to use of ICT in practical aspects of teacher-training also. Emphasizing on developing lessons, assignments etc. using ICT and implementing these in their practical work experience at various levels, the students are provided with an opportunity to assess the facilities available at workplace and effectively use their own skills to manipulate these facilities. Based on the concept that the pre-service teacher is a learner, manager, designer and researcher, he is expected to research their practicum school's ICT facilities, design ICT activities with their tutor-teacher, manage those activities in the classroom, and evaluate their effectiveness in terms of student learning ideally, an integrated approach is to be followed for developing ICT skills in teaching. Whatever may be the approach followed in the institutions to develop knowledge about ICT, it has its own limitations and coupled with other reasons, they are not making student-teachers fully confident of using ICT in their day-to-day classrooms and other situations. In the opinion of authors, all the four approaches are required to develop awareness of expert level skills in student-teachers.

ICT Training Inputs for Teachers Education

For the successful implementation of ICT, teacher trainees, teachers and teacher- educators need to be trained in the following dimensions. The commercially available training programs are designed to provide exposure only to system software, some of the application software and the basics of internet.

1. **Awareness phase**: The input should be to make the teachers aware of the importance and possibilities of ICT-the current trends and future projections.
2. **Learning theories and technology integration**: Traditional and modern view of learning, shift from teaching to learning, constructivism, role of ICT in lifelong learning.

3. **Basic hardware skills** : Hands on experiences in operating a) the PC and laptops-switching on, shutting down, and networking, b) storage devices- using floppy drive, CD ROM drive, flash drive, and burning CD-ROM, c) output devices-using printers and speakers, d) input devices-using keyboard (Including shortcuts), mouse, modem, scanners, web cam, digital camera, camcorders, date loggers and d) display devices-data projectors, and interactive white boards.

4. **Understanding system software**: Features of desktop, starting an application, resizing windows, organizing files (Creating, editing, saving and renaming), switching between programs, copying etc.

5. **Using application/productivity software**: Word processing, spreadsheet, database, presentation, publishing, creation of Portable Document Format (PDF) files, test generation, data logging, image processing etc.

6. **Using multimedia:** Exposure to multimedia CD ROMs in different subject, installing programs, evaluating CD ROMs, approaches to using CD ROMs, creating multimedia presentations.

7. **Using internet: e-mail, communities, forums, blogging, wiki**: subscription to mailing lists, e-mail and internet projects, web searching strategies (navigating, searching, selecting, and saving information) videoconferencing, designing web pages, freeware and shareware, evaluating website resources, virtual fieldtrips, learning opportunities using the web, and netiquette.

8 **Pedagogical application of ICT tools**: Specific use of application software in different subject, appropriate ICT tools and pedagogy, unit plan integrating ICT tools, approaches to managing ICT-based learning groups, assessment of learning, electronic portfolio and assessment rubrics, creating teacher and student support materials, supporting students with special needs.

9. **Introduction to open source software**: Concept, types, advantages, working on open sources application software.
10. **Social, legal, ethical and health issues**: Advantages and limitations of computer use, privacy violations, copyright infringement, plagiarism, computer security (hacking, virus, misuse, abuse and staying safe) healthy use (seating, light, sound, radiation, exercise)
11. **ICT for professional and personal productivity:** ICT for administration, record keeping, reporting and transfer of information, attendance, research, careers in computers and professional development opportunities.

As an advanced training website development, installation and use of server based applications, training in course management system, e learning course content development using various authoring tools, audio/video /image editing, animation etc. can be introduced. In addition to the hands on experiences every training program could include an ICT awareness /familiarity quiz, exhibitions of ICT books and multimedia CD ROMs by commercial agencies, poster session on success stories, case study presentations and analysis, ICT based demonstration lesson in the schools (whole class, small group, internet based, etc) exhibitions and presentations by commercial agencies on emerging technologies

8

Blended Learning

Introduction

Blended Learning refers to a mixing of different learning environments. Blended learning gives learners and teachers a potential environment to learn and teach more effectively. Our Blended Learning approach to instruction stems from the best practices, research, and experience available in the field of education today. We developed our revolutionary approach because we know that children learn best when exposed to different methods and approaches to instruction. The blended approach to instruction has seen a steady increase in the past years, and survey data indicates that administrators in higher education expect that trend to continue. An instructor can begin a course with a well-structured introductory lesson in the classroom, and then proceed with follow-up materials online. Blended learning can also be applied to the integration of e-learning with a Learning Management System using computers in a physical classroom, along with face-to-face instruction· Guidance is suggested early in the process, to be used more sparingly as learners gain expertise.

Blended Learning refers to a mixing of different learning environments. The phrase has many specific meanings based upon the context in which it is used. Blended learning gives learners and teachers a potential environment to learn and teach more effectively.

Whether a course should be proposed as a face-to-face interaction, an online course or a blended course depends on the analysis of the competences at stake, the nature and location of the audience, and the resources available. Depending on the cross-analysis of these 3 parameters, the course designer will opt for one of the 3 options. In his course scenario he/she will then have to decide which parts are online, which parts are offline? A basic example of this is a course of English as a second language where the instructor reaches the conclusion that all audio-based activities (listening comprehension, oral expression) will take place in the classroom where all text-based activities will take place online (reading comprehension, essays writing).

Blended learning increases the options for greater quality and quantity of human interaction in a learning environment. Blended learning offers learners the opportunity "to be both together and apart." A community of learners can interact at anytime and anywhere because of the benefits that computer-mediated educational tools provide. Blended learning provides a 'good' mix of technologies and interactions, resulting in a socially supported, constructive, learning experience; this is especially significant given the profound effect that it could have on distance learning.

Blended Learning is learning which combines online and face-to-face approaches. The following material resulted from an ANTA-funded project which set out to investigate blended learning through a series of interviews with teachers. A blended learning program uses a combination of e-learning and classroom instruction. Independent schools that teach English as a second language and TOEFL / TOEIC prep are using this learning solution to save time, lower costs, and improve quality of service to students.

Kaplan, one of the world's largest private education providers, sees blended learning as an essential part of its business strategy: Our Blended Learning approach to instruction stems from the best practices, research, and experience available in the field of education today. We developed our revolutionary approach because we know that children learn best when exposed to different methods and approaches to instruction.

Defining Blended Learning

There are brick and mortar options, such as coaching, classes, and mentoring. Then there are electronic options, ranging from e-learning classes, to on-line help systems, to templates, decision support tools, and knowledge bases. E-learning gurus Elliot Maisie and Brandon Hall recognize the many options and encourages combined systems, which they call 'brick and click,' or 'blended' learning" (Rossett & Sheldon, 2001).

Blended Learning can combine the positive aspects of the two learning environments, classroom-based learning and e-Learning (Bonk & Graham, 2006). However, some experts are now taking a broader view in that it goes beyond e-learning and classrooms:

Blended learning is a mix of delivery methods that have been selected and fashioned to accommodate the various learning needs of a diverse audience in a variety of subjects. This method can include any combination of any of the above delivery methods (McSporran & King 2002).

'The integrated combination of traditional learning with web based on-line approaches'. This is, arguably, the classic definition of the term. 'Traditional learning' here is classroom teaching or 'face-to-face' language lessons. The delivery of the online part of the course is usually through learning technologies, typically involving a Virtual Learning Environment (VLE) such as 'Blackboard' or 'Moodle' and comprising the use of synchronous and asynchronous electronic tools, such as, respectively, 'chat' and 'bulletin boards'.

'The combination of media and tools employed in an e-learning environment'. This definition could describe a purely distance learning course, where no face-to-face lessons occur. Communication between the learner and e-tutor may take place through any number of technologies, such as email and internet telephone.

'The combination of a number of pedagogic approaches, irrespective of the learning technology used'. A course that combines 'transmission' and 'constructivist' approaches would fit into this category, such as one involving elements of a present-practice-produce methodology as well as task-based learning.

The term continues to develop. A further possible conceptualization of BL is as 'a combination of real world plus in-world', where a teacher delivers a face-to-face lesson and then arranges to meet his or her student for a follow-up class in a virtual world such as 'Second Life'.

Furthermore, computer-assisted language learning in general has been described as 'context specific', and a number of local uses of the term 'BL' also exist within various educational settings, both national and institutional. For example, as some governments switch from course books to CD Rom or web-based material, the term has been applied to the blending (or combination) of print and digital materials.

There are also a number of 'dimensions' associated with definitions of BL, such as 'breadth' and 'connotation'.

Thus, *Blended Learning* is the use of two or more distinct methods of training. This may include combinations such:

1. blending classroom instruction with on-line instruction
2. blending on-line instruction with access to a coach or faculty member
3. blending simulations with structured courses
4. blending on-the-job training with brown bag informal sessions
5. blending managerial coaching with e-learning activities

The Growth of Blended Learning

The blended approach to instruction has seen a steady increase in the past years, and survey data indicates that administrators in higher education expect that trend to continue. According to the Handbook of Blended Learning, a majority of respondents in a 2006 survey expect a dramatic rise in the use of blended learning as an instructional format, eventually encompassing 40% of course offerings within the next 6 years.

Research from the University of Central Florida has indicated that faculty and student satisfaction with BL is high, and that the majority of both students and instructors would be willing to participate in future blended courses based on their past experiences with the format.

The Appeal of Blended Learning

Why has a blended approach been welcomed by faculty and students?

From a pedagogical perspective, blended learning's aim to join the best of classroom face-to-face learning experiences with the best of online learning experiences allows for:

1. An increase is learning outcome measures and lowering of attrition rates vs. fully online courses (Dziuban, Hartman & Moskal, 2004).
2. An opportunity for students to practice technology skills in navigating online course materials and possibility creating digital content for assignments.
3. An increase in student-instructor and student-student interaction through the use of course communication tools like discussion forums.
4. The ability to reserve face-to-face time for interactive activities, such as higher-level discussions, small group work, debates, demonstrations, or lab activities.

From a student perspective, the appeal of blended learning includes:

1. Flexibility of schedule: learn any-time, anywhere.
2. Control: students have some level of control over the pacing of their learning. Difficult concepts can be reviewed as often as necessary.
3. Convenience of an online class with many of the social aspects of a face-to-face class.

Format of Blended Learning

When choosing to explore blended learning as a course format, there are several dimensions to course planning and development that should be considered:

Technology Just like online courses, hybrid/blended courses are dependent on several technologies to function. These can include:

1. learning management systems
2. digital libraries
3. mobile technologies
4. streaming audio and/or video media
5. reusable learning objects and materials

Integration

Online materials are central to a blended course's success, and the students' work online must be relevant to the in-class activities. Aycock, Garnham, & Kaleta (2002) at the University of Wisconsin's blended learning effort revealed the importance of integration:

"The project's participants emphasized this point repeatedly. When asked, 'What would I do differently?' they were united in their response: 'I'd devote more attention to integrating what was going on in the classroom with the online work.' This was true even though the project's faculty development sessions repeatedly emphasized the importance of connecting in-class material with out-of-class assignments. One instructor responded emphatically, 'Integrate online with face-to-face, so there aren't two separate courses.' We found it impossible to stress integrating face-to-face and online learning too much."

Students can be critical of blended instruction if they felt the face-to-face and time-out-of-class components of the course were not well integrated.

Organization

For the most part, the blended format will be new to students, and they will benefit greatly from a clear rationale for its use.

Instructors may need to explain the model and why it was chosen. A carefully constructed syllabus can provide much of the information about course structure for students; information like when and where the face-to-face meetings will be held, when and how assignments should be submitted, and what exactly will occur during the class meeting times are all critical aspects of the course that may not be obvious to those students new to blended learning.

Interaction

Research indicates that student satisfaction with the blended format is highly dependent on the level of interaction with instructors and other students. Instructors can address interaction issues by providing time during the face to face sessions for discussion, in addition to using available online discussion tools such as ANGEL discussion forums.

Student Expectations

Blended learning students require a greater ability to regulate their work and manage their own time. This is because they have fewer in-class meetings, and thus may not realize that they are falling behind in the course. Many blended instructors report significant problems with students not taking responsibility for their courses and with students' poor time management skills.

In addition, some instructors have found that students occasionally assume that online and blended courses are inherently "easier" than traditional face-to-face courses. This can create problems when the rigors of the course surpass the expectations of some students. Again, a well-constructed syllabus can provide the essential details on what exactly is expected of students, thereby mitigating possible confusion on the part of students.

Role of Instructor in Blended Learning

The instructor can combine two or more methods of teaching method. A typical example of blended learning methodology would be a combination of technology-based materials and face-to-face sessions to present content. An instructor can begin a course with a well-structured introductory lesson in the classroom, and then proceed with follow-up materials online. Blended learning can also be applied to the integration of e-learning with a Learning Management System using computers in a physical classroom, along with face-to-face instruction· Guidance is suggested early in the process, to be used more sparingly as learners gain expertise

The role of the instructor is critical as this requires a transformation process to that of learning facilitator. Quite often, with the increase of baby boomers going back to school and pursuing higher education the skills required for technology use are limited. Instructors then find themselves more in the role of assisting students with computer skills and applications, helping them access the internet, and encouraging them to be independent learners. Blended learning takes time for both the instructor and learner to adapt to this relatively new instructional concept.

Conclusion

Learning requires some sort of experience to take place. And the experience may be quite different for each learner in that we have to consider differences in (Banathy, 1968):

1. interest spans
2. needs
3. aptitudes
4. achievements
5. variations of time needed to master a specific learning task
6. abilities to deal with abstractness or concreteness
7. degree to which a learner needs to be guided
8. abilities to deal with complexities
9. abilities to manipulate objects (such as equipment or machines)
10. the degree to which imaginations can be involved
11. degrees to motivate creativity
12. problem solving differences

A systems approach to instruction implies a scientific study of the kind of instruction required by each learner, the time when it is needed, and the appropriate design, organization, and operation of a system which can achieve behavioral goals. In its broadest sense, an instructional system is a set of interrelated components (not aids or adjuncts) in mutual interaction.

Thus, good instruction provides individual learning experiences within the learning environment by using a mixture of media, strategies, and methods. These learning experiences promote interactions that allow the learners to recall information so that it may be remembered and combine it with other experiences so that new knowledge bases may be formed.

References

1. Pellowe, Adams, Elliott, Murrell, and Cox, "The use of a blended learning infection prevention programme in the pre-registration nursing curriculum", Journal of Infection Prevention, v.11, UU, Pp.55 – 57, 2010.
2. Smeekens, Broekhuijsen-van Henten, Sittig, Russel, and Van de Putte., "Successful blended learning programme on the detection of child abuse in Emergency Departments: a randomised controlled trial", Arch. Dis. Child., 2011.
3. Zainab, "Book Review: Blended Learning: Tools for Teaching and Training by Barbara Allan 2007", Journal of Librarianship and Information Science, 2008.

9

Designing Learning Environment of Tomorrow

Introduction

Education is the moment to moment experience of the humanity at large. To envisage it, one needs to know the meaning of learning better. Learning depends mainly on three factors, student's interest, teacher's ability and their environment. Increasing the standard of learning means increasing student's interest, diversifying teacher's ability and providing a suitable environment or milieu. Can Innovation, Education and Technology be the Ingredients for a better Society in Generating Employment?

Innovation, Education and Technology

Innovation is a driver of growth and well-being. New technologies, products, services and organizations create jobs and rejuvenate industries – while making others obsolete (out-dated). To reap the gains of innovation, policy makers need to understand, how we innovate the way for change process and what this implies for education and training policies. There is a need for integration of technology in education for innovations and creativity to bloom out of the box. "We've been on the brink (threshold) of radical transformation in education for about 20 years now," says Eylan Ezekiel, digital engagement consultant for *ON School.* The benefits and restrictions of technology and its help in innovation on education are numerous and evident to all of us. But the question that remains us is "how" to do the integration of the same. One strategy can be a step-wise amalgamation of technology with innovation, thus progressively making the learning more productive and 'better'. This can be better said as enhancing the quality of education through increased personalization, precision and introduction of latest Ed-tech knowledge and practices.

Technology with the help of Internet today, gives the perfect personalization and exposure. Thus students can have more interactive sessions and a better environment. Competition is a great motivator and thus broadcasting is one method to bring students with various intelligence levels and combine them for one greater good, ***"Great brains work Miracles"***. This will help in increasing the interests of students all-round the year and making them thinkers, rather than just listeners. Today the task of integrating innovation and education for building a creative society and by the by generating employment-beyond digital age, one has to have more and more facilities and potentialities /nature with prompt methods and means to achieve the same. As discussed, for an improved learning one needs to have better environment/nurture /milieu too.

It is clearly evident that these three major ingredients **(Innovation, Education and Technology)** are highly needed together for any significant improvement in the learning of children. But the methods to do so, largely depends upon the situation and available resources for the institutions. The benefits and restrictions of technology and its help in innovation on education are numerous and evident to all of us. But the question of hour that remaining us is what about" and "how" that we have to make the 'Designing Learning Environment of Tomorrow'.

The Three Trends in Higher Education

There are three trends on the horizon in higher education. Leading educators shared their **insights and innovative programs** – three dominant themes emerged, 1) The competency based learning, 2) The personalized student learning and 3) The changing role of the instructor. Each presenter shared extensive research in an area of his or her expertise and details of an innovative educational program. That program provides a non-traditional education that defies the status quo. The summary of the trends so designed to provide the readers with a strong practico - practical ideas and ideals for application to their own area of study or work with specialization.

The Competency Based Learning Vs Seat Time

Western Governors University introduced the radical idea of competency based learning in 1997 and was one of the first fully online universitys that did not require classroom attendance; fast forward to 2012 and competency based learning appears to be in the future of higher education. Learning that focuses on measurable outcomes is becoming a reality as technology facilitates self-paced and adaptive learning platforms, and employers lament about the skill- gap that recent college graduates cannot fill. Responsive companies are partnering with education start-ups to create competency learning programs that address the skills needed for 21st century employees.

The Idea of 'Seat Time' is in peril. Key highlights for these are below

(1) Employers are coming up with innovative ways to address the skill-gap. Companies including **Google and Microsoft** have partnered with University to create classes in **3D graphics,** appropriate development and more– needed skills that they cannot find even in the recent college graduates **(Ripley, 2012).** Educomp and TATA Edge are the companies also recruit teachers for software preparations at present.

(2) Southern New Hampshire University [SNHU]-The goal of SNHU is to provide affordable quality education, "to reduce costs, increase access and provide transformational experiences for students who have been marginalized by traditional higher education".

(3) The colleges are partnering with employers to create programs that not only provide academic preparation but career skills. The New Community Colleges opened its doors with an innovative program designed to link classroom learning to career experiences in the community.

(4) Another new university that looks promising a platform to allow students to progress through course work at their own pace. Students learn by spending as little or as much time as needed to master the content. The goal of the schools is to provide affordable education to anyone, anywhere at any time.

Personalized Student Learning

'Learning, your way' is the new motto for numerous higher education institutions across the country, and significant ones too. The University of Central Florida [UCF] that allows students to choose between five learning modalities, customizing their learning based upon their needs. Students expect to be able to learn anytime and anywhere in their chosen institutions, and numerous schools including UCF are responding.

(1) At UCF and University of Wisconsin, Milwaukee (UWM) students customize their schedule from a choice of many learning modalities. The school's web page features the options for learning, "Flexible and Convenient Online, Evening, Weekend and Hybrid Classes to Accommodate Any Schedule."

(2) Research suggests that 'learning is learning' to students regardless of modality. To students, "a course, is a course, modality makes no difference" at all (Cavanaugh, 2012).

Therefore, the colleges will need to address the needs of the life-long learner, not just the college student where schools have traditionally told students when and where they need to go to learn. Students of all ages want to be able to learn anytime and anywhere at times convenient for them. Think of all students as life-long learners, and offer students' choices of learning when, how and where they want.

The Changing Role of the Instructor

To focus on this Microsoft issue, UNESCO convened a two-day meeting in November 2011 to bring together 30 knowledgeable participants from more than 10 countries to discuss about the accessible technology for students and report on practical solutions for educators. All participants were deeply knowledgeable about accessibility and technology use in schools, including teachers, school administrators and experts from the IT industry and representatives from organizations with a focus on disability issues also.

The professor is no longer the *only* source of knowledge for students. The traditional method of knowledge transfer–the lecture, where the course instructor transfers knowledge [content] to student, is being augmented or replaced by other 'nodes' of information. Nodes are content sources, and might be a video, website, textbook, subject matter expert, or e-resource. Subsequently the teaching paradigm is shifting, students can access content, can learn from a variety of sources (Downes, 2012). The instructor role is thus changing, and in some institutions, the instructor role is being replaced with a mentor or advisor. Students in this model tend to take charge of their learning and use mentors, peers and study groups as support mechanisms for their learning goals.

(1) University now, "*peer-to-peer learning communities where students share their knowledge and skills, and help each other obtain recognized degrees and credentials*".

(2) The program at SNHU (Southern New Hampshire University) about Innovation states that University *"won't have instructors in the traditional sense. Pathways (*program at Innovation) *will employ advisors to help students establish goals and set their learning pace*".

Therefore, higher education still needs experts, and students need role models, leaders and mentors. Acknowledging that students can access content and expertise from a variety of sources which suggests that the course instructor is no less important. Now the instructor's role shifts to one of *guide* or *mentor*, who is influencing, shaping and inspiring students to become educated, life-long learners.

3. The Time is Now to Move to Competency-Based Teacher Professional Development:

At the Recent Education World Forum in London, UNESCO's Director General Irena Bokova, recalled the attention that she announced a new version of the UNESCO ICT (information and communication Technology) Competency Framework for Teachers. This framework identifies key competencies that enable teachers to help prepare a 21st century workforce by using ICT in the classroom. The recent researches show that helping teachers in their challenge of combining ICT with innovative teaching practices that strongly predicts students' acquisition of 21st century skills, the challenge continues to be helping teacher's develop the competencies needed to combine great learning activities with meaningful and relevant use of ICTs.

There are many challenges to Effective Professional Development of ICT integration

(1) Many teachers are aware that they should integrate ICT into their teaching practices, but they are uncertain as to, what that actually it is meant for?

(2) The absence of a common internationally recognized standard in the area of ICT integration and the devoid of a training based on those standards that prevents in having a consistent method to assess teacher competency.

(3) "One size fits all" training fails to address the needs of individuals. Teachers within the one school itself will have very different needs. While some may have never used a computer, others will be using multiple devices and applications to achieve desired outcomes.

(4) Mandatory training which is not at all relevant. But the teacher's self-assessment and their personal planning of their own development, increases the likelihood that what is presented actually will result in a change in their teaching strategies by diminishing their resistance to training.

(5) The ability to have large scale of face-to-face effective professional development to reach all teachers in a country is a frightening and expensive endeavor.

One appreciable response to these challenges is the VERY NEW Partners in Teaching-Learning with Technology Curriculum, now offered via Microsoft IT Academy. Microsoft has worked in partnership with governments, colleges of education and subject matter experts from around the world, to create a curriculum which includes a range of learning scenarios and is associated with the global standards of the UNESCO ICT-CFT (computer facilitation technique) with Technology Literacy Approach.

Rethinking Innovation in Education

The renowned innovative ICT specialized educationist Anthony Salcito said that he had the pleasure of attending the Worldwide Innovation Summit for Education (WISE), held in Doha, Qatar recently. This is the third year Microsoft e-summit and it continues to be a very valuable K-20 conversation among the state of education around the world on, "Rethinking Innovation in Education." Here one of the things he (Anthony Salcito) tried to do in his comments was disconnect innovation with technology, because too often it's synonymous for schools...as people think about innovation, they jump too quickly to technology as the solution.

The opportunity to share information and get access to information anywhere, anytime, anyplace, is a game changer that fundamentally will have a huge role in the future. The great teaching that makes sure that the kids are properly motivated to succeed a holistic approach. Hence Technology can support, enable all of those things, but technology alone is not going to overcome a bad teacher or a bad environment.

The other issue we have to think about is as it relates to the technology itself, because in many cases the technology will evolve to create a new opportunity for learning. Most of what we have done with technology in schools all over the United States and the world has been to automate the passive learning models and modalities. So we have taken classrooms and turned them virtual. We have taken tests and turned them online. We have taken books and created electronic books. While all these transitions are valuable and helpful, they don't provide any transformative experience other than moving from a piece of paper to a digital screen or a phone conversation to a text message. And while the value and efficiencies can support schools and help budgets, but the learning process is not transformed so far.

Then what can make a change? How technology is applied to create much more responsive, reactive and personal learning environments? The answers to these questions are as such;

To create the settings to connect students to quality of content and information that previously was unavailable,

To refine learning to respond predictive to a learner's need based on learning styles, test scores, etc. And when all these aforesaid elements come into play, learning retention increases, test scores potentially increase, and we have more and more of engaged and motivated students with creativity and transformative talents in building a creative society for generating employment in this meta-digital age.

Accept Innovation with Open Arms

To Teacher

Teachers, you must explore your opportunities. Challenge your administrators to let you try new things. Teaching is all about learning, both for you and the students. Don't feel constrained by your textbooks or curriculum, but rather try to adopt new methods that so what complement them. You know your goals; the path you take to get to your goal is entirely up to you. We have said it before repeatedly and we too will say it again and again:

Teaching is an Art

To the Administrator

Administrators, you should know WHAT's happening now. The only thing certain is, if you are not innovating, you are losing your popularity in no time. You do not necessarily need to pioneer change, but do not be the force that holds your teachers back. You have hired great people and allowed them to set goals. Now let them go out and are great. If they come to you with new tools and ideas, and a burning look in their eye, certainly they are onto something. Do not take hold of every innovation insight, but listen and work with your teachers to move forward.

Observation

It is so correctly observed by Mr.Christensen that your best think is not layering technology on top of your current educational practices, but instead spinning off a few classes where technology is the primary driver of education. This is where true innovation can occur, and you can test the success on a small sample of audience and then extend it then and there.

Conclusion

That is why; this present inter-national Conference very rightly focuses its attention on building innovations for developing creative society and generating employability as it envisages that innovation is an indispensable one in the present day world. Like that creativity is the essence of human life that has made the progress ever since the inception of human beings in the world from Stone Age to Digital age. The time is now so reaped to think beyond digital age/meta-digital age.

Thus this meta-digital age has seen tremendous changes in the field of Education to have the high-tech classrooms. Teachers with software knowledge have become acquired the essential qualifications. The new kind of job demands the teachers to become the digital content developers, effective consumers, efficient disseminators for promoting meta- digital aged ultra-model creative society with E- content and digital learning materials, men, methods, modes, manners and modalities that may suit the ever-enshrining single global humanity with an ardent spirit and fervor in respecting the oneness of humanity.

References

1. The report of the redical idea of competency based learning, Western Governors University1997.
2. Cavanaugh, the Directions of UCF(Univercity of Centrral Florida) and UWM(University of Wisconsin, Milwaukee) on the Modality of learning Corses, 2012.

3. The report of Downes, on the teaching Paradigm shift from instructor to mentor or Advisor, 2012.
4. Report of the Microsoft IT Academy, the global standards of Unesco ICT – CFI, Technology Literary Approach, 20145.
5. Technology and Education, Mind springs Enrichment Centre, 2012
6. Anthony Salcito, A turning Point for Education? - Trends to watch in 2012.
7. Anthony Salcito,JP Sa Couto and Critical Links at CES, 2012.
8. Anthony Salcito, Navigating the World via Bing and Microsoft Translator, 2012.
9. Anthony Salcito, Microsoft Technology preserving Local languages and Cultures. 2012.
10. Anthony Salcito, Join the new Partners in Learning Network Today and start spreading Ideas to improve Worldwide, 2012.

10

Effectiveness of Multimedia Programme in Perceiving Human Anatomy Among Higher Secondary Students

Introduction

Research work is being continuously done in the field of science and also in the related teaching methods and materials. In order to keep pace with the development of science, the need for new instructional strategies was greatly felt. One such innovative teaching strategy, called multimedia programme, has been chosen and studied by the investigator in this research work. Upgrading Biology curriculum by introducing Human anatomy demands a change in the instructional strategy. The need for developing an instructional strategy for teaching Human anatomy and physiology is very important to make the teachers and students aware of the scientific principles that govern the advances being made in medicine. The functions of the internal organs of human body can be easily explained through a multimedia programme. This also saves the use of expensive chemicals and sophisticated instruments which are beyond the reach of higher secondary schools. In schools, the required equipment to explain the human anatomy is not available. In this situation, the working mechanism of internal organs can be explained by a multimedia programme, which when used as an instructional strategy will make the task of learning human anatomy easier, effective and less expensive. The present study aims to find out the effectiveness of multimedia programme in perceiving human anatomy among higher secondary students in Tindivanam. A samples of 100 higher secondary students selected randomly were studied. A questionnaire method of survey was used to find out the effectiveness of multimedia programme in perceiving human anatomy. The data were collected by using questionnaire as an instrument. Primary data were collected by conducting direct structured interview using questionnaire. All the respondents were asked the same questions in the same fashion and they were informed the purpose of study. Mean, SD, and t-test analysis was applied to test the hypotheses. The findings and observations are the result and outcome of the interpretations made during the study of analysis. The result found that majority of the higher secondary students satisfied about multimedia programme.

In view of growing importance of science education, old concepts of science teaching have therefore, rather become completely outmoded and an entirely new ethos and approach to science curriculum have come into existence. Moreover, unprecedented development of scientific research, new discoveries, and new methods of investigation, in the early twentieth century, has created a need and urge to examine and reorganize science teaching programmes at all levels in schools. Institutions are functioning in an era of rapidly emerging new technologies. Some of them, like information and communications technology, have fuelled a veritable explosion of rising expectations everywhere. When such is the pace of developmental processes, it becomes fairly imperative on the part of the students not only to possess sound knowledge and understanding of fundamental concepts, but also to understand and appreciate the ramifications of various developments in the field of science and technology, especially in the context of their future career. The situation underscores the significance of research in science education and it is time for the educationists to evolve a proper and appropriate strategy for teaching science.

At the Higher Secondary level, the science subject is divided into Physics, Chemistry, Botany, and Zoology according to Tamil Nadu State Board syllabus. Zoology deals with the life history, distribution, structure, reproduction, and importance of animals including Homosapiens, the human beings. 'Human anatomy' is one of the units of the Zoology subject. Human anatomy is the branch of anatomy devoted to the structure of the human body. In general the study of human anatomy helps the students to do their higher studies in Medicine, Physiotherapy, Nursing, Degree courses like B.Sc., Zoology, and Microbiology etc. Apart from acquiring the technical knowledge, it is necessary for human beings to know and control their own systems of their body for healthy life. Hence the investigator has selected the unit "human anatomy" to teach through multimedia programme for the higher secondary students in the present investigation.

An instructional or teaching strategy refers to a pattern of teaching act that serves to attain certain goals and to guard against others. An instructional strategy is a purposefully-conceived and determined plan of action. It also occupies a central position in formal education. Instructional strategies aim at establishing relationship between teaching inputs and learning outputs, mainly in terms of realizing the learning outcomes. Instructional strategies include teaching methods, approaches and techniques.

Methods of instruction may be teacher-centered such as Historical method, Biographical method, Lecture method, Lecture-demonstration method or pupil-centered method which includes group methods such as project method, discussion, seminar and workshop. The pupil-centered methods also include individual methods such as programmed instruction, Computer Aided Instruction, Instructional Modules and Multimedia packages.

Review of Literature

Chang, Kuo-En et al. (2008) studied the effects of learning support in simulation-based physics learning. The results of the study revealed that the outcome for learning about the basic characteristics of an optical lens was significantly better for simulation-based learning than for laboratory learning.

Djeassilane (2008) investigated the effect of computer aided instruction (CAI) in enhancing the academic achievement of higher secondary students in commerce. The findings of the study showed that the computer aided instruction was effective in helping the students of the experimental group to perform better in the post-test. It proved the effectiveness of the computer aided instruction in commerce developed by the investigator. And also it was found that the experimental students had more favourable attitude towards computer assisted instruction.

Garnett, Hackling and Oliver (2009) developed an interactive multimedia package to improve students' understanding of the particulate basis of chemical reaction, and their ability to interpret chemical equations and solve problems based on equations. The study showed that Interactive multimedia provided learners with access to a rich information source and appropriate activities to promote learning and understanding.

Junaidu, Sahalu (2009) studied effectiveness of multimedia in learning & teaching data structures online. This paper explores and reports on the importance of creating multimedia-rich course content and the important role that animations can play in creating a successful online learning experience. Results indicated that students consistently perform much better in questions requiring application of material taught in carefully animated algorithms. These results should carry over to other educational environments.

Liao, Yuen-kuang C., Chang, Huei-wen and Chen, Yu-wen (2009) compared the effects of computer applications (i.e., computer-assisted instruction, computer simulations, and Web-based learning) versus traditional instruction on elementary school students' achievement in Taiwan. The results suggest that computer application instruction is more effective than traditional instruction for elementary school students in Taiwan.

O'Day, Danton (2010) studied on "using animations to teach biology: past & future research on the attributes that underlie pedagogically sound animations". Multiple technical resources (commonly referred to as multimedia) are currently used by many instructors to communicate difficult topics and concepts to their students in meaningful ways. Various sources have shown that animations are more effective than static sequential images. This study evaluated how animations can be and have been used as effective teaching and learning tools in biology and what more needs to be done to understand their true value.

Ozmen, Haluk (2010) studied on "The influence of CAI on students' conceptual understanding of chemical Bonding and attitude towards chemistry: A case for Turkey". The results of this study suggested that teaching-learning of topics in chemistry related to chemical bonding can be improved by the use of computer-assisted teaching materials.

Ponraj and Nellaiyapen (2010) investigated the effectiveness of CAI in teaching Zoology. The major finding of the study showed that the experimental group performed better than the Control group in the post-test. The results of the study revealed that experimental method of teaching is more effective than the traditional method of teaching the topic 'Nucleus' in Zoology.

Pryor, Caroline and Bitter, Gary (2010) used multimedia to teach in-service teachers and studied its impacts on learning, application, and retention. The study found that the video modeling in the module was effective in helping teachers learn, and discourse strategies were learned, applied, and retained.

Rotbain, Marbach-Ad and Stavy (2011) used a computer animation to teach high school molecular biology. The achievements of the experimental group were compared with those of a control group. Analysis of the post-test showed that the mean score of the experimental group was significantly higher than the mean score of the control group.

Venkataraman (2011) prepared software packages (CAI) for XI standard physics and studied the effectiveness of it's among selected modes of CAI in physics in relation to learners' personality. The results of the study showed that the CAI is effective with different modes. Computer Assisted Instruction shows significant difference in the achievement of different instructional objectives. Further Computer Assisted Instruction enhances the retention of the learnt content.

Vernadakis et al. (2012) examined the effect of multimedia computer-assisted instruction (MCAI), traditional instruction (TI), and combined instruction (CI) methods on learning the skill of shooting in basketball. Additionally, a comparison of the students' attitudes towards the MCAI and TI methods was made. Students took pre-, post-, and retention written test covering techniques and rules of the games. Post-test results indicated no significant differences between the groups concerning the written test. Nevertheless, the attitude test scores of the CI group were more favourable to MCAI method than the TI method. Retention test results showed that groups retained the knowledge acquisition. However, the combined method of instruction tended to be the most effective for cognitive learning.

Victor, Adeosun Olufemi (2012) investigated the relative effects of three multi-media instructional packages on Nigerian students' achievement in social studies. The purpose was to determine which of the combinations of videotape recording presentation, pictures and the chalk and talk method; the combination of audiotape recording presentation, pictures and the chalk and talk method and the combination of pictures and the chalk and talk method. The study revealed that the combination of pictures and the chalk and talk method was most effective among the packages tested in the learning of social studies.

Objectives

1. To develop a Multimedia Programme for the unit of Human anatomy from XI standard Zoology subject in order to teach the higher secondary students.
2. To find out the effectiveness of Multimedia Programme in teaching Human anatomy among higher secondary students.

Methodology

The methodology adopted for the study is explained in detail. The sampling technique, size of the sample, variables of the study, description of the tool used and administration of tool are elaborated.

Sample

A samples of 100 higher secondary students in selected randomly were studied in Tindivanam Town.

Data Collection

The present study aims at developing and using Multimedia programme for perceiving human anatomy for higher secondary students to enable them to understand the concepts very easily through individualized instructional technique. It is maintained that the Multimedia programme may reduce monotony in the classroom by bringing out real life situations and motivate them for self-study and provides opportunities for individual pace and ability.

The study intends to develop a multimedia programme for human anatomy for XI standard Zoology subject prescribed by Tamil Nadu State Board Syllabus and find out the effectiveness of the Multimedia programme through experimentation in perceiving human anatomy among the higher secondary students. The study provides scope for the development and use of many Multimedia programmes in the concerned discipline as well as other disciplines for the benefit of learners of different categories. Hence the multimedia programme can be used as an individualized instructional technique for the students of different categories in the science subjects as well as other subjects.

Analysis and Interpretation

Performance of control group students between the pre test and post test in human anatomy.

The Mean, Standard Deviation and Co-efficient of Variation were computed for the control group students in their performance in human anatomy between the pre test and post test.

Table 1

Distribution of Mean, Standard Deviation and Co-efficient of Variation on the performance of control group students between the pre test and post test in human anatomy

Group	N	Mean	S.D	CV
Pre test	100	42.69	13.60	31.86
Post test	100	52.46	13.28	25.31

The Co-efficient of Variation of the pre test and post test for the control group students was found to be 31.86 and 25.31, which reveals that the control group students are more consistent in their performance in human anatomy in the post test than the pre test. It reveals that the control group students have improved in their performance in human anatomy in the post test than the pre test.

To find out the significance of the difference between the control and experimental group students in their performance in human anatomy in the pre test, the 't' test was used.

Table 2

Distribution of 't' value between the control and experimental group students in their performance in human anatomy in the pre test

Group	N	Mean	S.D	't' value	Level of Significant
Control	100	42.69	13.60	0.17	p>0.05
Experimental	100	43.31	12.59		

There is no significant difference between the control and experimental group students in their performance in human anatomy in the pre test.

The obtained 't' value 0.17 is not statistically significant since it is less than the table 't' value 1.96 for 50 df at 0.05 level of significance. Hence the null hypothesis is accepted. It shows that there is no significant difference between the control and experimental group students in their performance in human anatomy in the pre test. It is therefore concluded that both control and experimental group students have the same level of performance in human anatomy in the pre test.

To find out the significance of the difference between the control and experimental group students in their performance in human anatomy in the post test, the 't' test was used.

Table 3

Distribution of 't' value between the control and experimental group students in their performance in human anatomy in the post test

Group	N	Mean	S.D	't' value	Level of Significant
Control	100	52.46	13.28	14.38	p<0.05
Experimental	100	92.81	5.31		

There is no significant difference between the control and experimental group students in their performance in human anatomy in the post test.

The obtained 't' value 14.38 is statistically significant since it is greater than the table 't' value 1.96 for 50 df at 0.05 level of significance. Hence the null hypothesis is rejected. It shows that there is significant difference between the control and experimental group students in their performance in human anatomy in the post test. It is therefore concluded that the experimental group students performed significantly better in human anatomy than that of control group students in the post test.

To find out the significance of the difference between the pre and post test mean scores of control group students in the performance in human anatomy, the 't' was used.

Table 4

Distribution of 't' value for the pre and post test mean scores of control group students in the performance in human anatomy

Group	N	Mean	S.D	't' value	Level of Significant
Pre test	100	42.69	13.60	2.62	p<0.05
Post test	100	52.46	13.28		

There is no significant difference between the pre and post test mean scores of control group students in the performance in human anatomy.

The obtained 't' value 2.62 is statistically significant since it is greater than the table 't' value 1.96 for 50 df at 0.05 level of significance. Hence the null hypothesis is rejected. It shows that there is significant difference between the pre and post test mean scores of control group students in the performance in human anatomy. It is therefore concluded that the control group students have improved in their performance in human anatomy in the post test.

Suggestions

The present study aims at developing and using Multimedia programme for perceiving human anatomy for higher secondary students to enable them to understand the concepts very easily through individualized instructional technique. It is maintained that the Multimedia programme may reduce monotony in the classroom by bringing out real life situations and motivate them for self-study and provides opportunities for individual pace and ability.

Conclusion

The study intends to develop a multimedia programme for human anatomy for XI standard Zoology subject prescribed by Tamil Nadu State Board Syllabus and find out the effectiveness of the Multimedia programme through experimentation in perceiving human anatomy among the higher secondary students. The study provides scope for the development and use of many Multimedia programmes in the concerned discipline as well as other disciplines for the benefit of learners of different categories. Hence the multimedia programme can be used as an individualized instructional technique for the students of different categories in the science subjects as well as other subjects.

The present study reveals that the experiment group students who used multimedia programme performed significantly better than that of the control group students who did not use, which implies that the multimedia programme has tremendous impact upon the performance in human anatomy than the students learning through traditional method. This proves the effectiveness of the multimedia programme in human anatomy developed by the investigator.

The present study reveals that the performance of the control and experimental group students in the post test is significantly higher than the pre test. But the performance of the experimental group students in the post test is more significantly higher than the post test performance of control group students. Thus, it proves the supremacy of the multimedia programme over traditional method.

References

1. Chang, Kuo-En; Chen, Yu-Lung; Lin, He-Yan; Sung, Yao-Ting (2008). Effects of learning support in simulation-based physics learning. Computers & Education, 51(4): 1486-1498.
2. Djeassilane, N. (2008). Effect of computer aided instruction (CAI) in enhancing the academic achievement of higher secondary students in commerce. Unpublished Doctoral Dissertation, Alagappa University, Karaikudi.
3. Garnett, P., Hackling, M., & Oliver, R. (2009). Designing interactive multimedia materials to support concept development in beginning chemistry classes.
4. Junaidu, Sahalu (2009). Effectiveness of multimedia in learning & teaching data structures online. Turkish Online Journal of Distance Education-TOJDE, 9(4), Article 7. Retrieved March.
5. Liao, Yuen-kuang C., Chang, Huei-wen & Chen, Yu-wen (2009). Effects of Computer Applications on Elementary School Students' Achievement: A Meta-Analysis of Students in Taiwan. Computers in the Schools, 24(3-4): 43-64. Retrieved.
6. O'Day, Danton H. (2010). Using animations to teach biology: past & future research on the attributes that underlie pedagogically sound animations. The American Biology Teacher, 70(5):274-278. Retrieved March 20.
7. Ozmen, Haluk (2010). The influence of Computer-Assisted Instruction on students' conceptual understanding of chemical Bonding and Attitude toward chemistry: A case for Turkey. Computers and Education, 51(1): 423-438. Retrieved March.

8. Ponraj, P., & Nellaiyapen, N. O. (2010). CAI in teaching Zoology. Research and Reflections on Education, 6(2): 18-21.
9. Pryor, Caroline R., & Bitter, Gary G. (2010). Using multimedia to teach in-service teachers: Impacts on learning, application, and retention. Computers in Human Behavior, 24 (6): 2668-2681. Retrieved March.
10. Rotbain, Y., Marbach-Ad, G., & Stavy, R. (2011). Using a computer animation to teach high school molecular biology. Journal of Science Education and Technology, 17(1): 49 – 58. Retrieved March.
11. Venkataraman, S. (2011). Relative effectiveness among selected modes of CAI in physics in relation to learner's personality. Unpublished Doctoral Dissertation, Annamalai University. Chidambaram.
12. Vernadakis, N., Zetou, E., Tsitskari, E., Giannousi, M., & Kioumourtzoglou, E. (2012). Student attitude and learning outcomes of multimedia computer-assisted versus traditional instruction in basketball. Education and Information Technologies, 13(3): 167-183.
13. Victor, Adeosun Olufemi (2012). Relative effects of three Multi-Media Instructional Packages on Nigerian student's achievement in Social Studies. Pakistan Journal of Social Sciences, 5 (5): 415 – 420. Retrieved March.

11

Title of the Paper-learning Styles and Blended Learning

Introduction

Nowadays rapid and extensive developments in sciences and technology and emergence of modern perspectives on social, political, economic and cultural issues have brought essential changes in educational system and pedagogy methods. With the decline of behaviorist psychology and the advent of cognitive psychology, especially constructivist approach in learning, learners are considered as creators of their own learning and adopt their own learning styles rather than merely recipients of it. Learners must process information while receiving them and links it to previous experiences, organize their learning and apply them in new situations. Successful adaptation to information age and science and technology explosion requires one's ability and sufficient skills to pursuing information and analyzing it But the term 'blended learning' nowadays primarily means integrating the use of technology in course design and delivery. The most important features of the e-learning unfold as following: interesting, open access: any time-anywhere, varied information, self-learning mode etc: There are various concepts within e-learning.

Blended learning is one of them which can be used as a strategy of teaching.

Learning online nowadays has been growing as a mainstream educational approach 'maximizing access to and interactions with various knowledge sources' (Lee, 2002 including contents and human resources using the Internet. It has a range of new opportunities for learners and teachers.

Traditional classroom teaching methods are no longer effective to achieve current learning standards. Technological approaches alone can't provide students with deep and meaningful learning experience. But the combination of both can help an educational institution stand at the top. Students who have grown up with interactive technology do not pay attention to old traditional classroom lectures. What educators need to do is provide students with relevant and engaging learning experience. Traditional approaches become effective in enhancing education if and only if they are combined with technological approaches; for those educational institutions as well as educators who truly believe in the above principle, shifting to Blended learning is a very good solution.

Learning

Learning is a very complicated variable which is being affected by multiple factors such as intelligence, incentive, adequate environment, family and social parameters, quality of school and education, educator and etc. some type of intelligence e.g. emotional intelligence Learning can be defined by Burns (1995, p. 99) as "a relatively permanent change in behavior, including both observable activity and internal processes such as thinking, attitudes and emotions". Students have undertaken learning process by means of various processes such as reading, thinking, listening, observing, talking, writing etc. in both formal as well as informal ways. But the aforementioned description could not give neither how students learn nor do they account for why they teach (Brown, 2004).

Researchers have put more effort in the area of psychology in order to realize various perspectives and process of learning.

Behavioral psychologists like Pavlov, Tomdike, Watson and Skinner who made study on animal behavior supposed that the conditioning has believed to be a main reason for learning.

Learning in a structured educational setting may be thought of as a two-step process involving the reception and processing of informational. In the reception step, external information (observable through the senses) and internal information (arising introspectively) become available to students, who select the material they will process and ignore the rest. The processing step may involve simple memorization or inductive or deductive reasoning, reflection or action, and introspection or interaction with others. The outcome is that the material is either "learned" in one sense or another or not learned.

A learning-style model classifies students according to where they fit one a number of scales pertaining to the ways they receive and process information.

A student who favors intuitive over sensory perception, for example, would respond well to an instructor who emphasizes concepts (abstract content) rather than facts (concrete content); a student who favors visual perception would be most comfortable with an instructor who uses charts, pictures, and films.

Learning styles

Styles refer to a pervasive quality in a person's behavior, a component that persists even when the content changes (Fischer and Fischer 1979). People of all ages and intellectual capacities learn in a ways that differ dramatically (Dunn and Dunn, 1979). Some require virtually complete silence in their environment when they are concentrating, others can" block out"Extraneous sound: and still others need background sound when they are studying. Some students work and learn best alone and are distracted by other people: others achieve best in group settings with a large element of peer interaction. Some individuals appear to learn and remember best what they hear (an estimated 20to 30percent of school age children's are predominantly auditory): others are primarilyvisual (perhaps40%): still others are either tactual/kinesthetic, visual/

kinesthetic, or some combination of these senses(can estimated 30 to 40 percent)

Basic characteristics of learning styles

Recently, Reid (1995) reported the following basic characteristics of learning styles.

1. Learning style, learning strengths and weakness will vary from one individual to another. Thus each and everyone have a unique learning style.
2. Through the characteristics of learning style will be straight opposite to that of another learning style, they will exist on wide continuous.
3. Three styles are value – neutral in nature. As a result, no style is found to be inferior to another. However, the performance of the students from a US school system that gives importance to particular styles is identified to be better than students from other academic systems.
4. In general the learning styles of the students are determined by their learning strategies.
5. It is necessary to motivate the students to extend their learning styles to all situations so that they could deal with any kind of situations.
6. The teachers should support their students in identifying their learning strengths and weakness. This will be helpful to improve the performance of the students.

   Different types of dimensions and variable are associated with learning styles. As a result, the researchers face many challenges while examining the learning styles (Tyacke, 1998), the following challenges in analyzing the learning styles were reported by the researchers:

   Complex nature of the learning styles as well as the difficulties in analyzing the overall learning habits of an individual complicates the studies further.

7. Learners will not adopt the same learning style all the times. They will choose the style based on the context of learning.
8. The methodology involved in the process of knowledge transfer is biased in nature and it will be in favor of a particular type of learner (analytic) over another (global).
9. Despite these challenges, the researchers have attempted to examine the learning styles based on age, gender, field of study, educational qualification and culture.

Students learn in many ways – by seeing and hearing; reflecting and acting; reasoning logically and intuitively; memorizing and visualizing and drawing analogies and building mathematical models; steadily and in fits and starts.

How much a given student learns in a class I governed in part by that student's native ability and prior preparation but also by the compatibility of his or her learning style and the instructor's teaching style.Many people recognize that each person prefers different learning styled and techniques. Everyone has a mix of learning styles. Some people may find that they have a dominant style of learning, with far less use of the other styles. Others may find that they use different styles in different circumstances. There is no right mix. Hence the need arises that everyone may be of a great benefit to know what his or her particular style may be.

Using multiple learning styles and "multipleintelligence" for learning is a relatively new approach. Traditional schooling used (and continues to use) mainly linguistic and logical teaching methods. It also uses a limited range of learning and teaching techniques. Many schools still rely on classroom and book-based teaching, much repetition and pressured exams for reinforcement and review. So the need arises to know about the learning style that can help you plan learning strategies to better study, read effectively and get more out of our education

We meet these challenges through Blended learning

Blended learning is realized in teaching and learning environments where there is an effective integration of different modes of delivery, models of teaching and styles of learning as a result of adopting a strategic and systematic approach to the use of technology combined with the best features of face to face interaction. (Krause, 2007).

Blended learning

Blended learning is a formal education program in which a student learns at least in part through online delivery of content and instruction with some element of student control over time, place, path, and/or pace. The methodology behind blended learning is to combine classroom learning with mobile learning and online learning

Griffith has adopted the term 'blended learning' as the principal means of addressing the use of information and Communication Technologies (ICTs) to enhance its learning and teaching activities. In the Griffith context, the following definition is used to inform policy and practice in relation to blended learning.

A blended learning approach to instruction combines face – to – face classroom methods with computer-based/mediated activities, resulting in an integrated learning experience for students. Blended courses combine fact-to-face and online methods to varying degrees, depending on the discipline, the size of the class, student demographics, and the preferences of the instructor. There are no rules in place to prescribe what the ideal blend is.

For example, a blended approach to a traditional, fact-to-face course might mean that the class meets once per week instead of the usual three-session format. Learning activities that otherwise would have taken place during classroom time such as lectures, an in-class debate, and a quiz on audio and visual material can be moved online with the help of different tools.

Blended learning is about effectively integrating ICTs into course design to enhance the teaching and learning experiences for students and teachers by enabling them to engage in ways that would not normally be available or effective in their usual environment, whether it is primarily face-to-face or distance mode. In many cases the act of "blending" achieves better student experiences and outcomes, and more efficient teaching and course management practices. It can involve a mix of delivery modes, teaching approaches and learning styles.

Blended learning approaches and teaching:

Blended learning is gaining more and more attention from teachers. As schools adopt learning platforms, teachers want to know how to use them efficiently, and are turning to Blended learning in approaches for answer. Blended learning is a tool for every teacher. blended learning is gaining more and more attention from teachers. As schools adopt learning platforms, teachers want to know how to use them efficiently, and are turning to blended learning approaches for answer. Blended learning is a tool for every teach

Through many theoretical models of blended learning exist, at its core blended learning is incorporating the internet in the teaching and learning process. Many teachers already use the internet for communication and organization, but blended learning allows them to exploit its 'untapped potential' by using more advanced tools like online discussion boards and multimedia uploading.

"Blended learning is performing or conducting teaching in a combined classroom – the combination of the physical classroom and the virtual classroom. Use the traditional space and then add something to it". "Most teachers look at the two elements of blended learning – the physical and virtual classroom – as two separate things. But the value is in the combination, the combined classroom." Blended learning is about time management, but it's also a tool for getting to know the students better. It allows teachers to decide when and where to teach the curriculum. In short, blended learning gives teachers options, and it actually offers an extra classroom – the virtual one

Advances in technology provide new opportunities for teachers to design and deliver their courses in ways that support and enhance the teacher's role, the students' individual cognitive experiences, as well as the social environment; three key elements in successful learning and teaching. Blended learning technologies can:

1. Broaden the spaces and opportunities available for learning;
2. Support course management activities (e.g., communication, assessment submission, marking and feedback);
3. Support the provision of information and resources to students;

Engage and motivate students through interactivity and collaboration. So it is not just about using technology because it is available; blended learning is about finding better ways of supporting students in achieving the learning objectives and providing them with the best possible learning and teaching experiences, as well as supporting teachers in their role (including the management and administration of courses). Of course, the integration of blended learning in courses will naturally vary according to such factors as: discipline, year level, student characteristics and needs, course or program learning objectives, as well as the academic approach to teaching, and confidence and experience in using technology.

Advantages of blended approach

The goal of a blended approach is to leverage the best aspects of both fact-to-face and online instruction for the students, benefit. The advantage of using a blended approach is that instead of using classroom time for presentation of material, for example, teacher can use that time to engage students by handling and clarifying their questions, to help them apply what they view/listen to in lecture, and to work with each other in face-to-face or team problem – solving. As well, online activities and assessments can usually be completed at any time of day; anywhere the student has internet access.

Taking a blended learning approach to the course can be used to support face-to-face teaching, large group and small group learning self-directed learning, communication between the teacher and individual students or groups of students, as well as between students themselves. They can "blend" time (e.g., face-to-face vs. recorded lectures), place (small group tutorial on – campus vs. online discussion forum; traditional field trip vs. 'virtual' field trip using web sites and online chat with industry personnel), people (podcast of guest lecturers, or virtual classroom to include both on-campus and off-campus students), resources and activities (textbook vs., online readings; in-class vs. online quiz).

By using online web-based courses, several methods of instruction can be used and students can participate in identifying coursework according to the design that best suits their leaning style and preferences (White &Bridwell, 2004).

Conclusion

In recent years, many organizations have been investing heavily in integrating technology into the learning/teaching process. Nowadays, almost all corporate learners have access to computers and the Internet. When used in a structured way, blended learning can allow organizations to mix different teaching materials and tools into an effective, integrated learning experience, giving learners an opportunity to move from passive learning to active learning.

Human attributes are designed individually and collectively to encompass divergent degrees of learning and processing information. The ideology of learning styles was adapted to incorporate multiple ways of people respond, to think, see, hear, touch, rationalize, and formulate knowledge or learning (Dunn & Dunn, 1993). Learning styles have gained prime importance in our society

Once an individual's learning style has been identified using assessment tools, there is a reater appreciation, deeper insight, and a better understanding by professionals of the numerous ays individuals learn).an awareness of learning preferences and an understanding of individual learning styles can help educators develop instruction using multiple resources. The learner should also be knowledgeable of their learning styles or individual preferences of learning, so that optimum learning will occur and everyone who is involved in the learning process can feel successful (Honigsfeld& Dunn, 2006)..

Diversity is a key ingredient in the learning environment. Technology is a method of teaching used by educators to engage students in rich learning experiences and provide creative opportunities for learners to exercise a multitude of learning styles.

Colleges, universities, and instructors work cooperatively to design web-based courses to encompass students learning styles.

Adoption of blended learning in normal secondary schools is slow because the system is unreceptive to change and lacks the funds to properly implement the technological enhancements. Majority of the schools have not their own bildings. Students also tend to have limited access to the high-speed internet connections often required for the more sophisticated online learning programs.

Reference

1. A.V. NageshwaraRao.(2006), Effectiveness of Blended Learning, Journal of educational technology, I- manager, vol-3, p.30.
2. Badri Shahtalebi1, Hassan Javadi2, Relationship between Emotional Intelligence and LearningStyles of Students, 1Department of Educational sciences, Khorasgan (Isfahan) Branch, Islamic Azad University,Isfahan, Iran.
3. Blended Learningstategy(2009)-http//www.griffith.edu.au.
4. Charles R. graham,blended learning systems:definition, current trends, and future directions,brigham young university, usa.
5. GiaDaneka Kimbrough Johnson, (2008),learning styles and emotional intelligenceof the adult learner,Auburn University, Alabama.,May 10, 2008.
6. Shengjian Chen1, a ,Yun Lu2, The Negative Effects and Control of Blended Learning in University college,1Institute of Educational Technology, Qujing Normal University Qujing Yunnan,655011, China.

12

The Role of Virtual Classroom in Enhancing Teaching and Learning”

Introduction

With the ever-increasing popularity and accessibility of the Internet, it is only natural that the educational community should want to make use of this tremendous resource. Use of the Internet and Web are leading to significant changes in educational models. As this use of Internet is increasing, a traditional classroom has shifted to E-Learning. Thus, E-Learning can be defined an approach to facilitate and enhance learning by means of personal computers, multimedia components and the Internet. The growing popularity of E-Learning has introduced new terms to education, as Virtual Classroom, where student will be present with his professor and fellow learners in a classroom. They will not be present physically in the classroom but connected to the classroom via Internet. This new facet of life highly increases students of acquiring technological skills as they are exposed to the tools used for web-based learning, computer-based learning typically provided by Internet. This is extremely valuable since computers are becoming prevalent for future student. The present paper emphasizes on the role of virtual classroom in enhancing teaching and learning process.

With the advent of the Internet there has been much talk about how learning can now be delivered at a distance. With no need for individuals necessarily to attend face-to face courses. It is suggested that the Internet has the potential to open up learning to a wider audience by allowing a person to have greater flexibility regarding where, when and how they learn. This concept is often referred to in education as the *virtual classroom, virtual university* or *virtual learning environment.* A *virtual classroom* enables to bring learners from around the world together online in highly interactive virtual classes while greatly reducing the travel, time and expense of on-site teaching/training programs. It can be used as a solution for live delivery and interaction that addresses the entire process of creating and managing the teaching-learning process. It facilitates instructor and student in teaching-learning events, such as a seminar, online discussion or a live training for teachers or administrator in the school. In a traditional classroom, professor, students and fellow learners are present, similarly, the same set of participants are present in a virtual classroom. They can talk with each other alike the traditional classroom via chat. Similarly presenter uses whiteboard, gives notes/resources and gives presentation as given in traditional one. Thus, virtual classroom can be visualized as a classroom where a lecture or session is conducted using Internet. As this use of Internet is increasing, a traditional classroom has shifted to E-Learning. While advancements in communication tools were easily adapted to learning methods, it was the introduction of the personal computer and the development of the Internet that would create the most radical transformation in higher education.

Virtual Classroom

Virtual classroom is a computer medicated communication system. The need of gathering at one place for communication in traditional classroom is been overcome by virtual classroom, the main advantages of virtual classroom is that due to shrinking distance communication is improved. The architecture of virtual classroom is in *three* phase which include the normal instructor to classroom setup, classroom behind firewall setup and instructor to group of geographically dispersed student. The term virtual means a simulation of the real thing, *Virtual Classroom is a simulated classroom via Internet, which provides a convenient communication environment for distance learners just like traditional face-to-face classroom.* A virtual classroom allows learners to attend a class from anywhere in the world and aims to provide a learning experience that is similar to a real classroom. In a college setup, lectures are scheduled, students arrive on time; find their teachers, fellow learners, a blackboard or whiteboard, LCD projector, optionally a television screen with videos. Likewise, a Virtual Classroom is a scheduled, online, teacher-led training session where teachers and learners interact together using computers linked to a network such as the Internet. They will not be present physically in the classroom but connected to the classroom via Internet. Virtual classroom aims to simulate the experience of attending a class over the web. So everyone is able to see other participant virtually. *A virtual classroom is an advanced learning environment, created using internet, computers, supplicated video conferencing devices, in which either teacher is not physically present (for remote learning)or students are not present (distance education)in the classroom.* Virtual Classroom learning is an evolving way of learning where the learner attends LIVES lectures remotely on his/her computer terminal, given by the subject matter experts or instructors at other end, using Internet as the medium between the learner and instructor. As lectures are given LIVE on internet, the student gets to have the opportunity of asking his/her queries to the instructor at any instant. Most of the distance learning degree and training courses heavily rely on the concept of ***'Virtual Classroom'.*** As the learner is no more required to attend the lectures/sessions in person, this new method of learning helps keeping the lecture costs much lower than conventional classroom teaching without compromising on the quality of learning. This makes Distance learning much affordable compared to regular training courses. Virtual classroom is very multipurpose technology or platform which can be used for Webinars, Tuition, One-to-one training and tuition, mentoring, Interviews, Team meetings, Project meetings, demonstrations, staff or students meetings, Technical support, student service, On-line user communities. A virtual classroom enables to bring learners from around the world together online in highly interactive virtual classes while greatly reducing the travel, time, and expense of on-site teaching/training programs. It can be used as a solution for live delivery and interaction that addresses the entire process of creating and managing our teaching-learning process. In Virtual classroom commonly we find the tools like *Projector, LCDs, Server Machine, Video conferencing System and its accessories, High-Definition Multimedia Visualizer, Interactive Whiteboard or Touch Panel, Digital Canvas, High-Definition Cameras etc.* Thus, virtual classroom can be visualized as a classroom where a lecture or session is conducted using Internet. Rather than being built of steel and concrete, the Virtual Classroom consists of a set of group communication and work ***"spaces"*** and facilities that are constructed in software. Thus it is a ***"virtual facility"*** for interaction among members of class, rather than a physical space.

Objective of Virtual Classroom

The following are the objectives of virtual classroom:

1. To **support live on-line classes** for distance learning and remote education.
2. To **pool academic resources thereby** improving access to advanced educational experiences
3. To **improve the quality and effectiveness of education** by collaborative learning and teaching process.
4. To **hold and participate** in the meetings, webinars, Conferences/ Symposium /Workshop, interviews, etc. through video conferencing.
5. To **increase and improve** the accessibility of educational resources to the **persons with disabilities**

Different Users of Virtual Classroom

There are different classes of users of virtual classroom based on the roles that they play. When presenter enters in virtual classroom, he has different work to do than participant. Depending on the user type, virtual classroom takes different form for each user. These forms can be categorized depending on the user's role. These roles are as follows:

Facilities provided by presenter interface to Faculty

1. **Register new users :** Presenter as an administrator has to register new users that will be attending the session.
2. **Create a session :** Presenter has to decide the session time, users that will be invited for the session. While creating a session, he can specify the time and users of the particular session.
3. **Cancel a user registration :** If any registered user does not want to attend the session, presenter cancels his registration.
4. **Conduct Online presentation :** As a presenter, he conducts the session for participants. During presentation he performs various activities in the classroom. He can load the presentation slide that will be displayed to participants.
5. **Share Resources :** Presenter can add various resources to the session. It may be a file or just a simple web page link that participant can download at their end.
6. **Conduct Poll :** He can create a poll for participants. Also he can chat with participants.
7. **Explain concepts using Whiteboard :** He can use whiteboard to explain some of the topic, which may not be able to explain via presentations, or to solve any particular doubt asked by the participant.

Facilities provided by participant interface to students

1. **View online presentation:** When a participant joins the session, they can view the presentation (PowerPoint presentation slides or it may also include the snap of the whiteboard), which are conducted by the presenter in the virtual classroom.
2. **Public/Private Chat:** The participants can have a conversation with the fellow participants publicly or privately

via the chat feature available in the interface, the chat allows the participant to send the instant messages to the participants who are also attending the session. Participants can also send private messages to any of the participant but he is not allowed to send private messages to the presenter but can do so by using the hands up facility.

3. **Raise Hands:** Whenever any participant will have any doubt, then he can tell that to presenter by using the hands up facility available in the user interface of the participant, using this feature the participant can interact with the presenter via the private chat.

4. **Give Response to the polls:** The participants can answer the polls that are submitted by the presenter by using the "Submit Response" facility provided in the interface. The poll can be of type objective or it may be of Yes/No type. If the particular poll is public then participants can see response for that particular poll, else it will be kept hidden from the participant. The only presenter is able to see the response for private poll.

5. **Download Resources:** The resources that are been shared by the presenter can be downloaded by the participants at their machine. The resources can be the files which may include course material, e-book's etc, or it may be also web links which presenter may want the participants should refer.

Mode of Virtual Classroom Session

The presenter can create the session in the beginning & will conduct online presentation in the session. The participants can attend this session using the name of the session and view the presentation made by the presenter. In the session of the classroom, various functionalities that will be performed by the users are as follows:

1. **Agenda:** The presenter creates the agenda in the beginning of the session. This agenda specifies an outline of the session. The participants can only view the agenda in their main

window. The agenda will give him the idea about the topics that will be covered in the session.

2. **Presentation Area:** In the presenter interface, the presentation area allows presenter to upload the presentation file. It also allows him to navigate between the slides in the participant window, the presentation area will display the slide that the presenter is explaining.
3. **Whiteboard:** The presenter will be able to write, draw and highlight any particular area on the whiteboard. The white board will be consists of various components such as various shapes, lines, eraser, pointer, etc, using which he will be able explain the particular topic to the participants. The participants can view the whiteboard in their interface, but they will not be allowed to use it (they will not be allowed to make any changes to whiteboard). The changes made by the presenter on the whiteboard will be displayed to the participants.
4. **Shared Resources & Web links:** The presenter can share their resources using the load resources facility that will be present in the presenter interface. The resources will be files of type (doc, rtf, pdf) or web links (URL). The participants can download these shared resources on their machines, also they can refer the given web links using their web browser.
5. **Poll:** The presenter can ask the participant any question by using the poll functionality that will be of the objective or yes/no type question. The response of the poll will be public or private. If the response of any particular poll is private then the response will not be shown to the participants, only presenter will be able to see the response. The response will be shown in the vertical bar chart format. The participant will be able to submit his response to the poll submitted by presenter. Also, he can view the responses of the polls for which presenter has allowed permission to see the response by participants. The private responses will not be shown to the participants
6. **Chat:** The presenter will use the chat functionality to send text messages to the participants. He can send a message to

particular participant or to all participants. The participants will be able to send text messages to each other. But, he will not be able to send message to presenter directly. He can do it by using the hands-up facility.

7. **Hands-up:** The presenter interface will consist of hands-up list, which will display the names of the participants, which has raised their hands. Hands-up by participant indicates he has some doubt or question to be discussed with presenter. Participant will use the hands-up facility if he wants to ask some question or want to talk with presenter. He can use this facility to initiate the conversation with the presenter. After the participant uses the hands up facility, presenter will allow him to have a private chat with him.

8. **Participant list:** In the presenter interface, there will be the list of participants, which will consist of the names of the participants that will be attending the session. If the presenter has to eject any particular participant, then he can use the eject facility that will be available in presenter interface. In the participant interface, the list of participants will only show the names of the fellow participants that are attending the session.

Advantages of Virtual Classroom

Following are the advantages of Virtual classroom over traditional classroom model:

1. **Removal of geographical barriers (Anywhere learning):** A virtual classroom allows learners and teachers to attend a single live training session from any place in the world, provided they have a computer and Internet connection.

2. **Sessions can be recorded:** A virtual classroom has a facility to record the session so learners or teachers can replay it afterwards. Teachers can get an opportunity to review their own or their colleagues' performance. The entire classroom session can be recorded in video format and stored in library for future reference. This feature is extremely useful, especially for absent students, who can review the recordings later and

understand the concepts elaborated by the professors. Moreover, the students can also refer to the recordings for revision purpose, at their convenience.

3. **Quicker to organize:** Training can be organized more quickly than traditional classroom-based training. Classrooms and projectors do not need to be reserved; materials do not need to be distributed. The sessions are easier to schedule or reschedule since attendees will not be traveling to the venue of the session.

4. **Synchronous Learning:** In this type of learning process, students and professors connect and interact with each other in real time. This is indeed a very significant process where students get answers to their queries & questions then and there. Interaction with professors and peers makes the learning process interesting and enriching for students.

5. **Live Audio-Video Support:** Audio and video support both contribute towards the e-learning process in virtual classroom. Various tools are available for text-based chat- verbal interaction through audio conferencing and sharing of one's own video through web-camera. Professors can share their audio and video, thus establishing one-to-one relation with students. Moreover, the students asking questions can share their videos with the fellow students as well.

6. **White Board:** It is an alternative to the traditional blackboard method, used as a tool for drawing graphics or diagrams in virtual classroom. It comes handy when professor wants to visually explain any abstract concept.

7. **Sharing of Learning Resources and/or Desktop Screen:** The resource sharing feature in virtual classroom allows professors to share varied content in different formats with the students in real time while delivering lectures on various course topics. This resource sharing feature supports sharing of various file formats – MS-Word/Excel/ PowerPoint, PDF files, flash presentations, flash videos etc. While teaching, the professors can exhibit all the operations from the desk, by

sharing a particular application or the entire desktop. This resource sharing feature is extremely useful for sharing various course materials like topic notes, subject diagrams or graphs, explanatory videos etc. With this type of supportive and informative course material, learning becomes interesting and gives an interactive experience.

8. **Classroom Control by Professors & Active Student Participation:** In virtual classroom when professors deliver lectures to the students while explaining or elaborating concepts, ideally one sided process of communication is followed, and students are not permitted to talk/ express themselves at the same time in order to avoid chaotic situations. Though all the participants from the virtual classroom are connected through audio and/or video conference, the participation rights are controlled by the professors. During the lectures, in case the students come across a particular doubt or query, while the professors are explaining, the students can set their status to "raise hand" which indicates that the student has a question which needs to be addressed by the professor. However, only one student can ask question at a time, in order to avoid confusion as well as commotion and to maintain focus and clarity on queries asked. Since the professors have the control rights, they can respond to the question or else disable the status of "raise hand" and take the question at the end of the session.

9. **Multi-Level Fallback Mechanism for Class Continuation:** Virtual classroom is a web-based tool which is solely dependent on internet connectivity. If in the remotest possibilities, participants get disconnected from virtual classroom, there are various alternatives to keep the class active. The technical team operates the fallback mechanism. If the internet is intact, then with the pre-configured ***Skype*** accounts of all participants, a common Skype call is initiated to connect all participants to further carry on with the class. In case all the participants lose internet connectivity then the successive portion of the class is conducted through telephone.

10. **Live Tech Support:** With this feature, technical support representatives of the institutes or corporate organizations will be able to provide text based chat and live tech support to their users.
11. **Offers Any time Access:** Offer live classes, office hours, and group discussions at times that are convenient for instructors and students, not just when the physical facilities are available.
12. **Ensures Comprehension:** Ensure students understand their lessons by asking for immediate feedback, answering questions, and giving in-depth verbal explanations of complex material.
13. **Electronic whiteboard and polls, quizzes, and surveys:** A best practice of live instructions to regularly offer interactive exercises. By offering whiteboard exercises and asking polling questions, students will remain highly engaged.
14. **Flexible content area:** A variety of content types can be viewed such as PowerPoint, Word, Excel, HTML, WebPages, images, movie clips, PDF, Flash etc.
15. **Access to persons with disabilities:** Just because a student has a disability doesn't mean they shouldn't be able to attend live on-line class. Live and archived classes can be close-captioned for the **hearing impaired** persons while also reaching out to the **visually impaired persons** by offering numerous key board short cut keys, hotkeys and compatibility with most screen readers. These accessibility features will ensure this technology is inclusive to all.
16. **Create Community:** Create a sense of community among students and instructors who might not otherwise interact with one another.
17. **Public & private text chat:** Some students are more comfortable writing than speaking, and our chat messaging allows the shy student to communicate textually so they can participate with their more talkative classmates.

18. **For Participants**

    1. Offers the combined advantages of face-to-face interaction and distance learning.
    2. Enables working professionals who would like to acquire new skills and/or enhance their knowledge in their respective functions to do so without taking a career break.
    3. Offers those who missed obtaining a degree the chance to get one now from premier colleges without having to take leave from work or travel out of their hometown.
    4. Minimizes disruption to work as classes are conducted on weekends or at convenient timings during weekdays

19. **For Institutes**

    1. Increases the institute's reach to a vast and geographically dispersed pool of potential students across globe.
    2. Enables institutes to meet the demand for quality education, given the heavily skewed demand-supply ratio of students and educational institutes.
    3. Facilitates access to a network of Virtual Classrooms across different cities.
    4. Enables seamless delivery of lectures and supports display of PowerPoint/Audio/ Video/Animation presentations and usage of whiteboard.

Disadvantages of Virtual Classroom

Though it gives lots of advantages, it has some pitfalls also. *Following section describes some limitations of virtual classroom.*

1. **Teachers and students need to become familiar with the tools :** Teachers and students are familiar with the workings of a traditional classroom, that is, they understand the concepts of hand raising, the whiteboard, assignments, and so forth. With a virtual classroom, all attendees must become familiar with the way the virtual classroom works before virtual classroom based training starts.

2. **Time dependency for Live Sessions :** Attending virtual classroom training is restricted to a certain scheduled time.
3. **Infrastructure for the participants :** Personal Computer (PC) needs to be prepared Virtual classroom sessions need to be scheduled, teachers need to be invited, and participants' PCs need to be prepared.
4. **Technical Limitations :** Technical issues such as bandwidth, speed of the connection or power failure may create problem while presentation is going on.

Conclusion

The emergence of Virtual Classroom is arguably one of the most powerful tools available to the growing need for education. Virtual Classroom education is rapidly increasing and becoming as a viable alternative for traditional classrooms. A virtual classroom enables to bring learners from around the world together online in highly interactive virtual classes while greatly reducing the travel, time, and expense of on-site teaching/training programs. It can be used as a solution for live delivery and interaction that addresses the entire process of creating and managing our teaching-learning process. In the end, we can assume that the concept of ***'Virtual Classroom'*** is truly the way towards ***'Global learning'*** on web.

Reference

1. Aggarwal J.C. (1999), *Essential of Education Technology,* Vikas Publishers Pvt. Ltd., New Delhi.
2. Gupta Vikas (2004), *Comdex Computer Course kit,* Dreamtech, 19-A, Ansari Road, Daryganj, New Delhi-110002.
3. Jagannath Mohanty(1992), *Education Technology,* Deep and Deep Publication, F -159, Rajouri Garder, New Delhi-110027.
4. Mangal S. K. (2000), *Advanced Educational Technology,* Prentice –Hall of India Pvt. Ltd. New Delhi.
5. Meena Kumari Goswami (2008), *Educational Technology,* Asian Book Pvt. Ltd, New Delhi.

6. Microsoft Corporation-India (2003), *Partners in Learning*, Microsoft Corporation (India), Pvt. Ltd, 9th Floor, DLF Cyber Greens, Gurgaon-02.

7. NCTE (2009), *Organizing Teaching Learning Resources in Teacher Education Institution*, NCTE, New Delhi.

8. UNESCO (2012), *Information and Communication Technologies in Education: A curriculum for schools and Programme of Teacher Development*, www.unesco.org, Accessed from website.

9. Vanaja. M. (2009), *Educational Technology*, Neelkamal Publication Pvt. Ltd, Hyderabad.

13

Awareness on Digital Techniques Applying in Classroom Teaching for Present Generation Among Teacher Educators

Introduction

Education is the foundation stone of a Nation's intellectual power which steps its power profile. Thus, it is rightly said that it depends upon the quality of its Teachers. The destiny of India is being shaped in its classrooms. In class room Teaching, Digital Technology provides the opportunity to go beyond the class room boundaries to the outside world and events. Hence the Government is very keen in implementing the scheme of Teaching through computer in Government schools. When the Government is very much interested in the computer Teaching, It is essential that the Teachers must be well aware of the potentiality of the computer Technology. Hence the Investigators were interest to know the level of the Awareness on Digital Technology of Teacher Educators. It is a survey Research. The Investigators developed the opinion scale contains 40 statements with different dimensions such as Computer in Teaching Learning, Power point Presentation and Internet. Four points scale ranges from Strongly Agree, Agree, Strongly Disagree and Disagree was used.

Developed Opinionnarie was administered to 100 Teacher Educators who are working in various Colleges of Education in Perambalur and Trichy Districts. Gender, Locality and Subject they studied were taken as the variables. The collected data was using Statistical Analysis like Mean, SD and't' test which have revealed the varied results.

Modernization is generally regarded as a process of change of traditional society into a society based on technology. As Teaching has entered the Digital age over the last several years, Technology in the Classroom is an area that all Teachers and Students are Embracing. For Teachers who have taught many years before this can be a challenging one. There are many Computer lesson plans, CDs, DVDs, audio e -books and videos available that will help in the transition. Digital Technology in the Classroom involves a lot of time and focus in its infancy, but with the Computer Lesson plans mentioned, it will develop into a fun and creative learning experience for Students and new and exciting challenges for Teachers. The incorporation of Digital technology in the education sector is important to meet the challenges presented by new trends, especially with the Global Communication of Knowledge. It is essential that the Students become familiar with the concept and use of Computer Technology in order to equip them for future job market. Similarly, the teacher can achieve better quality in Teaching Methodology.

Rationale of the Study

Computer plays key role in Education. Learning through Computer is an interesting affair. Now–a-days Digital Technology in Education has become the essential part of the system. In fact Teacher must well aware of the potentiality of the Digital Technology. Government is very much interested in introducing Computer Technology in Class Room instruction in Teacher Education. Hence the Investigator was interested to know the level of Awareness on Digital techniques applying in classroom teaching for present generation among Teacher Educators.

Statement of the Problem

The important key words used in this problem were (i) **Awareness:**

Alertness, New Idea. (ii) **Digital Technology**: The Technology which is used to change the method of Class Room Teaching with the help of Electronic machines and Computer, (iii) **Teacher Educators** Teachers who are working in the Colleges of Education.

Overview of the Study Already Done

Asan(2003) studied on "Computer Technology Awareness by Elementary School Teachers: A Case Study from Turkey" and found that many Teachers were not computer users. At the same time Wheatley, (2003) also studied on increasing computer use in early childhood Teacher Education. The study was found that Teachers lacked a functional Computer Literacy Foundation to new Technology and skills. Nickish and Reinhard (1992) in their study "Teacher Anxiety toward Computer Technology" found that Urban Teachers are used Computer often than Rural Teachers. Sengamalam @ Vanathi (2013) Studied on Awareness on e learning among M.Ed scholars under Bharathidasan University, found that the awareness of scholars whose major subject is Science was found to be superior to the scholars with Arts as major subject.

Objectives of the Study

The objectives of the study were i) to measure the level of Awareness on Digital Technology among Teacher Educators. ii) To measure the level of significant difference on the Awareness on Digital Technology among Male and Female, Rural and Urban, Science and Arts group Teacher Educators.

Method and Materials

It is the Normative Survey method. Investigator constructed a Tool Awareness on Digital Techniques applying in Classroom Teaching for present generation among Teacher Educators. That consists of 40 statements with different dimensions such as Computer in Teaching Learning, Power point Presentation and Internet, which have four point scale such a Strongly Agree, Agree, Disagree and Strongly Disagree. After the Development of the Questionnaire, the Investigator distributed it to Teacher Educators for validation. Their valuable ideas were taken care. Then the questionnaire was given to 10 Teacher Educators by Test - Retest method. The obtained r value 0.84 reveals that the tool is reliable one. Investigators randomly selected 100 Teacher Educators from various Colleges of Education in Perambalur and Trichy Districts.

Analysis

The collected data was analysed by using different statistical technique like Mean, SD and 't' test. The results are given in the following Tables

Table: 1

Significant Difference on the Mean Scores of Male and Female Teacher Educators

S.No	Dimension	Gender	Mean	SD	t test	Remarks
1.	**Total**	Male Female	63.0 64.3	0.92 0.74	**7.38**	**S**
2.	**CTL**	Male Female	60.54 61.62	1.19 1.41	1.48	NS
3.	**PPT**	Male Female	65.04 61.24	3.89 0.98	**6.43**	**S**
4.	**INT**	Male Female	71.07 69.58	1.92 3.35	**2.38**	**S**

CTL – Computer in Teaching Learning **PPT** – Power Point Presentation
INT Internet **NS** - Not Significant **S** - Significant

From the above Table it is noted that the 't' values are significantly difference at 5% level of the Teacher Educators for Total, PPT(Power Point Presentation) and INT(Internet). Total, PPT (Power Point Presentation) and INT (Internet) the Mean score of Male Teacher Educators are higher than the Female Teacher Educators. In CTL(Computer in Teaching Learning) there is no significant difference at 5 % level of the Teacher Educators.

From the above Table, the calculated 't' values are revealing that there is no significant difference at 5% level for the dimensions CTL and PPT. But there exists significant difference at 5% level with respect to Total and INT. In the Total and INT the Mean score of the Rural Teacher Educators are higher having higher awareness on Digital Technology than the Urban Teacher Educators.

Table: 2

Significant Difference on the Mean Scores of Rural and Urban Teacher Educators

S.No	Dimension	Gender	Mean	SD	t test	Remarks
1.	**Total**	Rural Urban	64.76 3.07	0.837 0.823	**5.46**	**S**
2.	**CTL**	Rural Urban	60.74 63.18	1.61 0.989	1.69	NS
3.	**PPT**	Rural Urban	62.90 63.07	0.78 0.65	1.06	NS
4.	**INT**	Rural Urban	74.53 70.93	1.72 1.68	**3.62**	**S**

Table: 3

Significant Difference on the Mean Scores of Science and Arts Teacher Educators

S.No	Dimension	Subject	Mean	SD	t test	Remarks
1.	**Total**	Science Arts	63.83 64.31	0.929 0.779	1.21	NS
2.	**CTL**	Science Arts	62.43 61.28	1.06 1.11	**4.79**	**S**
3.	**PPT**	Science Arts	63.02 60.34	4.22 0.934	**3.27**	**S**
4.	**INT**	Science Arts	71.94 73.38	1.19 1.02	**6.03**	**S**

The Mean scores and the calculated 't' values from the above table shows that there is significant difference in all the mean score of CTL, PPT and INT at 5% level except Total. It can be understood that the level Awareness on Digital Technology among Teacher Educators are good in CTL , PPT and INT.

Results and Discussion

The salient findings of the study are i) All the Teacher Educators am having good Awareness on Digital Technology. ii) The Mean score of Male Teacher Educators are higher than the Female Teacher Educators towards Awareness on Digital Technology with respect to the dimensions such as Total, PPT and INT. iii) With regards to Locality, the Mean score of Rural Teacher Educators are higher than the Urban Teacher Educators towards Awareness on Digital Technology in Total and INT. iv) The Mean scores of Teacher Educators with respect to Science Subject are higher in CTL, PPT and Arts Teacher Educators are higher in INT.

The result shows that Gender, Locality and Subject of Teacher Educators were not the influencing factor in determining Awareness on Digital Technology. While considering the Gender, Male Teachers are having higher Awareness on Digital Technology than the Female Teachers. This is because Male Teacher Educators may have more time to work in the Computer but the Female Teachers have the commitment to look after their family. By this way Rural Teachers are having Good Awareness on Digital Technology than the Urban Teachers. This is due to the fact that Rural Teachers may show more interest to know about the new things. As well as Science Group Teacher Educators are show more awareness than Art Group Teacher Educators. It may be due to their subject knowledge.

Recommendations for Policy Makings

The result of this study shows that the Teacher Educators are having Good awareness on Digital Technology. Hence the usage of Computer must be increased to develop their practical knowledge. They are having more involvement in using Digital Technology in their class room Teaching. Effective teaching to promote better learning, proper orientation training Programme must be provided them to develop their knowledge in Digital Technology. The Government must ensure proper training to Teacher Educators to maintain Computers and Electronic things. Educational Authorities should create, improve and sustain the Awareness of Teacher Educators about Computer Knowledge. Teacher Educators should be encouraged by Administrators to use the stand alone Computer Applications in their Teachings. Using Internet application should be given special concentration, because, it empowers and enhance creativity. Digital Technology acts as a catalyst to support change in Teacher Pedagogy.

Conclusion

The Good Awareness on Computer Technology among Primary and Middle School Teachers will show the Conducing Climate towards

Educational Technology. The Instruction through Computer has been making wonders in the Class Room Activities. Hence Teachers must have Awareness on Computer Technology to get success and enjoy their Professions.

Reference

1. BEST,J.W,(2003). *Research in Education,* Prentice - Hall of India (P) Ltd., New Delhi.
2. LOKESH KOUL.(2005). *Methodology of Educational Research,* Vikas Publishing House (P) Ltd, New Delhi.
3. SINGH.Y.K,(2005). *Instructional Technology in Education,* P. P. H Publishing Corporation,NewDelhi-110002.
4. SAREEN.N, (2005). *Information and Communication Technology,* Anmol Publication Pvt.Ltd, New Delhi-110002.

14

Life Skill Learning for Mental Health

Introduction

Today's youth facing many problems similar to lack of self-esteem, self-confidence, anxiety and drug abuse, etc. There are many factor accomtable for the problems. Decreasing joint family structure, present examination system, Job opportunities, etc. This paper is focused towards the discussion of life skill learning to maintain mental health on the background of present scenario.

Life skills learning based education (LSLBE) has a long History of supporting child development and health promotion. In 1986 Ottawa charter for health promotion recognized life skills in term of making better health choices. The 1989 convention on the right of child (CRC) linked life skills to education by stating that education shows be directed toward the development of the child's fullest potential. The zoo Dakar world education conference took a position that all young people and adults have the human right to benefit from an education that include Learning to know, Learning to do, Learning to be, Learning to live together and Life skills in two out of the six goals.

Life skills learning based is now recognized as a methodology to address a variety of issues of child and youth development and the matic responses including as expressed in UNGAS on HIV/AIDS (2001) World Health Report (2003) World Programme for Human rights education (2004) undecided on education for sustainable development (2005), Un Secretary general's study on Violence against children (2006), 51th commission on the status of women (2006), and the world development report (2007). All these say that adults have the human right to benefit from an education that includes learning to know.

Definition of Learning

Our ability to learn from experience is the most fundamental process in the study of human behaviour. All our deeds and thoughts come out of our learning. Learning makes us to accumulate Knowledge which we pass on from one generation to the other. The world learning is a synonym of study and scholarship etc. Learning is a life lone mental process.

Psychologist defines learning in a broader sence (i.e) it is a process that results in any relatively permanent change in behaviour or behavior potential. That occurs as a result of practice or experience.

Life Skills

Self-awareness, empathy, decision making, problem solving, effective communication, Interpersonal relations, creative thinking, dealing with emotions, critical thinking, coping with stress.

Social Skills	Thinking Skills	Emotional Skills
Self-awareness, Effective communication, Interpersonal Relationship, empathy	Creative Thinking, Critical thinking, Decition Making, Problem Solving	Coping with emotion, Coping with stress

This classification shows us that life skills are fore the cognitive, effective and spiritual development of students. Today student's opposite many problems. This problem makes him mentally feeble. She/he lost their self confidence, self esteem. She/He is Intellectual but not have of emotional intelligence. All of us read/watch the news in paper/television that students make the suicide. When his father scrolled he or he gets low marks in the exam. Students look toward the parents and teacher for proper guidance but they are not capable for this because of many reason. Decrease of combined family, Cable culture, and revolution in technology, memory foundation examination system and social atmosphere disturbs the student's mental health. Life skill learning gives the proper direction to him about how to handle stress full situation without losing his mental health.

Sl.No.	Category of Life Skills	Sub Skills	Characteristics of mentally health Students
1.	Social Skills	Self-esteem and confidence awareness about strength and weakness goal setting self evolution, Self assessment and Self Monitoring verbal and non-verbal communication, Expressing respect for others contribution and different styles.	1. Health and easy going attitude towards their own selves fathers. 2. Realistic awareness of their own strength and weakness. 3. Optimistic about Life structure. 4. Healthy work habits and attitude towards work. 5. Capable of greeting along with people and develop healthy social relationship.
2.	Thinking Skills	Information gathering Skills, evaluating future consequences of present actions for self and others.Determining alternative solution to problems analyzing peer and media influences.	1. Able to solve the problems of daily life. 2. Ready to face challenges. 3. Try to learn new things and develop their capabilities.
3.	Emotional Skills	Anger management dealing with grief and Anxiety time management, Positive thinking, Confect Management.	Control over their own impulses, Thoughts, Habit and Emotions, Enjoy life and manage time well enough to relax and work, Enjoy Work, Play, and Entertainment and relaxation activities healthy sense of humor.

Definition of Mental Health

Above mention definition tells us that mental health is not a mere absence of disease or illness. Mental health has been progressively conceived as a psycho-social process in which the positive aspect takes centre stage rather than average behavior or illness, mental health is the feeling of well-being.

Conclusion

Life skills learning which are essential for students to live happy in his everyday life. With the help of these skills students will handle his pressure full situation with assurance. When Students take on mastery over these life skills. Learning this mental health will stay good. When their mental health leftovers good then can do this work qualitatively.

References

1. WHO (2004) 'Skills for Health' an important entry point for health promoting child, friend schools, Geneva.
2. Self learning key to new syllabus, artick in times of India.
3. Psychology for nursing students.

15

Blended Learning- A New Horizon of Holistic Education

Introduction

The education sector, where student-centric learning is the core aspects to take into consideration, is highly influenced by technology. There are two forms of affective learning methodologies, i.e., face to face learning methodologies and online learning methodologies. While each of these two modes of instruction has its advantages and disadvantages, the need would be for a method that will combine the positive features of both, and would provide both the educational institution and the student with competitive and learning advantages respectively. This need is being satisfied with the emergency of a new wave of learning called "hybrid or blended learning". Blended learning can make use of the powerful internet technology, and at the same time, provide the elements lacking in web based instructions such as engagement and social contact. Blended learning within a flexible-learning framework offers a unique opportunity to fully integrate pedagogy and technology with teaching and learning. It should also provide a wide choice to learners as per their self regulatory perception. It is essential to provide a good support and training model and should keep the cultural components also in mind. A blend which make the right balance between innovation and mass utility as well as which bridge the digital divided will be the successful blended learning model.

Blended learning which is also called hybrid learning is a blend of both class room or face to face learning and online learning (Garrisen and Kanaka, 2004). It is commonly known classroom instruction, learning takes place inside the classroom, where students gather in a physical place (the classroom), listen to lectures, hand in homework assignments and take scheduled examinations. Blended learning offers more choices to benefit educators and learners than either classroom based or web based learning alone (Singh, 2003). According to him blended learning can make use of the powerful internet technology, and at the same time, provide the elements lacking in web based instructions such as engagement and social contact. Blended learning can improve student retention in higher education.

Blended learning includes face to face learning, E-learning and self paced instructions. It is the learning which offers learners the opportunities "to be both together and apart".

Face to face +E-learning (synchronous or asynchronous conversation) =Blended learning

Thus blended learning courses are:

1. Not traditional "distance education" courses,
2. Not entirely online
3. Not simply traditional classes with a Web site

1. Online time replaces some classroom time,
2. Not just transferring information to the Web
3. Involves an extensive course redesign
4. Many different formats and schedules are possible

Dimensions of Blended Learning

The dimensions of blended learning are Pedagogical, Technological, Interface Design, Evaluation, Management, Resource Support, Ethical and Institutional Dimensions.

Promises of Blended Learning

Among the electronically instructional strategies blended learning is fast picking up with the following benefits.

1. It addresses the different learning styles, methods of information delivery to reinforced lessons
2. It offers improved pedagogy as it increases the level of active learning strategies peer to learning strategies and learning centered strategies.
3. Boundless information in the world wide web can be accessed instantly; social interaction is relatively more in blended learning then e-learning
4. For self motivated adult learners it offers the benefits of self regulatory learning in case of revision.
5. Designing the blended learning modules is not a costly affair too.

Elements of Blended Learning

As per the learners demand and expected learning out comes the blended learning experience is designed by the experts. Bersin and Associates (2004) have identified the following elements related to blended learning.

1. Instructors led/ lecture/training.
2. Webinars
3. Web-based courseware
4. Simulations
5. CD-ROM based courseware
6. Internet delivered videos
7. Offline videos
8. Electronic performance support system
9. Rapid e-learning courseware
10. Collaboration system(chat room, discussion board)
11. Video conference

12. Conference calls
13. Job aids
14. Work books
15. Books
16. On the job exercise

Variants of Blended Learning Models

The various structural and functional variants of blended learning models are

1. Program flow blend
2. Core -spoke blends
3. Concentric blends
4. Branching blends
5. Enabling
6. Enhancing
7. Transforms
8. Knowledge driven
9. Skill driven
10. Attitude driven
11. Competency driven

Kinds of Blending/ Components of Blend Learning

1. Blend learning environment
2. Blending instructional strategies
3. Blending instructional media

Blending in Teaching Learning Process

Although blended learning environment differs from place to place, there are some similarities among them. The commonly used models of blended learning are:

Rotation Model: In this type of blending, students are rotated within a given course, on a fixed schedule between learning modalities, at least one of which is an online leering and other modalities might include activities such as small group instruction, projects, individual tutoring etc.

Flipped Model: in this model within a given course students are rotated on a fixed schedule between face to face teachers guided practice in school and online delivery of content and instruction of same subject from a remote location after school.

Flex Model: It is a model in which content and instructions are delivered primarily by the internet and the teacher–of–record is available, students move on an individually customized schedule among modalities.

Self Blend Model: In this, students choose to take one or more courses entirely online to supplement their traditional courses. Students self blend some individual online courses with courses at campus with face to face teachers.

Enriched Virtual Model: It involves a whole school experience in which within each course, students divide their time between attending the traditional class and learning remotely using online delivery of content and instruction.

Teachers' Role in Blended Classroom

Role of Teachers in Blended Classroom is

- Help to guide students
- Manage their activities
- Direct their learning
- Help develop their skills.

Teachers are essential in the success of the classroom

Advantages of Blended Learning

There are some obvious advantages to the use of digital media for content delivery

1. Students have greater time flexibility, freedom, and convenience by working part of the time online from home due to decreased commuting and parking hassles.

2. Students are likely to interact more with the instructor and fellow students since there are numerous opportunities to do so both in class and online.
3. Students have access to unlimited up-to-date resources available via the Web.
4. Students often develop or enhance skills in time management, critical thinking, and problem solving.
5. Students enjoy increased success as measured by fewer course withdrawals and somewhat higher grades.
6. Students can participate more in class discussions since they can choose environment — online or face-to-face — in which they feel more comfortable.
7. Students have more time to reflect and refer to relevant course and other research materials when working and writing online than when responding in class.
8. Students typically have 24/7 access to online course materials.
9. Students usually receive more feedback, and more frequent feedback, from their instructors.
10. Students can acquire useful skills from using the Internet and computer technology.

Challenges Ahead

6. Negative attitude towards new technology among the instructors and learners.
7. Cost of many on-line components is high
8. Teachers and learners should be made accustomed with modalities
9. Lot of e-content in various topics should be developed
10. Bandwidth needed for the fast access of internet should be improved
11. Server with better capacity needed for congestion free learning
12. Developing adequate technological and human resources

13. Developing adequate contingency plan in case of technical problem

Conclusion

The success of blend largely depends on the right mix of the elements it posses. A good blend should provide optimum role of live interaction. It should also provide a wide choice to learners as per their self regulatory perception. It is essential to provide a good support and training model and should keep the cultural components also in mind. A blend which make the right balance between innovation and mass utility as well as which bridge the digital divided will be the successful blended learning model. So blended learning may be considered as "the right mix of various media to maximize learning experience with minimum utility of resources to ensure optimum realization of educational objectives, by making the perfect blend of information technology and instructional technology

Reference

1. Atken, J (2006) *Education and assessment; update on changes*. Accountancy Ireland Vol. 38, 1
2. Singh. H (2003) *Building effective blended learning programs.* Educational Technology (43), 51-54.
3. Mohana sundaram, K and Siva kumar, A (2010). B.L; *A new Horizon*, University News. Vol. 47, No. 50. pg14-17
4. Bersin, J (2004) *The blended learning book: Best practices, proven methodologies, and lessons learned* San Francisco: Pfeiffer.
5. Kurtus, R (2004) *Blended learning* http://www.school-for-champions.com/elearning/blended.htm
6. Valiathan; P (2002) *"Blended learning models"*, ASTD Learning Circuits,2002 http://www.learning circuits.org2002/june 2002/elearn.htm.retrieved on April 21.
7. Warrier,B.S(2006)*"The perfect blended learning"* www.thehindu.com/thehindu/edii 2006/05/08/stories/ 2006050800250700.htm.

16

Principal In-charge Nadar Saraswathi College of Education, Theni

Introduction

Blended learning can be thought of as a pedagogical approach that combines the effectiveness and socialization opportunities of class room with the technologically advanced active learning possibilities of the online environment. Research has shown that high level of student and instructor satisfaction can be produced in the fully online environment. But both faculty and students lament the loss of face-to-face interaction.

Blended learning models comprise of the following elements like learning through information, learning through interaction, learning through collaboration and learning through classroom experiences mixed in varied proportions according to an organization's requirements. Dziuban, Hartman and Moskal (2004) in a research brief for EDUCAUSE titled "Blended Learning" noted "Blended learning should be viewed as a pedagogical approach that combined the effectiveness and socialization opportunities of the classroom with the technologically enhanced active learning possibilities of the online environment, rather than a ratio of delivery modalities.

In recent years, ICT has paved the way for accelerating the paradigm shift through providing more flexible ways of learning. The students can do self-learning using enormous potentials of Internet and providing them with several online exercises. The main focus should be on learning rather than on technology.. Blending of face-to-face instruction with various types of non-classroom technology mediated delivery has been practiced within the academy for more than four decades. A good blend would provide optimum role of live interaction. It is essential to provide a good support and training model and should keep the cultural components in mind. It is the responsibility of authorities to provide necessary learning support in providing access to online learning so that out students become 'blended learners' with self-regulatory authentic learning experience.

Blended learning can be thought of as a pedagogical approach that combines the effectiveness and socialization opportunities of class room with the technologically advanced active learning possibilities of the online environment. Blended learning models comprise of the following elements like learning through information, learning through interaction, learning through collaboration and learning through classroom experiences mixed in varied proportions according to an organization's requirements.

What is Blended Learning

Blended Learning means many things to many people, even within our relatively small online learning community. It is referred to as both blended and hybrid learning, with little or no difference in the meaning of the terms among most educators. In general terms, blended learning combines online delivery of educational content with the best features of classroom interaction and live instruction to personalize learning, allow thoughtful reflection, and differentiate instruction from student-to-student across a diverse group of learners. Definitions of blended learning range from some so broad that practically any learning experience that integrates some use of educational technology might qualify, to others that focus on a specific percentage combination of online curriculum and instruction in a face-to-face setting. A few of the many definitions of blended learning include:

1. The integration of face-to-face and online learning to help enhance the classroom experience and extend learning through the innovative use of information and communications technology. Blended strategies enhance student engagement and learning through online activities to the course curriculum, and improve effectiveness and efficiencies by reduction lecture time.
2. A course that blends online and face-to-face delivery. Substantial proportion of the content is delivered online, typically uses online discussions, and typically has some face-to-face meaning. "The sloan Consortium defines blended courses as having between 30 percent and 79 percent of their content delivered online, with the remaining portion of the course content delivered by face-to-face instruction or other non web-based methods, such as paper textbooks.
3. The combination of multiple approaches to learning. Blended learning can be accomplished through the use of 'blended' virtual and physical resources.

Dziuban, Hartman and Moskal (2004) in a research brief for EDUCAUSE titled "Blended Learning" noted "Blended learning should be viewed as a pedagogical approach that combined the effectiveness and socialization opportunities of the classroom with the technologically enhanced active learning possibilities of the online environment, rather than a ratio of delivery modalities. Blended learning redesign the instructional model with the following characteristics.

1. A shift from lecture to student centered instruction in which students become active and interactive learners.
2. Increases in interaction between student-instructor, student-student, student-content, and student-outside resources;
3. Integrated formative and summative assessment mechanisms for students and instructor.

Blended learning consists of two features

1. It is a planned combination of online learning and Face-to-face (F2F) instruction using a variety of learning resources.

2. It is an educational format that integrates online learning techniques including online delivery of materials through web pages, discussion boards, and e-mail with traditional teaching.

Ingredients of Blended Learning

1. **Live Events**

   Synchronous, teacher-led learning environment in which all learners participate at the same time. It can be in real classroom or can be virtual.

2. **Self-paced learning**

   Recorded live events, Internet based or CD ROM based, which helps the learner to learn at his own pace.

3. **Collaboration**

   It implies a more dynamic communication and interaction among many learners that brings about knowledge sharing.

4. **Assessment**

   It is both live and online measure of learner's knowledge to determine prior knowledge as well as to measure learning transfer.

5. **Performance Support**

   These are reference materials that enhance learning, retention and transfer. It may be printable references, downloaded multimedia learning objects, documentations etc.

Smart Classrooms

Smart Classrooms are technology enhanced classrooms that foster opportunities for teaching and learning by integrating learning technology, such as computers, specialized software, and audience response technology, networking, and audio/visual capabilities. The smart classrooms demand learning initiative that assists educators to make ICT integral to learning. The strategy is about engaging the digital generation, improving individualized learning opportunities, sparking innovation in learning, enhancing teachers' digital pedagogy and getting the best from schools ICT investment.

Smart Classrooms Vis-À-Vis Blended Learning

Smart classroom uses following elements, mixed in varied proportions according to an organization's requirements of blended learning:

Learning through Information

Material based information is the first coherent step towards starting a learning program. Web based material can now be handed to the learners, thanks to e-learning techniques, which can render the learning program easy to deliver and fasters to implement. Making the information accessible all the time will give learners the liberty of scrolling through the content at their own convenience, which, in turn, will enhance understanding and enthusiasm.

Learning through Interaction

The learner instructor, learner-content, learner-learner, and learner-infrastructure interactions become all the more important in a blended-learning environment. Web can assist all the above mentioned forms of interaction, which together, help retain the knowledge that is acquired through information. Web simulations of real life situations allow learners to apply their knowledge practically, without the possibility of them affecting your business directly.

Learning through Collaboration

Collaborative learning includes peer-to-peer discussions, conference calls, chat, team rooms and instant messaging. Technology has enhanced the concept of collaboration manifold, where learners, even though geographically remote, can communicate in real time. The collaborative environment also heightens the chances of collaboration between e-learners and subject matter experts (SMEs).

Learning through Classroom Interactions

Conventional, tested and, by far, one of the most effective approaches to learning, classrooms are the best places to personally connect to peers and instructors. No technology can replace the advantages of this approach, which is exactly why no e-learning or blended-learning model will skip this element for any reason. But, as one would like to believe, blended learning has never attempted to replace classroom-based learning.

Potential Constituents of a Blended Learning Approach

The notion of blending is nothing new. Good classroom teachers have always blended their methods – reading, writing, lecture, discussion, practice and projects, to name just a few, are all part of an effective blend.

Virtual Fieldtrips

Blended learning Virtual Fieldtrips can be used in any number of ways to serve a variety of educational goals. Using blended learning through the virtual fieldtrip is a wonderful opportunity. The virtual fieldtrip experience is an excellent model of a teaching strategy that was not possible before the advent of computers in the classroom.

Blogs

Blog is a term coined for the combination of two words, web and log. As part of a blended-learning project, it is an asynchronous form of online discussion. A blog is a publicly accessible website which contains a journal or diary of sorts. Anyone can initiate a blog either as a part of another website or personal web page or a blog can stand alone.

Blogs offer a forum for many people to state their opinions or comment on others opinions. Blogs could provide a great medium to enhance student writing through the use of technology.

A good blend would provide optimum role of live interaction. It is essential to provide a good support and training model and should keep the cultural components in mind. A successful blend would strike the right balance between innovations and mass utility. Some of the basic factors which should be considered in identifying the blend are:

1. Course instructional goals
2. Student profile

3. Hours of learning/training
4. Teacher experience and teaching style
5. Cultural dimensions
6. Resource availability
7. Budgetary requirement for training implementation

What Kind of Learners We Require?

1. Demonstrate creativity and intellectual curiosity resulting in enjoyment, fun and resilience.
2. Exhibit a sense of self-confidence and enjoyment
3. Are self directed and can work independently, collaboratively and cooperatively to learn and to develop products of use with themselves and others.
4. Display innovation and entrepreneurship.
5. Continually develop communication and collaboration skills.
6. Communicate globally through e-learning spaces.
7. Are able to research effectively and have information fluency.
8. Have developed digital literacy and understand technology operations and concepts.
9. Have developed digital proficiency to work effectively in 21st century environments.
10. Understand digital citizenship and work on issues and challenges that are real and relevant, that make a difference to them and to others.
11. Demonstrate accountability and adaptability.
12. Have developed skills to design, create, share and publish.
13. Build critical and systems thinking enabling problem identification, formulation and solution, and decision making.
14. Use ICT purposefully to engage in real research
15. Explore new ideas and tools in authentic contexts.

What Kind of Teachers We Require?

1. Demonstrate an ongoing commitment to professional knowledge, professional practice, professional relationships and professional values.
2. Have understanding of the transformative role of ICT for 21st Century curriculum design/interpretation, pedagogy and student learning.
3. Make conscious decisions about student learning based on an understanding of digital learners.
4. Are lifelong learners who are willing to take risks, fail and explore areas outside his or her expertise.
5. Employ a variety of methodologies, current learning theories and practices.
6. Constantly collaborate with colleagues and practicing professionals in order to consolidate understanding and to share and reflect on their learning, wonderings and discoveries.

Challenges

The challenges in a blended-learning environment can be looked in two different perspectives learners' perspective and teacher perspective. In focusing on the learner perspective, there is a need to consider the learning style and perceptual skills and abilities of students while designing blended-learning strategy. Learner's proficiency in using ICT is also important in a blended-learning environment. Therefore determining the skills and the ways students acquire and construct knowledge online is very important while designing blended-learning strategy.

One of the major challenges the teachers faces while designing a blended-learning strategy is to determine the balance between online and face-to-face instruction. There is a need of great expertise on the part of the teacher to design the strategy by considering both the educational provisions of the institute and the learner's needs in a blended-learning environment.

Conclusion

A good blend would provide optimum role of live interaction. It is essential to provide a good support and training model and should keep the cultural components in mind. A successful blend would strike the right balance between innovations and mass utility. It is the responsibility of authorities to provide necessary learning support in providing access to online learning so that out students become 'blended learners' with self-regulatory authentic learning experience.

17

Building Innovations for Creative Society on Blended Learning

Introduction

In recent years, ICT has paved the way for accelerating the paradigm shift through providing more flexible ways of learning. The demand of new technologies and the 24/7 global environment can't be satisfied with the only source of classroom instruction, with its inherent classroom limitations (Warrer, B. S.).The students can do self-learning using enormous potentials of Internet and providing them with several online exercises. Some of the researches show that focusing purely on the technology would be wrong (Russel, Jonasson & Ehrmamm, 1999). The main focus should be on learning rather than on technology. It is critical that research should explore not only the development of ICT to be used, but also the role of effective pedagogy that can maximize students' learning using ICT tools (Lim, Ping& Tay Yong, 2004). It has been widely recognized that harnessing the power of ICT requires appropriate learning strategy to harmonize effectiveness in learning with technology role. (Keams & Papadopoulous, 2000). On the other hand the significance of face- to- face instruction can't be ignored since the live human interaction in 'teaching' (or learning) can't be denied to a large extent. Keeping all these in view, a consensus has emerged among educationists working in the area that there is a need for tapping the wide applicability of online learning with face-to-face instruction and then evolve 'Blended Learning'. In actuality, blending of face-to-face instruction with various types of non-classroom technology mediated delivery has been practicsed within the academy for more than four decades. Dezure, Buckley, Barr and Tagg and others note that the confluence of new pedagogies, new technologies and new theories of learning are enabling entirely new models of teaching and learning and that this change is of sufficient magnitude to be described as a paradigm shift.

Blended Learning

Blended Learning means many things to many people, even within our relatively small online learning community. It is referred to as both blended and hybrid learning, with little or no difference in the meaning of the terms among most educators. In general terms, blended learning combines online delivery of educational content with the best features of classroom interaction and live instruction to personalize learning, allow thoughtful reflection, and differentiate instruction from student-to-student across a diverse group of learners. Definitions of blended learning range from some so broad that practically any learning experience that integrates some use of educational technology might qualify, to others that focus on a specific percentage combination of online curriculum and instruction in a face-to-face setting. A few of the many definitions of blended learning include:

1. The integration of face-to-face and online learning to help enhance the classroom experience and extend learning through the innovative use of information and communications technology. Blended strategies enhance student engagement and learning through online activities to the course curriculum, and improve effectiveness and efficiencies by reducing lecture time.

2. A course that blends online and face-to-face delivery. Substantial proportion of the content is delivered online, typically uses online discussions, and typically has some face-to-face meetings." The Sloan Consortium defines blended courses as having between 30 percent and 79 percent of their content delivered online, with the remaining portion of the course content delivered by face-to-face instruction or other non web-based methods, such as paper textbooks.
3. The combination of multiple approaches to learning. Blended learning can be accomplished through the use of 'blended' virtual and physical resources.

Dziuban, Hartman and Moskal (2004) in a research brief for EDUCAUSE titled "Blended Learning" noted "Blended learning should be viewed as a pedagogical approach that combines the effectiveness and socialization opportunities of the classroom with the technologically enhanced active learning possibilities of the online environment, rather than a ratio of delivery modalities. In other words, blended learning should be approached not merely as a temporal construct, but rather as a fundamental redesign of the instructional model with the following characteristics:

1. A shift from lecture to student centered instruction in which students become active and interactive learners
2. Increases in interaction between student-instructor, student-student, student-content, and student-outside resources;
3. Integrated formative and summative assessment mechanisms for students and instructor.

Most importantly, in this view, blended learning represents a shift in instructional strategy. Just as online learning represents a fundamental shift in the delivery and instructional model of distance learning, blended learning offers the possibility to significantly change how teachers and administrators view online learning in the face-to-face setting. Thus, it can be said that blended learning consists of two features:

1. It is a planned combination of online learning and Face- to-Face (F2F) instruction using a variety of learning resources.

2. It is an educational format that integrates online learning techniques including online delivery of materials through web pages, discussion boards, and e-mail with traditional teaching.

Ingredients of Blended Learning

1. **Live Events:** Synchronous, teacher-led learning environment in which all learners participate at the same time. It can be in real classroom or can be virtual.
2. **Self-paced learning:** Recorded live events, Internet based or CD ROM based, which helps the learner to learn at his own pace.
3. **Collaboration:** It implies a more dynamic communication and interaction among many learners that brings about knowledge sharing.
4. **Assessment:** It is both live and online measure of learner's knowledge to determine prior knowledge as well as to measure learning transfer
5. **Performance Support:** These are reference materials that enhance learning, retention and transfer. It may be printable references, downloaded multimedia learning objects, documentations etc.

Smart Classrooms

Smart Classrooms are technology enhanced classrooms that foster opportunities for teaching and learning by integrating learning technology, such as computers, specialized software, audience response technology, networking, and audio/visual capabilities. The smart classrooms demand learning initiative that assists educators to make ICT integral to learning. The strategy is about engaging the digital generation, improving individualized learning opportunities, sparking innovation in learning, enhancing teachers' digital pedagogy and getting the best from schools' ICT investment. The challenge lies in shifting from teaching and learning about ICT to teaching and learning with and through ICT. This means rather than using technology to do old things in new ways, we want to do new things in new ways and use technology to enable and transform teaching, learning and the curriculum.

Smart Classrooms Vis-À-Vis Blended Learning

Smart classroom uses following elements, mixed in varied proportions according to an organization's requirements of blended learning:

Learning through information: Material based information is the first coherent step towards starting a learning program. Web based material can now be handed to the learners, thanks to e-learning techniques, which can render the learning program easy to deliver and faster to implement. Making the information accessible all the time will give learners the liberty of scrolling through the content at their own convenience, which, in turn, will enhance understanding and enthusiasm.

Learning through interaction: The learner-instructor, learner-content, learner-learner, and learner-infrastructure interactions become all the more important in a blended-learning environment. Web can assist all the above mentioned forms of interaction, which, together, help retain the knowledge that is acquired through information .Web simulations of real life situations allow learners to apply their knowledge practically, without the possibility of them affecting your business directly.

Learning through collaboration: Collaborative learning includes peer-to-peer discussions, conference calls, chat, team rooms and instant messaging. Technology has enhanced the concept of collaboration manifold, where learners, even though geographically remote, can communicate in real time. The collaborative environment also heightens the chances of collaboration between e-learners and subject matter experts (SMEs).

Learning through classroom interactions: Conventional, tested and, by far, one of the most effective approaches to learning, classrooms are the best places to personally connect to peers and instructors. No technology can replace the advantages of this approach, which is exactly why no e-learning or blended-learning model will skip this element for any reason. But, as one would like to believe, blended learning has never attempted to replace classroom-based learning. On the contrary, technology-based learning takes care of the basic, mechanical and mundane aspects of learning to allow classroom-based training centre around discussions on already learnt subject matter and behavioral and psychological modifications.

E-learning technology can be put to good use while learning through information, interaction and collaboration. This not only reduces cost attributed to enlarged periods of

Non-productive activity on the part o the employees, commuting and employing instructors, but also creates reusable content, and reiterates core messages and concepts to ingrain them in the minds of the learners. At the same time, the classroom sessions develop interpersonal skills and the ability to communicate face-to-face.

Potential constituents of a blended learning approach: The notion of blending is nothing new. Good classroom teachers have always blended their methods -reading, writing, lecture, discussion, practice and projects, to name just a few, are all part of an effective blend. As has already been discussed, blended-learning arrangements tend to combine an electronic learning component with some form of human intervention; the constituents may vary in different settings. As is clear, the medium is not limited to technology and can include: Stand-alone, Asynchronous, or Synchronous online learning/training; Performance support tools (knowledge management tools); Traditional classroom, labs, or other 'hands-on' experiences; Reading assignments, CD-ROM or other self-paced learning; Teletraining/Telelearning, or Other media. Here is a table that categorizes the type of learning that may be used:

Video/DVD: Blended learning can include technology as common place today as using a video/DVD clip, segment, or movie. Videos used in classroom settings, regardless who produced them, can be educational, promotional, training, event, and evaluative.

Virtual Fieldtrips: Blended learning Virtual Fieldtrips can be used in any number of ways to serve a variety of educational goals. Using blended learning through the virtual fieldtrip is a wonderful opportunity. The virtual fieldtrip experience is an excellent model of a teaching strategy that was not possible before the advent of computers in the classroom.

Interactive Websites: Blended learning often includes the use of interactive websites. The use of interactive websites requires computer and Internet access in the learning situation. These sites provide another opportunity for teachers to use technology in their classroom, thus promoting blended learning. Interactive websites can be utilized within the class for those students who do not have Internet access and can give other students the opportunity to expand knowledge if access is available privately.

Websites for Teachers: Classroom websites help facilitates the creation of a blended-learning environment. Teachers use classroom websites to post assignments, receive homework submissions, and administer tests, and post grades and classroom policies. Teachers also use classroom websites as the medium to link to blended-learning sites such as external websites, videos, software, graphics, audio feeds, and virtual fieldtrips.

Live face-to-face (formal) Instructor-led classroom Workshops Coaching	Live face-to-face (informal) Collegial connections Work teams Role modeling
Virtual collaboration/asynchronous Live e-learning classes E-mentoring.	Virtual collaboration/synchronous Email Online bulletin boards Listservs
Self-paced learning Web learning modules Online resource links Simulations Scenarios Video and Audio CD/DVDs Online self-assessments Workbooks.	Performance support Help systems Print job aids Knowledge databases Documentation Performance/decision support tools

(Source: Strategies for Building Blended Learning by Allison Rossett, Felicia Douglis, and Rebecca V. Frazee) Some of these have been discussed below owing to their newness as a learning resource:

Course Management Systems: The use of a Course Management System (CMS) can assist a teacher when he or she is creating a blended learning environment in the classroom. In addition to using a classroom website to communicate and administer classroom activities (as described in the previous section), a CMS can better assess student work, share course content and help develop a community among the teachers, students, and parents. A CMS allows for the administration of blended activities into the classroom through various tools included with the software.

Synchronous and Asynchronous Discussions: Blended learning combines technology with face-to-face instruction. Synchronous and asynchronous discussions are both types of Internet communication that can be utilized in blended learning to fulfill the technology requirement. Both synchronous and asynchronous discussions utilize the Internet to provide forums for use by the classroom teacher to either give instructions or facilitate conversation among students that would normally take place in a classroom setting. Asynchronous and synchronous discussions can be teacher or student led and can be guided by a pre-set format or take place in a more open setting, just like a classroom discussion. While both synchronous and asynchronous discussions have advantages and disadvantages, their use together in a blended learning situation is critical to the development of the online learning community.

Blogs: Blog is a term coined for the combination of two words, web and log. As part of a blended-learning project, it is an asynchronous form of online discussion. A blog is a publicly accessible website which contains a journal or diary of sorts. Anyone can initiate a blog either as a part of another website or personal web page or a blog can stand alone. The author of the blog can choose to write in this journal as she pleases with no filters or censorship. Blogs span a wide variety of topics. There are reportedly over 11 million blogs on the web. Blogs offer a forum for many people to state their opinions or comment on others opinions. Blogs could provide a great medium to enhance student writing through the use of technology.

The success of a blend largely depends on the right mix of the elements. A good blend would provide optimum role of live interaction. It is essential to provide a good support and training model and should keep the cultural components in mind. A successful blend would strike the right balance between innovations and mass utility. Some of the basic factors which should be considered in identifying the blend are:

1. Course instructional goals
2. Student profile

3. Hours of learning/training
4. Teacher experience and teaching style
5. Cultural dimensions
6. Resource availability
7. Budgetary requirement for training implementation

What Kind of Learners we Require?

1. Demonstrate creativity and intellectual curiosity resulting in enjoyment, fun and resilience.
2. Exhibit a sense of self-confidence and enjoyment
3. Are self directed and can work independently, collaboratively and cooperatively to learn and to develop products of use with themselves and others.
4. Display innovation and entrepreneurship.
5. Continually develop communication and collaboration skills.
6. Communicate globally through e-learning spaces.
7. Are able to research effectively and have information fluency.
8. Have developed digital literacy and understand technology operations and concepts.
9. Understand digital citizenship and work on issues and challenges that are real and relevant, that make a difference to them and to others.
10. Demonstrate accountability and adaptability.
11. Have developed skills to design, create, share and publish.
12. Build critical and systems thinking enabling problem identification, formulation and solution, and decision making.
13. Use ICT purposefully to engage in real research.

What Kind of Teachers we Require?

1. Demonstrate an ongoing commitment to professional knowledge, professional practice, professional relationships and professional values.

2. Have understanding of the transformative role of ICT for 21st Century curriculum design/ interpretation, pedagogy and student learning.
3. Make conscious decisions about student learning based on an understanding of digital learners.
4. Are lifelong learners who are willing to take risks, fail and explore areas outside his or her expertise.
5. Employ a variety of methodologies, current learning theories and practices.
6. Constantly collaborate with colleagues and practicing professionals in order to consolidate understanding and to share and reflect on their learning, wonderings and discoveries.

Challenges

The challenges in a blended-learning environment can be looked in two different perspectives -learner perspective and teacher perspective. In focusing on the learner perspective, there is a need to consider the learning style and perceptual skills and abilities of students while designing blended-learning strategy. Learner's proficiency in using ICT is also important in a blended-learning environment. Therefore determining the skills and the ways students acquire and construct knowledge online is very important while designing blended-learning strategy. From the perspective of pedagogy, teaching and learning in a blended-learning environment can be highly unstable and fluctuating. One of the major challenges the teacher faces while designing a blended-learning strategy is to determine the balance between online and face-to-face instruction. There is a need of great expertise on the part of the teacher to design the strategy by considering both the educational provisions of the institute and the learner's needs in a blended-learning environment. But the issue arises in deciding the balance between online and face-to-face components. There is no unique model and the difficulty resides in identification of the balance point. Therefore it demands high attention on the part of a teacher to design learning environment with appropriate ingredients in correct proportions. It is the responsibility of authorities to provide necessary learning support in providing access to online learning so that our students become 'blended learners' with self-regulatory authentic learning experience.

References

1. Allison Rossett, Felicia Douglis, and Rebecca V. Frazee. Strategies for Building Blended Learning, http:// www.learningcircuits.org/2003/ jul2003/rossett.htm
2. Chopra, V. and Bisht, D. (2011) E-learning vis-a vis face to face delivery models. Paper presented in Twelfth International Seminar on Globalization of Higher Education: Challenges & Opportunities held at January 4- 5, 2011 at New Delhi.
3. Dutta, Subrat. (2003) "Impact of Information Communication Technology on Society." Yojna. 47, no. 7: 24. Ibid. (2003) Yojna. 47, no. 7: 30.
4. Foster, Jonathan and Bowskill, Nicholas. (2004). Preparing for networked collaborative learning. I managers journal of education technology, 1(3), 54-59.
5. Garrison, D.R. & Vaughan, N.D. (2008) Blended learning in higher education: Framework, principles and guidelines, John Wiley and Sons: USA.
6. Kant Ravi. (2009). E-education: A shifting paradigm. Edutracks, 8(8), 14-15.
7. Krishnan Dhanya and Phalachandra B. (2010). Promises and challenges in Blended Learning. Edutracks, 9(6), 23-24.
8. Kumar Sattheesh and John Sagy J. (2008). E-learning possibilities in education. Edutracks, 7(8), 13.
9. Lever-Duffy, Judy, McDonald, Jean B.and Mizell, Al P. (2003). Teaching and learning with technology: Allyn and Bacon.
10. Mohansundaram, K. & Kumaran, D. (2001). Web-based instruction: An innovative teaching strategy, University News, Vol. 39, No. 47, pp8-11.

11. NCERT (2005) National curriculum framework 2005, New Delhi: NCERT.
12. Nambiar, Vijayan K.K. (2005). Psychology of learning and instruction Hyderabad, India: Neelkamal publications Pvt Ltd.
13. Sonkambl, C. & Pagare, P. (2010). Use of blended learning approach in teacher education. In Z. Abas et al. (Eds.), Proceedings of Global Learn Asia Pacific 2010 (pp. 3978-3981). AACE.
14. Talawar, M.S. & Pradeep Kumar, T. (2009). Podcasting: A new trend of web-based technology in education, University News, Vol. 47, No.30, pp13-15.
15. Takwale, Ram: “Challenges and opportunities of globalization for higher education in India” Alternative through e-education.
16. UNESCO (2005) .ICT in schools-A handbook for teachers. Bangkok: UNESCO.
17. Valiathan, P. (2002). “Blended learning models”, ASTD Learning circuits, 2002 http:// vv-ww.learningcircuits.org/

18

21st Century Learning Environments

Introduction

This white paper has been created to provide an overview of research and expert opinion on 21st century learning environment. Its purpose is to offer a descriptive view of 21st century learning environments. To further guide schools and communities in designing dynamic 21st learning environments.

The term "learning environment" suggests place and space – a school, a classroom, a library. In today's interconnected and technology-driven world, a learning environment can be virtual, online, remote; in other words, it doesn't have to be a place at all. Perhaps a better way to think of 21st century learning environments is as the support systems that organize the condition in which humans learn best – systems that accommodate the unique learning needs of every learner and support the positive human relationships needed for effective learning. Learning environments are the structures, tools, and communities that inspire students and educators to attain the knowledge and skills the 21st century demands of us all.

It is worth emphasizing, too, that these support systems are valuable not as ends, but as means to a greater goal – to helping children grow emotionally, socially, physically, and academically. Academic achievement, as research from the Association for Supervision and Curriculum Development (ASCD) shows, is inextricably intertwined with social, emotional, and physical health. Thus, 21st century learning environments address the multiple and interconnected learning needs of the whole child. 21st century learning environment as an aligned and synergistic system of systems that:

?Creates learning practices, human support and physical environments that will support the teaching and learning of 21st century skill outcomes.

Supports professional learning communities that enable educators to collaborate, share best practices, and integrate 21st century skills into classroom practice.

?Enables students to learn in relevant, real world 21st century contexts (e.g., through project-based or other applied work)

?Allows equitable access to quality learning tools, technologies, and resources. ?Provides 21st century architectural and interior designs for group, team, and individual learning. ?Supports expanded community and international involvement in learning, both face-to-face and online.

Structures for Learning

Most classrooms today are undeniably more flexible, more colorful, and more engaging than their 20th century counter parts. Students may no longer sit in rows of chairs bolted to the floor. Student work may be on display. Technology may be present, perhaps in the form of a whiteboard at the front of the room or a few computers in the back. In some schools, there may even be a laptop for every student. The Organisation for Economic Co-operation and Development (OECD) has considered learning needs around the globe in recommending that schools "accommodate both the known and identifiable needs of today, and the uncertain demands of the future.

They should provide an environment that will support and enhance the learning process."

Connecting with the Wider World

Over a century ago John Dewey, the noted American philosopher and educator, observed that learning that endures is "got through life itself." While the physical space of many 21st century learning environments may be small, the learning they engender extends out into the local community and the world at large. Students and community members may work together on service projects and internships. Learners may connect with their peers across the globe to share data on a common problem like climate change or wildlife preservation. Teachers and students may seek the advice of world-renowned experts to guide them in their inquiry-based projects.

Sustainability and Re-use

For schools these days, as with any construction project, the watchword is sustainability. While going green may once have been felt to be a luxury, it is now seen as a common-sense strategy. School officials see value in investing in slightly higher construction expenses to realize lower operating costs over the lifespan of the building. To help educational authorities sort out their options, experts advise them to focus on green design elements – like air quality, temperature control, and lighting – that have a proven positive effect on learning, and pay for them through long-term resource efficiency.

Green schools also provide rich opportunities for students to explore sustainable planning and design, and learn about the impact that design and operations decisions have on the environment. Sustainable schools also serve as positive examples to students, educators, and community members, encouraging everyone to "think green" in all areas of their lives. A wonderful example is found at St. Pancreas Primary School in southern England, where students have turned the building of a new environmentally sustainable addition into an opportunity to learn 21st century skills. By documenting the planning and construction process, students are deepening their understanding of environmental issues, while gaining IT and video production expertise and honing their narrative skills by documenting their compelling story.

Re-conceiving the Library

Twenty-first century design is also influencing another traditional learning space – the school library. As more and more content moves into virtual form, many schools are wondering how the library should respond. Yet even as information becomes digital, kids still need space, says Julie Walker, the executive director of the American Association of School Librarians (AASL). The library media center should be the nerve center of the school, a place where kids gather to get and create information, a place where they can get excited about learning and where they can escape from the pressures of the day.

The 21st century library media center must play multiple roles: carrying out its traditional role of bringing information resources to learners, of course, but also providing the tools and infrastructure that enable learners to analyze, synthesize, and evaluate resources in ways that demonstrate learning and create new knowledge. It must offer places for formal learning in which large groups can gather for presentations; places for social learning where teams can collaborate on projects; and places for individual learning where individuals can find a quiet space for reading, reflection, or relaxation. By providing the audio and video communications technologies that build bridges between people and places all over the globe .Many school libraries are creating portals that link their holdings to other appropriate sites and afford 24/7 access to information for their school community. These new spaces show the promise of the 21st century school library – as a gateway to information resources and services, a design studio to spur creativity and collaboration, and a calm and orderly place to make sense of a data-flooded world.

Time for Learning

Flexibility of design needs to extend to time as well. Twenty-first century learning cannot fully flower when embedded in a rigid 19th century calendar. More malleable units of time than the typical 50-

minute class period are required for project-based work or interdisciplinary themes. Many schools are turning to block scheduling to create bigger, more adjustable time slots for student learning, and for teaching planning and professional development. Establishing time during the day for collaboration and planning is another way to advance 21st century teaching practice. In earlier eras, teachers had little structured time during the day for interaction with other adults. Today, though, the challenges of preparing all students for success require the collaborative efforts of all the professionals in a school. To ensure that this time is used productively, school leaders at Upper Merion Area Middle School in Pennsylvania have developed comprehensive planning guide that helps teachers move from collegial conversations to critical dialogue. According to Assistant Principal Jabari Whitehead, the guidelines, based on principles of action research and Malcolm Baldriges „Plan, Do, Study, Act model, enable teachers to use data to drive decision making as well as develop appropriate interventions.

Other states and districts are experimenting with extended school days and school calendars to provide more opportunities for learning and more durable linkages between students, families, and the community. But merely lengthening the school day or school year does not guarantee the desired results. Professor Lawrence Baines has pointed out that U.S. students attend school on average over 1,100 hours per year, while students in most developed nations, most of whomoutperform U.S. students on international tests, go to school an average of 701 hours per year.

This statistic suggests that relationship between time and learning is not a simple one. A 2007 Education Sector report acknowledged this fact, while noting that "improving the quality of instructional time is at least as important as increasing the quantity of time in school..." and observing that "the addition of high-quality teaching time is of particular benefit to certain groups of students, such as low-income students..." Thus, it is not just how much, but how time is used that matters.

According to a recent study on education and time sponsored by the Mott Foundation too often school systems pay insufficient attention to the many ways that students learn outside of the classroom, “from forming cultural bonds to multi-tasking with technology tools.”

But what seems certain is that learning does not happen on the clock. What is needed is a seamless approach to integrating all the forms of learning that occur in a Childs typical day. Powerful learning can happen outside of schools through internships, online learning, and community service. The ASCD High School Reform Proposal sums it up: “What counts is not the time spent in the school building, but the learning that the student masters.” Twenty-first century learning environments promote this integration of formal and informal learning, for “when it comes to learning, there is no final bell.

Technology In Support of Learning

A number of professional associations provide valuable guidance on the many ways in which technology can enhance education. The Software & Information Industry Association recently released its Vision K-20 website and report, which calls for every K-20 educational

Institution to fully embrace technology and e-learning by the end of the decade. On the industry side, Cisco has commissioned a comprehensive literature review on the effectiveness of various educational technologies. In 2008, the Consortium for School Networking (CoSN) launched Empowering the 21st Century Superintendent, a resource-rich website to help superintendents and other district leaders build their knowledge, skills, and confidence about educational technology. The International Society for Technology in Education (ISTE) offers a wealth of resources on its website, including their award-winning Center for Applied Research in Educational Technology (CARET), which features research-based resources that address critical educational technology questions.

As a first step in the technology planning process, policy makers and school officials should consider the technological options in light of the needs and resources of their state, district, or school. Having a clearly articulated instructional strategy is essential for sorting through the possibilities and making informed decisions. As a CoSN brief reminds readers, “technology is not the end goal – it is but one component in an educational program." It is how we use it that counts. Towards that end, what follows are some of the most notable ways that technology can enhance student learning and promote mastery of 21st century skills:

1. Promoting greater student achievement
2. Increasing student engagement
3. Assessing student performance
4. Facilitating communication and collaboration
5. Maximizing administrative effectiveness
6. Building student proficiencies in 21st Century skills

Students Supporting Technology

Networks and devices need maintenance to stay robust and current. Individuals need training and ongoing support to maximize technology's benefits. Creative school systems have turned this problem into a21st century learning opportunity by establishing programs like MOUSE that organize and train student-led squads to provide much of the technical support in their schools. Students learn valuable technical skills, while also honing other critical workforces skills like teamwork, project planning, and time management. Such programs have paid off in valuable corporate internships for their young participants, and even more importantly, in their enhanced self- confidence and capacity for leadership.

At the school or district level, the LAN should be designed to support the following (in order of deployment priority):

1. Core network: routing and switching; network security; wireless access
2. Building controls: physical security (video monitoring)
3. Communications (audio, then video): telephony and its applications; videoconferencing; rich media on-demand; telepresence

Administrator scan conduct online assessments and retrieve data to facilitate decision making; teachers can tap into educational portals and curriculum- resource sites; and all learners can benefit when school, public, and academic libraries share electronic resources. With high-speed broadband, educators, students, and families can fully experience media-rich educational resources and participate in anytime/anywhere learning community.

In addition to local area networks, states and countries need to consider deployment of a broadband network linking schools together with their central administration or ministry of education. It may also be advantageous to link such a broadband network to higher education institutions, thereby creating national research and education networks. Data centers, located on the broadband network and centrally running multiple academic and administrative applications, can enable economies of scale and lower servicing costs across a number of educational institutions, while facilitating research, scholarship, and learning at all levels.

Communities for Learning

From Isolation to Connection

The George Lucas Foundation cites numerous studies showing that strong home- school connections result in the following outcomes:

?Children do better in school when their parents are involved in their education

?After-school learning opportunities promote student achievement

?Community youth development programs spur academic performance

Accountability: Inside and Out

Today, we hear a lot about accountability in education. Generally, this is understood to be a system of external measurement – often accompanied by sanctions for non-performance – designed to ensure that a school system meets the expectations of external stakeholders like the general public, employers, or parents. Such accountability systems have their place in helping schools track the progress of the students in their care, and in enabling educators to monitor school progress, spurring them to greater achievement.

Citizens of the 21st century need to think critically and creatively, embrace diversity and ambiguity, and create as well as consume information. They need to be resourceful and self-reliant, while also skilled at collaboration and group process. They need to understand the many "languages" of modernity – such as mathematics, science, and technology – and be fluent in varied forms of communication – such as persuasion, presentation, and self-expression.

Conclusion

Many schools today still reflect their Industrial Age origins with rigid schedules, inflexible facilities, and fixed boundaries between grades, disciplines, classrooms, and functional roles. The 21st century, though, requires a new conception of education – one that breaks through the silos that separated schools from the real world, educators from each other. The modern world demands learning environments that embrace the wide world of people, places, and ideas, and are flexible in their arrangements of space, time, technology, and people. These connections will foster healthy cultures of mutual respect and support among students, educators, families, and neighbor hoods, serving their lifelong learning and recreational needs, and uniting learners around the world in addressing global challenges and opportunities. We shall have the deepest and best guarantee of a larger society which is worthy, lovely, and harmonious.

19

Designing Learning Environment of Tomorrow

Introduction

In the race to achieve Education for All (EFA) goals by 2015, the importance of creating optimal conditions to enable and sustain learning has sometimes been overlooked as a 'peripheral' factor in the provision of quality education. However, a rapidly expanding body of research on the conditions of learning suggests that physical, social and organizational environments in which teaching and learning processes take place have a more central role than previously acknowledged. As the evidence gathered for this report asserts, the design and management of learning spaces is fundamental to the achievement of positive learning outcomes as well as to the health and well-being of learners. Simply put, good learning environments foster quality learning, and bad learning environments do not.

This exhaustive review of the literature on learning environments aims to provide all those who wish to fulfill the promise of EFA with evidence-based suggestions for creating and sustaining 'good learning environments. Whether applied to formal schooling, alternative learning, or non-formal education contexts, the reflections and findings contained herein offer a rich and varied knowledgebase for policy makers, educators and communities to develop strengthened policies and actions that meet local needs in the creation and maintenance of enabling places to learn.

Definition

Learning environment – the complete physical, social and pedagogical context in which Learning is intended to occur. The term most often refers to school classrooms but may include any designated place of learning such as science laboratories, distance learning contexts, libraries, tutoring centers, teachers' lounges, gymnasiums and non-formal learning spaces. The components and attributes of a learning environment are conceptualized in relation to their impact on learning processes and outcomes in both cognitive and affective domains. This term may also refer to the natural environment surrounding school buildings4 when they are used as a learning space.

Objectives of learning environment of tomorrow:

The goal of Learning Environments for Tomorrow is to provoke and collectively explore interdisciplinary insights on two overarching questions:

1. What are the principles of effective pedagogy and design for the coming decade?
2. How can new visions of learning environments be shaped by the latest research and practices in learning theory, emerging technologies, environmental sustainability, child/adult collaboration and community engagement?

In answering these questions, the program aims to achieve the following learning objectives:

1. Understand the principles of effective pedagogy and design for the coming decade
2. Learn the latest thinking in the areas of learning theory, child/adult collaboration, student and community engagement, social media technologies and environmental sustainability

3. Speculate on the modes of creativity and productivity which education will need to address in the coming decade
4. Consider the implications that the areas noted above have on designing effective learning environments
5. Critique learning environments and educational facilities that are seen as models of effective design

Principles of innovative learning

1. Learners have to be at the center of what happens in the classrooms with activities focused on their cognitive and growth.
2. Learning is a social practice and cannot happen alone emotions are an integral part of learning
3. Learners are different and innovative learning environment reflect the various experience and prior knowledge that each student bring to class.
4. Student need to be stretched but not too much
5. Assessment should be for learning not of learning
6. Learner needs to be connected across discipline.

How the learning environment should be

Learning environments should also be healthy, safe and protective. This should include:

(1) Adequate water and sanitation facilities,

(2) Access to or linkages with health and nutrition services,

(3) Policies and codes of conduct that enhance physical, psycho-social and

Emotional health of teachers and learners, and

(4) education content and practices leading to knowledge, attitudes, values, and life skills needed for self-esteem, good health and personal safety, friendly and easily accessible facilities; well-motivated and professionally competent teachers;

Learning Environments for Tomorrow will explore four key themes emerging as defining elements of 21st century education: collaboration; technology; engagement; and sustainability. Through a research-based understanding of current and emerging best practices, participants will work with Harvard faculty and leading practitioners to envision how school buildings can most effectively support learning in the coming decade and beyond.

As a specialized field, LER takes the position that the creation and maintenance of enabling conditions for learning is both a means and an end. All the components that are essential to the quality of the outcome are interdependent and all are measurable using different sets of tools. Teaching and learning processes are shaped by their physical, social and organizational environment, and the design of learning environments is, in turn, influenced by the processes that take place within them. Both are important to measure and to continuously adjust in order to improve the quality of education

What constitutes learning in the 21st century?

Should reading, watching, memorizing facts, and then taking exams be the only way to learn? Or could technology (used effectively) make learning more interactive, collaborative, and constructive? Could learning be more engaging and fun? The ultimate goal of this project-based course is to promote systematic design thinking that will cause a paradigm shift in the learning environments of today and tomorrow.

Student engagement in learning and catering for 21st century learners was the original impetus for whole school cultural change. Personalized learning enabled through team teaching in flexible open plan environments is the focus of Bellaire's innovative learning environment. This is strongly supported by teacher coaching and goal setting. The school works to engage students in learning communities through the personalized learning focus.

Conceptualizing the physical learning environment

The concept of "learning environment" will become increasingly significant as schools of the future Become centers of lifelong learning.

"Learning environment" is a term used liberally in educational Discourse because of the emerging use of information technologies for educational purposes on the one hand and the constructivist concept of knowledge and learning on the other It has been demonstrated that international comparisons of education can be achieved through Comprehensive quality management and quality criteria (Finnish National Board of Education, 2008; OECD, 2006). As a result, the emphasis is shifting from developing physical learning environments using norms and regulations to comparing these environments on the basis of qualitative improvement.

The future of the physical learning environment

School facilities that supports the user learning space and its operational environment as such. Within it, flexible and modifiable learning spaces and their related learning environments are formed through Pairs of dimensions. They are all interactive and totally supportive of one another, as shown below.

Supportive learning contexts

1. Social
2. Individual
3. Physical learning environment
4. Formal teaching
5. Informal learning

The Innovative Learning Environments

Research Study takes the position that focusing on the social practices of teaching and learning and the use of learning spaces and technologies is the next step in research on Innovative Learning Environments (ILEs).

The key question for this study is

- To what extent do innovative learning environments contribute to improved cognitive, affective and social learning outcomes for students?

The sub-questions are:

- To what extent do innovative learning environments contribute to changes in behavior and Pedagogical practices?
- How are teachers, students and the community using innovative learning environments, particularly new learning spaces?
- How have schools prepared for the transition to new learning spaces or other innovative Learning environments?
- To what extent have schools consolidated and evaluated the effectiveness of new learning and teaching practices in innovative learning environments?

The OECD 'Innovative Learning Environments Project (2010) characterizes an ILE as

- Learner-centered: focus of all activities
- Structured and well-designed: role of teachers in supporting inquiry and autonomous

  Learning
- Profoundly personalized: sensitive to individual and group differences in terms of

  Background, prior knowledge, motivation and abilities
- Inclusive: sensitive to individual and group differences in terms of learning needs
- Social: learning most effective when cooperative and in group settings.

Engage Students with Lectures

The engaging lecture can be a rewarding experience for our students. Lectures that open up a window on the teachers mind or relate exciting research experiences can be highly motivating.

To keep students engaged you can build variety into your delivery by "chunking" the class into sections of around 15 minutes. Use a shift in energy, change the focus, change the stimulus, or change the means of delivery.

1. Include music, visuals, pictures, quotes, and stories to tap into students' emotions
2. Show a short video clip to relate the material to the real world
3. Move to a different part of the room
4. Use electronic devices to ask students to reflect on what has been said in the last 15 minutes
5. Use clickers to check for common misconceptions
6. Ask students to talk to the person next to them to tell them what they have learned in the last 15 minutes
7. Bring in a guest speaker, either physically or virtually

When planning an engaging lecture, ask yourself: **"And what will my students are doing?"** Consider how the students will be involved in their learning and what you can do to facilitate the best learning.

Engage Students with Activities

You, as the expert, can design activities to help students think more critically about the content. This can be achieved inside the classroom while you are there to facilitate discussion and correct misconceptions. Activities can help the students' link disparate pieces of information together, scaffold the skills and concepts they need to construct knowledge, facilitate and guide questions, and link the knowledge to its application in the outside world. Have students:

2. Brainstorm an idea at the beginning of the class before you present the material, then debrief and the end of class
3. Fill in instructor-prepared system charts using the information presented
4. Develop a matrix of key concepts presented in the lecture. Give them one minute to write after each main idea
5. Answer short open-ended questions by writing a few sentences and then discussing with a partner
6. Draw concept maps to link together pieces of information
7. Write predictions about an outcome you are about to reveal

8. Chose the "best" answer from among different outcomes to a short case study
9. Walk the instructor through the steps needed to solve a question for the day
10. Evaluate writing or problems that have been written by someone else (anonymous, maybe even you).
11. Develop a rubric for an excellent paper.

The more you can apply what you are teaching to students' day-to-day lives or what's going on in the world today, the more motivated and engaged students will be. Real-life applications can tap into or awaken curiosity and give more value and meaning to what they are learning.

Consider the following ways to provide opportunities for authentic encounters with the material

1. Invite guest speakers to talk about how the course content is used in the field
2. Relate some of the interesting aspects of your own or other research around UT
3. Feature relevant articles in newspapers, journals or magazines to make connections to current events and the culture.
4. Introduce case studies where students have to grapple with the "messy" real-world issues

How can I make my class interactive?

Beyond making your class active for each individual student, another way to enhance the learning experience is to get students interacting with each other. You can do this by adding a layer of social engagement around the ways you are already guiding students' learning. For example:

1. Modify a question for individual student reflection into a prompt for class discussion
2. Turn a problem to solve into a collaborative project

3. Use a multiple-choice question as the basis for a group decision to be made
4. Take a student-generated question and turn it into an opportunity for peer assistance and feedback

Going further, you can strategize your entire teaching approach around maximizing these opportunities to have students exchange ideas and engage multiple perspectives. To find out more about this important characteristic of the UT learning experience, visit

How can I engage students during Discussions?

Good discussions hinge on well-crafted questions. Meaningful questions stimulate students to reflect on the content they have learned and extend it to a higher level. Different types of questions require different levels of thinking. Asking questions to test memorization of content evokes low-level recall thinking, whereas questions that require students to predict, analyze or evaluate evoke higher-order critical thinking skills and more meaningful discussions.

Ask questions that

1. Require student input: "What questions do you have about this specific part of the process? Or "What do you think the author of our book would say to that?
2. Are open-ended even if there is a correct answer: "When we multiply two numbers together will the answer always be greater than the multiplicand?" "If this were to happen in a vacuum how it would be different?"
3. Stimulate thinking from different perspectives: "Should smoking be banned from the UT campus?" From the perspective of a smoker and a non-smoker.

Thought-provoking questions developed within a good environment for exchanging ideas elicit richer discussions.

Discussions can be initiated with

1. Reflection guides that students complete before class
2. Key questions from a text or video that have multiple answers

3. Examples that fit or do not fit a particular model or theory
4. Challenges that extend the content
5. Personal experiences, yours or theirs, that fit or complicate a concept
6. A video vignette that stimulates inquiry
7. A poll of students' views or experiences (e.g., "Would you would tell a store assistant if she gave you too much change?")
8. "What if" questions
9. Intriguing stories, paradoxes, or problems that expand possibilities as more information is revealed
10. Multiple-choice questions where all the answers are correct possibilities, but with one answer considered the BEST answer. Have students explained why or rank order the possible answers.

How Can I Engage Students Through Peer Collaboration?

Effective engagement with peers has proven itself a successful and powerful learning method. Giving space in a lesson for students to build knowledge together can lead to deeper understanding of the material in addition to other positive outcomes.

When students are given questions or problems to solve while interacting with other students they:

1. ask questions to improve their own or their peer's understanding
2. explain, elaborate, clarify, and justify their reasoning
3. reflect on their knowledge
4. encourage and motivate team members
5. and build peer relationships

Students can work in pairs by collaborating with the person sitting next to them, or with a group of students sitting around them. Some instructors form permanent teams at the beginning of the semester and these teams sit in designated seats where they work together all semester.

Some examples of peer-to-peer learning are

1. **Peers Instruction** - students formulate an answer to a conceptual question, and then share it with a partner to compare their reasoning and come to agreement before submitting their answer again.
2. **Team-Based Learning** - students work in the same teams all semester, taking group quizzes and using in-class application activities to reach consensus on complex decisions.
3. **Problem-Based Learning** - students work together to solve a complex problem.
4. **Project-Based Learning** - students compose questions then find methods to answer their question.
5. **Case-Based Learning** - students explore factually based scenarios and evaluate a given course of action.
6. **Inquiry Learning** - students work in groups to generate their own problem, then research and explore answers.

For those teaching large classes, hear how some UT faculty designed their large class courses to be interactive and engaging.

The Future of Learning: Preparing for Change

This report aims to identify, understand and visualize major changes to learning in the future. It Developed a descriptive vision of the future, based on existing trends and drivers, and a normative vision outlining how future learning opportunities should be developed to contribute to Social cohesion, socio-economic inclusion and economic growth.

The overall vision is that personalization, collaboration and informalisation (informal learning) are at the core of learning in the future. These terms are not new in education and training but will have to become the central guiding principle for organizing learning and teaching in the future. The central learning paradigm is thereby characterized by lifelong and life-wide learning, shaped by the ubiquity of Information and Communication Technologies (ICT). At the same time, due to fast advances in technology and structural changes to European labour markets that are related to demographic change, globalization and immigration, generic and transversal skills become more important, which support citizens in becoming lifelong learners who flexibly respond to change, are able to pro-actively develop their competences and thrive in collaborative learning and working environments.

Many of the changes depicted have been foreseen for some time but they now come together in such a way that is becomes urgent and pressing for policymakers to consider them and to Propose and implement a fundamental shift in the learning paradigm for the 21st century digital World and economy. To reach the goals of personalized, collaborative and informalised learning, Holistic changes need to be made (curricula, pedagogies, assessment, leadership, and teacher Training, etc.) and mechanisms need to be put in place which make flexible and targeted lifelong Learning a reality and support the recognition of informally acquired skills.

Conclusion

Creativity is the essence of life. Innovation make things cozy comport in the world. A teacher with monotonous teaching style has been replied by multimedia approach.Transfering or importing knowledge is equally important as generating knowledge. Knowledge transferred in a down to earth manner will simplify the learning process and help the student to retain what is thought and to recall learned lesson as and when needed. Fruitful transfer of knowledge can be achieved by employing various student friendly teaching learning method. Student friendly teaching learning method always consider the interest, needs and level of students.

Technology explosion has yielded several new machines, material and media, which have great potential for youth in the educational enterprise. A judicious use of these together with new functions and rolls of educational personal in order to bring about more efficient and effective teaching learning to the development of new branch of study, namely educational technology.

20

Effective Usage of Technological Advancement in Class Room

Introduction

The innovative teachers are to be supported in kind or time as they provide the basis for schools to move forward and may even lead the appointment of ICT integrators, who help, shape and evolve a school's approach to use traditional and emerging teaching learning technologies by providing ideas on how best to use the technologies your institution has and provide ideas on how to use such technologies in Teaching learning.

With the development of technologies, teachers are able to create their own material and thus have more control over the classroom than they have in the past. Rather than deskilling teachers as some scholars claim, it seems that technology makes inspiring teachers to be more creative in customizing their own material. It is witnessed the fact that technology can be used to compliment other aspects of good teaching rather than replacing them. It is evident that involving students in the creation of useful material, as a part of learning experience is a way to make school, more meaningful for students.

The use of peripheral devices on learning process helps students to focus higher level concepts rather than less meaningful tasks.

Hurdles in the Use of Technology

Generally teachers thought that it was more beneficial to the educational process and should be continued to use technology for the day today classrooms. Irrespective of the benefits there are some hurdles. i.e.

1. Disparities between students who have access to computers at home and those who do not.
2. Maintenance of the Equipment needed to operate technologically enhanced school or College.
3. Teachers provided evidence of the importance of need for training for using technology in classrooms.
4. Teachers recognized that some times students are overloaded with the amount of information available.
5. Teachers had a hard time keeping up with the pace of change.
6. Now a days, we witnessed the problem of plagiarism because technology was making easy to reproduce and revise some other's work.
7. Another emerging issue, is the possible loss of the educational process to business partners.
8. Teachers generally noted that extra time was needed to learn new software and also to create new things for teaching because greater expectations were being placed on them.

Effective Usage of Technological Advancements

Besides of all these hurdles we can use the technological advancement effectively in teaching learning. Information and technology is an umbrella term that includes all the technologies for the manipulation and communication of information. It deals mainly with the usage of tools and techniques to enhance the effectiveness of teaching learning process.

Note Worthy

In recent years, integration of technologies into the schools and colleges has become a significant part of education. As such resource for education and assisting faculty in this new arana has become note worthy.

Accessibility

Teachers and learners no longer have to rely solely on printed materials in physical media, with the internet and World Wide Web, a wealth of learning materials in almost every subject and in a variety of media can now to be accessed any where ever at any time of the day and by an unlimited number of people.

Improving the Quality

Improving the quality and training is a vital issue, particularly during the educational expansion. Technologies can enhance the quality of education in many ways, by increasing learner motivation and engagement, by facilitating the acquisition of basic skills and by enhancing teacher training. Technologies are also transformational tools which, when use appropriately, can promote the shift to be learner centered environment.

Workshops

Workshops on how to use the software are not always enough. Teachers need to understand the way in which these new tools can make a significant difference in student learning

Transcent Time And Space

One defining feature of technologies is their ability be transcends time and space. Technologies make it possible achievements learning or bearing characterized by a time lag between the delivery of instruction and its receptions by learners. Online course materials may be accessed 24 hours a day 7 days a week. Additionally certain type of educational technologies like teleconferencing, enable instruction to be received, geographically dispersed learners.

Motivating Factor

Technologies such as videos, television and multimedia computer software than combine text, sound and colorful moving images can be used to provide challenging and authentic content that will engage students in learning process networked computers with internet connectivity can increase learner motivation as it combines the media richness to connect the students with real world events.

Acquiring the Required Skills

The transmission of the basic skills and concepts can be facilitated by technologies through drill and practice. Most of the early users of computers were, for computers based learning that focused on mastery of skills and content through repetition and reinforcement.

Updated and Dynamic Information

Information from the internet is more dynamic than the printed materials. Reference materials on CD-ROMs and curriculum assistance from high quality software offer many more resource opportunities than most classrooms and school libraries could provide. The depth and breadth of such information posses its own challenge. Internet content is less structured and manageable than material outlined by a printed material.

Enhancing the Training

Technologies have also been used to improve the access to and the quality of the training. The institutions like Cyber Teacher Training centers in developed countries are taking advantage of the internet to provide better teacher professional development opportunities to in-service teachers. They offer self directed, self faced, and web based courses for primary and secondary schools teachers.

The Virtual University

Applying the ICT Principles, the virtual university plans programs develop the study materials and ensures the delivery of these student support services through the internet. Students and teachers are connected together for their educational programs through internet or online connectivity.

Self Learning Packages

The self learning packages are prepared in such a way as to encourage students to discover learning. Extra reading material can be obtained from the internet WebPages.

Changing Teaching

A number of things were being done with websites. Several teachers were mentioned that they used power point and other computer programs to improve their presentation of materials to class. Teachers explained that technology enabled teacher to deliver more material to student and eliminated several basic problems such as poor handwriting, poor artistic skill, contrast, lighting and visibility.

Conclusion

Educational technology deals mainly with broad theoretical base for class room teaching. Some of the path breathing developments seen in recent years are: a whole new generation of sophisticated computer hardware and software, broadband internet access with line streaming video capability display and projection technologies, online real time information and interactive learning capabilities, Wi-Fi connectivity, distance e-learning program, video conferencing and so on. Thus the fact that new technologies are effectively used in the real class room teaching learning situation is witnessed. Teacher plays a prominent role in molding up future citizen. The teacher's shoulder posses training in using most modern technologies in the field of education.

References

1. Satija.B.R (1996).Trends in Education. Anmol publication (P)Ltd. New Delhi
2. Robinson.k (1999) All our futures. Creativity, Culture and Education. London, Department for Education and Employment
3. R.C.Misra (2005) Teaching of Informational Technology. A.P.H Publishing Corporation, New Delhi.
4. K.L.Kumar (2006) Educational Technology

21

Flipped Classroom vs Traditional Classroom

Introduction

The flipped classroom describes a reversal of traditional teaching where students gain first exposure to new material outside of class, usually via reading or lecture videos, and then class time is used to do the harder work of assimilating that knowledge through strategies such as problem-solving, discussion or debates. A traditional classroom is a learning room with desks in rows and a teacher in front. This room is usually overcrowded with students and one teacher. The mode of teaching in this class is generalized and does not focus on individual performance.

While some studies show online students slightly outperforming their traditional classroom counterparts, most indicate that there is little difference in overall performance between the two formats. One major difference is that student-learning style plays a role in each format's success. Students who are highly self-directed, organized and autonomous will likely thrive in an online environment, while those who tend to rely on instructors for direction may struggle.

Similarly, extroverted students who enjoy face-to-face classroom interactions may do best in a traditional environment, while introverted students may welcome the solitary qualities of online classes. Some students excel in online classes. They like the freedom to come and go as they please. They like being able to use their computer skills. They enjoy sitting at the computer to read their class lecture and do their coursework. Other students prefer the traditional classroom, thriving on the set schedule, the physical textbooks, and the face-to-face interaction with peers and their instructor. There is no right or wrong learning environment. It really does depend on the type of learner one is and what kind of classes fit into his lifestyle. Fortunately, in this day and age, students have lots of choices.

The flipped classroom describes a reversal of traditional teaching where students gain first exposure to new material outside of class, usually via reading or lecture videos, and then class time is used to do the harder work of assimilating that knowledge through strategies such as problem-solving, discussion or debates. The flipped classroom at its most basic level is the creation of online video lectures to quickly share lessons on concepts studied in class. These video lessons can be accessed from anywhere by students and can be used by students to move along at their own pace. Using the flipped model, has provided many opportunities to further advanced student learning by making students responsible for their learning. In essence, "flipping the classroom" means that students gain first exposure to new material outside of class, usually via reading or lecture videos, and then use class time to do the harder work of assimilating that knowledge, perhaps through problem-solving, discussion, or debates.

A traditional classroom is a learning room with desks in rows and a teacher in front. This room is usually overcrowded with students and one teacher. The mode of teaching in this class is generalized and does not focus on individual performance. The traditional classrooms are a schoolroom with a large chalkboard, a teacher's desk and several rows of student desks. This type of structured environment has many advantages over its online counterpart for students of any age. Some of these advantages include teacher-student interaction and instant feedback, which online components are not able to provide. The social and communication aspects of traditional classroom learning are another advantage that cannot be ignored.

Key differences between the Traditional Classroom and the Online Classroom

A really good teacher can make the traditional classroom an exciting place, and the same is true for the online classroom. The specific goals of any class, or course, must be clear in the mind of the teacher, as well as the best methods for the type of classroom, and type of content presented.

Traditional education and online education each have unique advantages. The emotively supportive face-to-face environment of the classroom allows immediate feedback, and an immediate social environment, which has been viewed as essential to a quality educational experience. Facial expressions and body language are vital clues to the level of student understanding and engagement, and fundamental to recognizing those “teachable moments!”.

The traditional classroom usually requires everyone travel to a single location, and there is a fixed amount of time for interaction. Larger class sizes limit the opportunity for interaction and the true individual attention students receive. Private interaction between teacher and student is often severely limited in a busy classroom. Due to diversity of background, attitude, and other factors, the ideal of Socratic small group interaction at a high level is often beyond practical attainment in many traditional classrooms.

The online classroom can also be emotively supportive, but in a medium that is so new as to be poorly understood - interactive reading and writing. Not all students are equally prepared to function well in the online classroom. An online classroom allows anyone, anywhere, anytime the opportunity to participate, without pressure from limited time or public speaking in front of a group.

While there are too many subtle advantages and disadvantages to list here, the reality is that both the traditional classroom and the online classroom have very real advantages and disadvantages, which require a teacher to think clearly about specific student and curriculum needs and the most effective means for presenting different types of content.

The issue becomes: when does use of the online classroom most benefit the student, and when does the traditional classroom most benefit the student? We now have alternatives to the traditional classroom which, when used wisely, benefit students and teachers, alike. As we gain more experience, and confidence, with use of the online classroom, our expectations will become clearer. Most teachers would agree our goal is to teach the love of learning, and to do the very best we can for our students.

Whether using online activities within a traditional classroom, or as out-of-class "homework" activities, combining online activities to create whole online courses presents additional possibilities and issues. The availability of online courses at anytime, from any location, supports the current boom in home-based learning. Home-based Internet access supports ongoing opportunities for lifelong learning, group dialogue, participation in communities of interest, and access to local community and global expertise.

Inverted Classroom

To make their course more compatible with the students' varied learning styles, they designed an inverted classroom in which they provided students with a variety of tools to gain first exposure to material outside of class: textbook readings, lecture videos, PowerPoint presentations with voice-over, and printable PowerPoint slides.

To help ensure student preparation for class, students were expected to complete worksheets that were periodically but randomly collected and graded. Class time was then spent on activities that encouraged students to process and apply economics principles, ranging from mini-lectures in response to student questions to economic experiments to small group discussions of application problems. Both student and instructor response to the approach was positive, with instructors noting that students appeared more motivated than when the course was taught in a traditional format.

Peer Instruction

Peer model requires that students gain first exposure prior to class, and uses assignments (in this case, quizzes) to help ensure that students come to class prepared. Class time is structured around alternating mini-lectures and conceptual questions. Importantly, the conceptual questions are not posed informally and answered by student volunteers as in traditional lectures; instead, all students must answer the conceptual question, often via "clickers", or handheld personal response systems, that allow students to answer anonymously and that allow the instructor to see (and display) the class data immediately. If a large fraction of the class (usually between 30 and 65%) answers incorrectly, then students reconsider the question in small groups while instructors circulate to promote productive discussions. After discussion, students answer the conceptual question again. The instructor provides feedback, explaining the correct answer and following up with related questions if appropriate. The cycle is then repeated with another topic, with each cycle typically taking 13-15 minutes.

By providing an opportunity for students to *use* their new factual knowledge while they have access to immediate feedback from peers and the instructor, the flipped classroom helps students learn to correct misconceptions and organize their new knowledge such that it is more accessible for future use.

"A 'met cognitive' approach to instruction can help students learn to take control of their own learning by defining learning goals and monitoring their progress in achieving them".

Although students' thinking about their own learning is not an inherent part of the flipped classroom, the higher cognitive functions associated with class activities, accompanied by the ongoing peer/ instructor interaction that typically accompanies them, can readily lead to the met cognition associated with deep learning.

The key elements of the flipped classroom

Provide an opportunity for students to gain first exposure prior to class. The mechanism used for first exposure can vary, from simple textbook readings to lecture videos to podcasts or screen casts. Video lectures prior to class. Videos can be created by the instructor or found online from YouTube.

The purpose of flipping the classroom is to shift from **passive** to **active learning** to focus on the higher order thinking skills such as analysis, synthesis and evaluation. Students access key content individually (or in small groups) prior to class time and then meet face-to-face in the larger group to explore content through active learning and engagement strategies.

In the flipped classroom, the **roles and expectations** of students and teachers change where:

1. students take **more responsibility** for their own learning and study core content either individually or in groups before class and then apply knowledge and skills to a range of activities using **higher order thinking**,
2. Teaching 'one-to-many' focuses more on **facilitation** and moderation than lecturing, though lecturing is still important. **Significant learning opportunities** can be gained through facilitating active learning, engaging students, guiding learning, correcting misunderstandings and providing timely feedback using a variety of pedagogical strategies,
3. There is a greater focus on **concept exploration**, **meaning making** and **demonstration** or application of knowledge in the face-to-face setting.

Important feature of the flipped classroom

1. **capture key content** for students to access at their own convenience and to suit their pace of learning (e.g. lecture material, readings, interactive multimedia),
2. **present learning materials** in a variety of formats to suit different learner styles (e.g. text, videos, audio, multimedia),
3. **provide opportunities for discourse** and interaction in and out of class (e.g. polling tools, discussion tools, content creation tools),
4. **convey timely information**, updates and reminders for students (e.g. micro-blogging, announcement tools),

5. **provide immediate and anonymous feedback** for teachers and students (e.g. quizzes, polls) to signal revision points,
6. **Capture data** about students to analyze their progress and identify 'at risk' students (e.g. analytics).

The Flipped Classroom IS

1. A means to INCREASE interaction and personalized **contact time** between students and teachers.
2. An environment where students take **responsibility for their own learning**.
3. A classroom where the teacher is not the "sage on the stage", but the "**guide** on the side".
4. A **blending** of direct instruction with constructivist learning.
5. A classroom where students who are **absent** due to illness or extra-curricular activities such as athletics or field-trips, don't get left behind.
6. A class where content is permanently **archived** for review or remediation.
7. A class where all students are **engaged** in their learning.
8. A place where all students can get a **personalized** education.

The Advantages and Disadvantages of the Traditional Classroom

The advantages of the classroom setting most students are familiar with include, of course, surroundings that students feel more comfortable in. In classrooms with a smaller teacher-to-student ratio, students can even get more direct assistance. Because there is real time interaction and students and their instructor speak instead of typing, more ground can be covered in less time.

There is also a physical space that can be utilized. An instructor or student can point to a page in their text. The instructor can write information down on a white board. Students can discuss information with each other, and because they are speaking in person, there is less chance that one of them will be misunderstood.

Interaction

One of the main advantages to traditional classroom learning is the students' ability to openly interact with both the teacher and other students in the classroom and allows her a better opportunity to properly engage and inspire her students.

Social Interaction

In a traditional classroom setting, students can correspond with and learn from other children who are both like and unlike them in many different ways. Students learn better communications skills, which will lead to better writing and speaking skills, which wouldn't be possible in a virtual classroom setting. Colorful Worksheets-Engage & Learn. Much Cheaper than Printable Sheets

Structure

Traditional classrooms hold a bit of comfort. This traditional structure these systems also teach students, children and adults alike, time management and discipline when they know they must get something done by the next day and bring it into the class.

Fewer Technology Requirements

Many students do not have access to technology, such as computers or the internet that would make learning in a non-traditional classroom possible for them. In this, traditional classrooms have a major advantage because students do not need constant access to either a computer or the internet.

The traditional classroom does have some disadvantages when compared to online instruction. The noisy students in the back of the room can be distracting to other students, just as noise in the hallway might detract from the professor's lecture. Quieter students also may not ever have a chance to participate if there are other students who tend to never give up the floor. Shy or marginalized students may not feel like they should speak up. The online environment is a more level playing field in that everyone can ask a question and be recognized, no matter how "quiet" she is.

Advantages and disadvantages of Flipped classroom

The best reason than to attend an online university would be if one cannot uproot her life, if she must maintain the job she has in the place where she already lives. Online students also don't have to worry about commuting or carrying heavy textbooks around a large campus. Their living room is their classroom.

When a student takes online classes, he must not only be able to attend class online, but he will also need to do his research online (often through the campus' virtual library). He also needs to have a computer or at least have access to one.

Obviously, he must be self-disciplined; he won't have classes on a set schedule and will have to be responsible. He should also feel that he is competent in email communication, and he should have a basic understanding of netiquette rules. Finally, the online student should be a fairly competent typist. If he types slowly, it will take him longer to "speak" online. Online colleges also tend to cost a little more than traditional schools.

Internet classes aren't for everyone. Some students feel a sense of isolation because they never really get to know any of their classmates. Sometimes if a student needs extra help, he doesn't quite know how to go about asking or how to communicate his needs online. Some students do better in a traditional classroom setting.

Significance of Both the System

Time Management

Both Flipped and traditional classes require students to manage their time wisely. In traditional classes, students structure their time outside of the classroom to allow for studying, projects and homework.

Participation

Both Flipped and classroom-based courses also assess student participation. In traditional classes, students voluntarily participate in discussions or ask and answer questions. In online courses, participation is mandatory, usually through written discussions in chat rooms or on message boards. Students, therefore, have the opportunity to hear a wider range of perspectives, including those of people who may struggle with participating in a traditional environment.

Student and Teacher Relationships

In a classroom-based course, face-to-face communication creates a different dynamic for every class. Online classes, however, lack this interaction, requiring teachers to use forums, chats and other online discussion media to build community. Students also lack the opportunity to get to know the instructor in-person. While traditional classrooms let students gain support and personal relationships from teachers, online courses only offer electronic communication.

Assignments and Tests

Traditional classroom instructors can offer virtually every type of assessment, from written work to tests to oral examinations and presentations. However, online classes are more limited in the types of assignments students can complete. Typically, online instructors grade students through papers, open-book examinations and student contributions to online discussions. Because online students must be self-directed, online instructors usually design assignments that are practical in nature. Many students find this approach more effective than cramming for tests and quizzes.

Conclusion

While some studies show online students slightly outperforming their traditional classroom counterparts, most indicate that there is little difference in overall performance between the two formats. One major difference is that student-learning style plays a role in each format's success. Students who are highly self-directed, organized and autonomous will likely thrive in an online environment, while those who tend to rely on instructors for direction may struggle. Similarly, extroverted students who enjoy face-to-face classroom interactions may do best in a traditional environment, while introverted students may welcome the solitary qualities of online classes. Some students excel in online classes. They like the freedom to come and go as they please. They like being able to use their computer skills. They enjoy sitting at the computer to read their class lecture and do their coursework. Other students prefer the traditional classroom, thriving on the set schedule, the physical textbooks, and the face-to-face interaction with peers and their instructor. There is no right or wrong learning environment. It really does depend on the type of learner one is and what kind of classes fit into his lifestyle. Fortunately, in this day and age, students have lots of choices.

References

1. Anderson LW and Krathwohl D (2001). *A taxonomy for learning, teaching, and assessing: a revision of Bloom's taxonomy of educational objectives.* New York: Longman.
2. Berrett D (2012). How 'flipping' the classroom can improve the traditional lecture. *The Chronicle of Higher Education,* Feb. 19, 2012.
3. Bransford JD, Brown AL, and Cocking RR (2000). *How people learn: Brain, mind, experience, and school.* Washington, D.C.: National Academy Press.
4. Crouch CH and Mazur E (2001). Peer instruction: Ten years of experience and results. *American Journal of Physics* 69: 970-977.
5. DesLauriers L, Schelew E, and Wieman C (2011). Improved learning in a large-enrollment physics class. *Science*332: 862-864.
6. Fitzpatrick M (2012). Classroom lectures go digital. *The New York Times,* June 24, 2012.
7. Hake R (1998). Interactive-engagement versus traditional methods: A six-thousand-student survey of mechanics test data for introductory physics courses.
8. Lage MJ, Platt GJ, and Treglia M (2000). Inverting the classroom: A gateway to creating an inclusive learning environment. *The Journal of Economic Education* 31: 30-43.

9. Mazur E (2009). Farewell, Lecture? *Science* 323: 50-51.

10. Novak G, Patterson ET, Gavrin AD, and Christian W (1999). *Just-in-Time Teaching: Blending Active Learning with Web Technology*. Upper Saddle River, NJ: Prentice Hall.

11. Pashler H, McDaniel M, Rohrer D, and Bjork R (2008). Learning styles: Concepts and evidence. Psychological Science in the Public Interest 9: 103-119.

12. Walvoord BE, and Anderson VJ (1998). *Effective grading: A tool for learning and assessment*. San Francisco: Jossey-Bass.

22

Hyper Diversed Teacher and Digital Skills

Introduction

Social media have risen to prominence in recent years, beginning first with sites like Classmates in the mid-1990s, followed by Friendsterin 2003. The most significant growth of social media has occurred since 2004 when Facebook.com was introduced. Today there are over 550 million Facebook users alone, along with millions more using sites such as Twitter, MySpace, Plaxo, LinkedIn and others. While early adopters of these sites were digital natives (i.e., those born and/or raised in the internet era), all age groups are now embracing these sites. Teacher Educators and Student teachers always find it easier to use the already made teaching aids for teaching practice for preparation of lessons and in their theory learning and submission of assignments .in such situation the modern technology i.e. internet is challenging them to be more innovative , explorative and modern in their teaching and learning experiences . Teaching faculty is challenged by the digital world to be in pursuit of skills development. At present there is a gap between campus pedagogy and social media usage among students and faculty. Teaching community need to be skilled digitally. This paper works to examine that chasm, and to draw some conclusions as to why it may be time to incorporate this technology into our classrooms. The researcher used the self constructed tool HYPER ADOPTION SCALE (HAS) to achieve this motive. The samples were 100 teacher educators and 200 student teachers. In methodology the statistical used were MEAN, Standard Deviation and 't' test. The findings show that the level of hyper diversification among the samples is high, and there is no significant difference among the samples based on the variables Locality, Residence, Status(teacher educators/student teachers) and Educational qualification(UG/PG) . However there exists a significant difference in term of Browsing habit. The educational implications suggest ways to diversify the teaching community and empower them digitally.

Social media have risen to prominence in recent years, beginning first with sites like Classmates in the mid-1990s, followed by Friendsterin 2003. The most significant growth of social media has occurred since 2004 when Facebook.com was introduced. Today there are over 550 million Facebook users alone, along with millions more using sites such as Twitter, MySpace, Plaxo, LinkedIn and others. While early adopters of these sites were digital natives (i.e., those born and/or raised in the internet era), all age groups are now embracing these sites. At present there is a gap between campus pedagogy and social media usage among students and faculty. Teaching community need to be skilled digitally. This paper works to examine that chasm, and to draw some conclusions as to why it may be time to incorporate this technology into our classrooms.

Need For the Study

Social media sites such as Face book and Twitter have come to dominate internet usage in recent years. Face book alone has over 550 million users as of fall 2010, while Twitter claims over 100 million users. While academia was fairly quick to adopt online education models in the 1990s, it has thus far not yet embraced social media portals as a way to deliver course content and engage students. This may be due to uncertainties regarding student perceptions about social media, its purposes, and its applications. Teacher Educators and Student teachers always find it easier to use the already made teaching aids for teaching practice for preparation of lessons and in their theory learning and submission of assignments in such situation the modern technology i.e. internet is challenging them to be more innovative, explorative and modern in their teaching and learning experiences. Teaching faculty is challenged by the digital world to be in pursuit of skills development. Hence the need for the study.

Background of the Study

The researcher is involved in the educational institution which is in the forefront to promote quality of pedagogy. The experience of the researcher has often been frustrating with lack of digital climate. Since the Tamil nadu Teachers Education University has created a platform for such pondering this study found its way out to reach out to the professional mob to leverage the educational system through virtualization of the academia. The HD (Hyper Diversified) Classroom is the need of the hour. Just as the digital divide vanished over time (males once dominated all computer and internet usage), it is possible that similar usage divides will also disappear. Online college courses, for example, have broad-based appeal, and even traditional campus-based courses often have high computer usage expectations. Given that social media are now part of the cultural fabric, it is necessary to explore if and how social media might find their place in academia. Therefore the researcher undertook this study.

Sample for the Study

300 Samples Comprising Teacher Educators and Student Teachers (100 teacher Educators and 200 Student Teachers)

Objectives of the Study

1. To construct a tool to find out the level of hyper diversification among teacher educators and student teachers
2. To realize the importance of hyper diversification and developing digital skills among teacher educators and student teachers.

3. To find out whether any difference exists among teacher educators and student teachers in their hyper diversification and digital skills in terms of the following variables:
    1. Locality
    2. Residence
    3. Status(teacher/student)
    4. Educational qualification(UG/PG)
    5. Browsing habit

Hypotheses of the Study

1. The level of hyper diversification among teacher educators and student teachers is high.
2. There is a significant difference among teacher educators and student teachers in their hyper diversification and digital skills in terms of the following variables:
    6. Locality
    7. Residence
    8. Status(teacher/student)
    9. Educational qualification(UG/PG)
    10. Browsing habit

Methodology

In order to carry out the study the researcher used the following statistical

Techniques

MEAN, STANDARD DEVIATION and 't' test

Mean

Mean was calculated by the formula

$\overline{X} = \frac{\Sigma x}{N}$ Where X = Score, N = Total Number of the scores.

Standard Deviation

Standard deviation was calculated by the following formula

$$\sigma = \frac{\sqrt{(X - \bar{X})^2}}{N}$$

Where $\bar{X}$ = Mean

X = Individual score

N = Total Number of the scores

Test of significant difference ('t' test)

Since the groups were large independent samples, the 't' test was applied through the statistical package by using the following formula:

$$t \quad \frac{M_1 \quad M_2}{\sqrt{\frac{\sigma_1^2}{N_1} \quad \frac{\sigma_2^2}{N_2}}}$$

Where M_1 - denotes mean of group 1

M_2 - denotes mean of group 2

$\acute{o}_1$ - denotes standard deviation of group 1

$\acute{o}_2$ - denotes standard deviation of group 2

N_1 - denotes total number of respondents in group 1

N_2 - denotes total number of respondents in group 2

Hypothesis 1

The level of hyper diversification and digital skills among teacher educators and student teachers is high.

Table 1 showing the analysis of hyper diversification and digital skills among teacher Educators and student teachers.

Entire Sample	N	Mean	S.D
Hyper Diversification	300	109.1	2.79
Digital Skills	300	24.21	3.40

The above table 1 shows that the mean and standard deviation on hyper diversification of the entire sample of teacher educators and student teachers' scores are 109.1 and 2.79 respectively. As 109.1 is higher than the mid-value of 64.1 (maximum score 129), it is concluded that the teacher educators and student teachers have a high level of hyper diversification. The mean and standard deviation on digital skills of the entire sample of teacher educators and student teachers' scores are 24.21 and 3.40 respectively. As 24.21 is higher than the mid-value of15 (maximum score 30), it is concluded that the teacher educators and student teachers have a high level of hyper diversification and digital skills.

HYPOTHESIS 2(a): There is a significant difference among teacher educators and student

Teachers in their hyper diversification and digital skills in terms of Locality.

The details of the results of the't' test in the level of hyper diversification and digital skills among teacher educators and student teachers based on Locality is given in table no.2.

Table- 2 Difference in the level of hyper diversification and digital skills based on Locality

Variables	Sub variables	N	Mean	SD	't' value	Level of Significance	Result
Locality	Urban	160	21.31	3.12	**1.13**	**0.05**	**NS**
	Rural	140	23.52	2.86			

It is evident from table no.2 that the calculated't' value 1.13 is less than the table value 1.96 at 0.05 level. This shows that there is no significant difference among teacher educators and student teachers in their hyper diversification and digital skills in terms of Locality.

Hence, there is no significant difference between the samples (teacher educators and student teachers) that live in Urban and Rural areas in their hyper diversification and digital skills.

Hypothesis 2(b): There is a significant difference among teacher educators and student teachers in their hyper diversification and digital skills in terms of Residence.

The details of the results of the 't' test in the level of hyper diversification and digital skills among teacher educators and student teachers based on Residence is given in table no.3.

Table- 3 Difference in the level of hyper diversification and digital skills based on Residence

Variables	Sub variables	N	Mean	SD	't' value	Level of Significance	Result
Residence	Hostel	130	22.42	3.40	**1.049**	**0.05**	**NS**
	Home	170	25.63	4.60			

It is evident from table no.3 that the calculated 't' value 1.049 is less than the table value 1.96 at 0.05 levels. This shows that there is no significant difference among teacher educators and student teachers in their hyper diversification and digital skills in terms of Residence.

Hence, there is no significant difference between the samples (teacher educators and student teachers) who reside at hostel and at home in their hyper diversification and digital skills.

Hypothesis (2C): There is a significant difference among teacher educators and student teachers in their hyper diversification and digital skills in terms of Status (teacher educator/student teacher).

The details of the results of the 't' test in the level of hyper diversification and digital skills among teacher educators and student teachers based on Status((teacher educator/student teacher) is given in table no.4.

Table- 4 Difference in the level of hyper diversification and digital skills based on Status (teacher educator/student teacher)

Variables	Sub variables	N	Mean	SD	't' value	Level of Significance	Result
STATUS	Teacher Educators	100	20.24	3.98 3	**1.61**	**0.05**	**NS**
	Student Teachers	200	22.57	3.79 3			

It is evident from table no.4 that the calculated 't' value 1.61 is less than the table value 1.96 at 0.05 levels. This shows that there is no significant difference among teacher educators and student teachers in their hyper diversification and digital skills in terms of Status.

Hence, there is no significant difference between the samples (teacher educators and student teachers) in Status in their hyper diversification and digital skills.

Hypothesis 2(d): There is a significant difference among teacher educators and student teachers in their hyper diversification and digital skills in terms of Educational Qualification (UG/PG).

The details of the results of the 't' test in the level of hyper diversification and digital skills among teacher educators and student teachers based on Educational Qualification(UG/PG)

Is given in table no.5.

Table – 5 Difference in the level of hyper diversification and digital skills based on Educational Qualification(UG/PG)

Variables	Sub variables	N	Mean	SD	't' value	Level of Significance	Result
Educational Qualification	UG PG	100 200	22.35 21.50	3.902 3.340	**1.21**	**0.05**	**NS**

It is evident from table no.5 that the calculated 't' value 1.21 is less than the table value 1.96 at 0.05 levels. This shows that there is no significant difference among teacher educators and student teachers in their hyper diversification and digital skills in terms of Educational Qualification(UG/PG).

Hence, there is no significant difference among teacher educators and student teachers in their hyper diversification and digital skills in terms of Educational Qualification (UG/PG).

Hypothesis 2(e): There is a significant difference among teacher educators and student teachers in their hyper diversification and digital skills in terms of Browsing habit. The details of the results of the 't' test in the level of hyper diversification and digital skills among teacher educators and student teachers based on browsing habit is given in table no.6

Table – 6 Difference in the level of hyper diversification and digital skills based on Browsing Habit

Variables	Sub variables	N	Mean	SD	't' value	Level of Significance	Result
Browsing Habit	Frequently	120	17.73	3.679	**5.820**	**0.05**	**S**
	Rarely	180	19.28	3.431			

It is evident from table no.6 that the calculated 't' value 5.820 is higher than the table value 1.96 at 0.05 levels. This shows that there is a significant difference among teacher educators and student teachers in their hyper diversification and digital skills in terms of Browsing habit.

Hence, there is a significant difference among teacher educators and student teachers in their hyper diversification and digital skills in terms of Browsing habit.

Hypotheses Verification

1. The level of hyper diversification among teacher educators and student teachers is high - **Accepted**
2. There is a significant difference among teacher educators and student teachers in their hyper diversification and digital skills in terms of of Locality - **Rejected**
3. There is a significant difference among teacher educators and student teachers in their hyper diversification and digital skills in terms of Residence - **Rejected**
4. There is a significant difference among teacher educators and student teachers in their hyper diversification and digital skills in terms of Status(teacher/student) - **Rejected**
5. There is a significant difference among teacher educators and student teachers in their hyper diversification and digital skills in terms of educational qualification(UG/PG) - **Rejected**

6. There is a significant difference among teacher educators and student teachers in their hyper diversification and digital skills in terms of Browsing habit - **Accepted**

Educational Implications

1. The result of the study leads to encourage Teacher Educators Student teachers to be hyper diversified and digitally skilled .
2. The usage of virtual world can be enhanced in colleges to develop skills and build capacity as part of professional life.

   Therefore Teacher Educators and Student Teachers can:

3. create and edit digital audios
4. use Social bookmarking to share resources with and between learners
5. use blogs and wikis to create online platforms for students
6. Exploit digital images for classroom use
7. Use video content to engage students
8. Use infographics to visually stimulate students
9. Use Social networking sites to connect with colleagues and grow professionally
10. Create and deliver asynchronous presentations and training sessions
11. Compile a digital e-portfolio for their own development
12. Have a knowledge about online security
13. be able to detect plagiarized works in students assignments
14. Create screen capture videos and tutorials
15. Curate web content for classroom learning
16. Use and provide students with task management tools to organize their work and plan their learning
17. Use polling software to create a real-time survey in class
18. Understand issues related to copyright and fair use of online materials

19. Exploit computer games for pedagogical purposes
20. Use digital assessment tools to create quizzes
21. Use of collaborative tools for text construction and editing
22. Find and evaluate authentic web based content
23. Identify online resources that are safe for students browsing
24. Use digital tools for time management purposes
25. Learn about the different ways to use YouTube in your classroom
26. Use note taking tools to share interesting content with your students
27. Annotate web pages and highlight parts of text to share with your class
28. Use of online graphic organizers and printables
29. Use of online sticky notes to capture interesting idea
30. Use of screen casting tools to create and share tutorials
31. Exploit group text messaging tools for collaborative project work
32. Conduct an effective search query with the minimum time possible
33. Conduct A Research Paper Using Digital Tools
34. Use file sharing tools to share docs and files with students online
35. Reduce Infrastructure Costs Through Consolidation
36. Virtualize the Most Demanding Workloads
37. Virtualize for High Availability
38. Improve Security and Reliability with Microkernelized Hypervisor
39. Protect Important Data Using Live Backup
40. Minimize Downtime with Quick Migration
41. Delegate Virtual Machine Management
42. Reduce Support Time with Integrated Management

43. Save Time and Money with a More Flexible Test Environment
44. Take Advantage of Broad Compatibility
45. Reduce Support Time with Integrated Management
46. Save Time and Money with a More Flexible Test Environment
47. Take Advantage of Broad Compatibility
48. Exploit Facebook,Youtube,Flickr andSocial networking Sites(SNS) for sharing eduinformation
49. Use Smartphones, iphones, tablets as educational resources.
50. Accomplish content delivery and student engagement by creating and maintaining a Fan Page, at no cost to anyone involved, and completely away from the limitations of course management systems such as Bloackboard, Angel and WebCT.

Bibliography

1. Baird, D., Fisher, M. (2005). Neomillennial user experience strategies: Utilizing social networking media to support "always on" learning styles. Journal of Educational Technology Systems. 34 (1) 5 - 32.
2. Bimber, B. (2000). Measuring the gender gap on the Internet. Social Sciences Quarterly, 81 (3):25-32.
3. Broos, A. (2005). Gender and information and communication technologies (ICT) anxiety: Male self-assurance and female hesitation. Cyber psychology & Behavior8(1):21-31.
4. Dennis, A.R., Kinney, S.T., & Hung, Y.T.C. (1999) Gender differences in the effects of media richness.Small Group Research . 30 (4): 405-437.
5. Dillon, D. (2001). E-books: The University of Texas Experience. Library Hi Tech. 19 (4) 350-62.
6. Gefen, D. & Straub, D. W. (1997) Gender differences in the perception and use of email: an extension to the technology acceptance model. MIS Quarterly 4: 389-400.
7. Horowitz, R. & Mohum, A. (1998). His and Hers: Gender Consumption & Technology. University of Virginia Press.

8. Jackson L.A., Ervin, K.S., Gardner, P.D. & Schmitt,N. (2001). Gender and the internet: women communicating and men searching.

9. Lenhart, M. (2010). Teens and Social Media, An Overview. Pew Internet and American Life Project.

10. Summerfield, M., Mandel, C., Kantor, P. (1999). Online books at Columbia: Early findings on use, satisfaction, and effect. Technology and Scholarly Communication. Berkley; University of California Press 282-308.

11. Wilska, A. (2003). Mobile use as part of young people's consumption styles.

23

Learning with Cloud Computing Technology

Introduction

'Swami Vivekananda voice education is the process of bringing out the potential that is latent is every human being India's educational system is the most ancient in the world's history teaching and learning is as old as human race'. Education is closely bound with the intellectual, economic, cultural, emotional and social life of the community. Education is one of the important instruments for improving the quality of people, society nation and it also helps in meeting challenges of fast developments in the world. Innovation in education is a means to enhance quality in education.

Innovations societies at large will make the fortune innovative centric teaching learning process need to be promoted in schools, colleges, institutions and universities. Education is a challenging academic discipline, learning with cloud computing is become a dominant model in information technology (IT). Field these days, this paper focuses on integrating and enhancing the learning using cloud computing technique.

Cloud computing has refers to the applications delivered as services over the internet and the hard ware and system software located in the data centers that provide the services. Cloud computing in an internet-based technology through which information stored in servers and provided as a service on-demand to clients. This technology has made the software more attractive as a services and shaped various industries.

Many students would likely cite a desire to learn. Students assume that, because they have read their text and memorized facts, they have learned something. Definition of 'learn' in a dictionary step, Step1. To acquire knowledge of a subject or skill through education or experience, Step2. To gain information about somebody or something. Step3. To memorize something. This definition is not particularly insightful, although it reminds us that the word can be used to describe the acquisition of both knowledge and skill, and that acquisition can be by a variety of means. Including education experience, or memorization.

Effects of educational Technology with multiples Intelligence

1. Educational technology has a significant positive impact on achievement in all subjects' area, across all levels of school and in regular classroom as well as those for special-needs students.
2. Educational Technology has positive effects on student attitudes.
3. Technology makes instruction more student-centered, encourages co-operative learning and stimulated increased teacher/ student interaction.
4. Positive changes in the learning environments evolve over time and do not occur quickly.
5. Educational games which challenge fine motor coordination while developing logical thinking skills and mastery over abstraction.

Learning

Learning is modifying the existing knowledge behavior skill etc., this can be achieved through continuous process and the change that and individual exhibit in relatively permanent. Psychologists explain many theories when an individual acquire difference patterns in behavior.

1. Conditioning learning theory
2. Cognitive learning theory
3. Social learning theory

Conditioning learning theory

Pavlov (1927) Pavlov conducted an experiment with a dog by providing it with piece of meat bone and by introducing bell sound to test its stimulus and response. Behavior can be learned by repetitive association between a stimulus and response. This is law of exercise.

B.F. Skinner (1938) operant conditioning learning theory: It is a type of conditioning in which desired voluntary behavior leads to a reward or prevents a punishment. This theory status that behavior is voluntary and it is determined maintained and controlled by its consequences.

Cognitive Learning theory: Edward c. Tolman (1948) an American psychologist stress the importance of perception problem solving and insight. Tolman found that learning in corporate relationship between cognitive environmental cues and expectation.

Social learning theory: this theory proposed by Albert (1977). Individual can learn through observation and direct experience.

In common the above three theories states that learning is done by observation, response and stimulus though which an individual reacts.

We have two type of learning one is horizontal learning and other one is vertical learning. Horizontal learning is eye view over a concept. But vertical learning is deep study is not done in totality but focuses on specific topics. Integrating IT advanced techniques in all fields will enhance their proficiency. An individual can attain proficiency only by continuous learning.

Cloud computing is an emerging process in IT Industries. The process is carried out over internet integrating cloud computing and vertical learning can bring tremendous change in knowledge.

Different kinds of thinking and learning

In cognitive theory and education have used Bloom's (1956) taxonomic of learning. Bloom and colleagues identified three learning domains. The cognitive domains involve thinking of all sorts. The affective domain includes feelings, emotions, attitude, values and motivations.

The psychomotor domain of learning includes physical movement, coordination, motor, and sensory-skills. When a learning experience has a profound effect on a student, it can result in a greater sense of caring for the subject, for them, other or learning in general. Greater caring can lead to new interests, energy for learning, or a change in values. 'To learn how to learn' this includes learning how to diagnose one's own need for learning and how to be a self-learner. Then type of learning enables students to continue learning with greater effectiveness and is a particularly important skill with the recent explosion of knowledge and technology.

Cloud Computing: Cloud storage is a network-based service which does not exist physically rather it's a virtualiesed pool of networking for sharing data over network. Cloud computing is mostly hosted by third parties and its limits the user to work with given configuration and storage. Hence individual can create their own cloud. Own cloud is a free, open-sources and powerful web application for data synchronization file sharing and remote storage of files. It is written in java script languages.

Uses: Vertical Integrated teaching and learning makes teaching learning process fruitful and is carried out by creating own cloud install own cloud storage in Linux, create cloud database.

1. Students or learner are allowed to access the cloud to upgrade their knowledge that shapes an individual. Students can access their account any time any where depending on their conveniences.

2. Individuals are provided with username and password. Even user can undelete the accidentally deleted data's from trash.
3. Uploading Videos, images in the cloud excites their interest and thinking process of the learners.

Conclusion

Technology is a tool for teachers to deliver knowledge and a tool for students the acquire it in the best and most efficient way. It will create different atmosphere in education program. Students will acquire knowledge and new way of learning by using technological resources. As education is a wide sector in today world, integrating it with IT techniques will enhance nation's development towards ICT and individual to be an optimistic learner' Education plays on important role in growth of a nation and hence a developed India by 2020 can be achieved.

Bibliography

1. AACU, 2002, Greater Expectations: A New Vision for Learning as a Nation Goes to College: National panel Report, American Association of Colleges and Universities, Washington, DC62p.
2. Atkinson,R.L Atkinson R.C Smith, E.E and Bem D.J., 1993, Introduction to Psychology, Harcourt Brace Jovanovich, Fort Worth, TX, 11 the edition
3. Cuesta College, 2004, Characteristics of a Successful Student: Cuesta College. Available at: http://academic. Cuesta.edu/accasupp/as/201.HTM.
4. Johnson, D.W., Johnson, R.T., and Smith, K., 1991, Active Learning: Cooperation in the College Classroom Interaction Book Company, Edina, MN.
5. Krathwohl, D.R.Bloom, B.S, and Masia,B.B., 1964, Taxonomy of Educational objectives. The classification of Educational Goals, Handbook II: Affective Domain. David McKay Company,Inc
6. Teaching Goals Inventory,2004, Available form: http://www.uiowa.edu/-centeach/tgi/.

24

Implementation of Cloud Computing in Education

Introduction

Innovation is necessary to ride the inevitable tide of change and one such hot recent area of research in Information Technology (IT) is cloud computing. Cloud computing is a distributed computing technology offering required software and hardware through Internet. It also provides storage, computational platform and infrastructure which are demanded by the user according to their requirement. Due to the growing need of infrastructure educational institutes, organizations have to spend a large amount on their infrastructure to fulfill the needs and demands of the users. Cloud computing is a next generation platform that allows institutions and organizations with a dynamic pools of resource and to reduce cost through improved utilization.

In the present scenario, many education institutions are facing the problems with the growing need of IT and infrastructure. Cloud computing which is an emerging technology and which relies on existing technology such as Internet, virtualization, grid computing etc. can be a solution to such problems by providing required infrastructure, software and storage. In this paper a basic research has been carried out to show how cloud computing can be introduced in the education to improve teaching, agility and have a cost-effective infrastructure which can bring a revolution in the field of education. It also tries to bring out its benefits and limitations.

The concept of cloud computing dates back to 1960, when John McCarthy opined that "computation may someday be organized as a public utility". The term 'cloud computing' is confusion to many people as the term can be used to mean almost anything. 'Cloud' is used as a metaphor for Internet and its main objective is customization and user defined experience. In other words cloud computing provides shared resources, software and information through Internet as a PAYGO (Pay-as-you-go) basis. In the recent years, where educational institutes, universities, industries are giving their full contribution in transforming the society and entire world economy. Various researches are carried out to update the present IT infrastructure especially in the area of education.

Cloud computing can be a welcomed optioned in the universities and educational institutes for higher studies. It gives a better choice and flexibility to the IT departments by building multipurpose computational infrastructure once and then Manuscript received. Uses it for several purposes for several times. Amazon, Google have already started providing their facilities for large business group. With the help of cloud computing the platform and application the user uses can be on-campus or off-campus or combination of both depending on the institutions need. Due to the evolution of cloud computing number of services have migrated from the traditional system to the online form. At present, as many universities are trying to update their IT infrastructure and data, but they are facing few challenges.

Defining the cloud

Broadly, the cloud can be described as on-demand computing, for anyone with a network connection. Access to applications and data anywhere, anytime, from any device is the potential outcome.

The consumer-level cloud is a good starting point for this – sites like Flickr and Face book act as digital repositories for data and we can access this data from any internet-enabled device, from our iPhones to our desktop computers. In the case of Flickr and the like, storage of our digital images is, from the consumer point of view, somewhere in the cloud. We don't need to know where specifically, we just need our Flickr login credentials and a web connection. We can see this model as evident in web-based email too.

The starting point (the bottom layer) is the physical hardware – the servers in data centers, whether owned by a firm or university for internal use or by the likes of Amazon or Google for public access. The next layer is virtualization. Virtualization allows a single physical server to run many independent virtual servers and is a necessary part of gaining the efficiencies (built on economies of scale) that cloud computing can offer those running the data centers. Automating the allocation of computing resources amongst the virtual servers and tracking user (customer) resource use requires a management layer. As Naone (2009a) highlights, this allows "true pay-as-you-go" billing which is part of the appeal of the cloud for users.

The cloud, however, doesn't stop here. The provision of software (services) to end-users mediated by the web is what has come to be known as Software as a Service (resulting in the rather clumsy acronym SaaS). This builds a further layer – the software running in the cloud and being accessed by users through their browser or other web-compliant tool. Firms like Salesforce.com have successfully built their business model entirely around providing web-based software, with the users' data storage and the processing of that data taking place in the cloud, rather than on the clients' own servers or their local machines.

Which can be solved by cloud computing. The challenges are;

Cost: choose the subscription or PAYGO plan.

Flexibility: cloud computing allows to dynamically scale the investment in infrastructures as demand fluctuate.

Accessibility: making the data and services available publicly without losing the sensitive information

Services of Cloud

With an aim of reducing the expenditure of the universities for IT infrastructure and the complexity faced by universities and institutions, the traditional installed software on the campus computers are now replaced by cloud computing. With the power of cloud, today higher education can gain significant flexibility and agility and can migrate the sensitive data into remote and world wide data center 'the cloud' itself. To use the cloud services the universities and the institutions has to first define their requirements and has to take a special attention for the privacy and critical issues.

There are several cloud services as follows

1. Software as a Service (**SaaS**): the application service provider is hosting the application which runs and interacts through web browser, hosted desktop or remote client. It eliminates the need to install and run the application on customer own computer and simplifying maintenance and support.
2. Infrastructure as a Service (**IaaS**): can be used to satisfy the infrastructure needs of the students, faculties or researcher globally or locally with some specific hardware configuration for a specific task.
3. Platform as a Service (**PaaS**): certain providers are opening up application platforms to permit customer's to build their own application without the cost and complexity of buying and managing the underlying hardware and software layers.
4. Computing as a Service (**CaaS**): providers offer access Implementation of Cloud Computing in Education – A Revolution.

Cloud Architecture for Education

Due to the higher accessibility, availability and efficiency of cloud services many universities, businesses are trying to make use of these services. Today's cloud computing providers are offering higher education, the opportunity to substitute their data and information in the 'cloud' for universities with existing data centers, servers and application replacing these traditional campus machines. Developing a cloud architecture for education can be distinct according to the purpose and infrastructure of the institution and can be challenging. The universities has to follow all the rules and regulation of the state and country for developing a cloud for education as many countries are very strict in cross broader transfer of information. Once the university establishes where their data will reside and gives the measure of data security an agreement called SLA (Service Level Agreement) can be made with the cloud service provider.

The SLA is a document which can ensure educational cloud users regarding the services provided by the cloud. It tries to identify the users need and simplifies complex issues and creates a relationship between the user and the service provider. It helps to specify the privacy, consistency and integrity. Privacy is one of the important factors which have to be taken care for cloud computing, as the service provider may require some personal information which is related to the data on what the user is trying to store in the cloud. So the universities should be very careful before disclosing the data and it should not lose the integrity of educational data.

There are many solutions that can ensure the security and protection of sensitive data in the cloud. These are;

1. Mask or de-identify of the data
2. Firewalls
3. Encryption and decryption
4. Authorization identity management.

Institutes can develop their own cloud called as 'private cloud' by making use of their existing Resources or multiple universities can come together and can develop a hybrid cloud called as 'educational cloud', in which they can share all the resources from the various universities. Private cloud makes use of the local network whereas the educational cloud makes use of public network to access the services provided by the cloud. Both private and educational cloud which is developed for education has to specify the services provided by them. Following table shows the differences between private and educational cloud.

Benefits and Limitations of Cloud Computing

Due to the recent development in IT technologies, infrastructure and continuous upgrades in software and hardware has put a great deal of pressure on the budgets and expenses of universities and educational institutes. Cloud computing development provides many universities with an opportunity to take advantage of new IT technologies at an affordable cost. Allows the lecturer to get their work done in their web browsers rather storing and carrying it on the hard drive.

1. Flexibility

The second a company needs more bandwidth than usual, a cloud-based service can instantly meet the demand because of the vast capacity of the service's remote servers. In fact, this flexibility is so crucial that 65% of respondents to an InformationWeek survey said "the ability to quickly meet business demands" was an important reason to move to cloud computing.

2. Disaster recovery

When companies start relying on cloud-based services, they no longer need complex disaster recovery plans. Cloud computing providers take care of most issues, and they do it faster. Aberdeen that businesses which used the cloud were able to resolve issues in an average of 2.1 hours, nearly four times faster than businesses that didn't use the cloud (8 hours). The same study found that mid-sized businesses had the best recovery times of all, taking almost half the time of larger companies to recover.

3. Automatic software updates

In 2010, UK companies spent 18 working days per month managing on-site security alone. But cloud computing suppliers do the server maintenance – Including security updates –themselves,

Freeing up their customers' time and resources for other tasks.

4. Cap-Ex Free

Cloud computing services are typically pay as you go, so there's no need for capital expenditure at all. And because cloud computing is much faster to deploy, businesses have minimal project start-up costs and predictable ongoing operating expenses.

5. Increased collaboration

Cloud computing increases collaboration by allowing all employees – wherever they are – to sync up and work on documents and shared apps simultaneously, and follow colleagues and records to receive critical updates in real time. A survey by Frost & Sullivan found that companies which invested in collaboration technology had a 400% return on investment.

6. Work from anywhere

As long as employees have internet access, they can work from anywhere. This flexibility positively affects knowledge workers' work-life balance and productivity. One study found that 42% of working adults would give up some of their salary if they could telecommute, and on average they would take a 6% pay cut.

7. Document control

According to one study, "73% of knowledge workers collaborate with people in different time zones and regions at least monthly". Cloud computing keeps all the files in one central location, and everyone works off of one central copy. Employees can even chat to each other whilst making changes together. This whole process makes collaboration stronger, which increases efficiency and improves a company's bottom line.

8. Security

Some 800,000 laptops are lost each year in airports alone. This can have some serious monetary implications, but when everything is stored in the cloud, data can still be accessed no matter what happens to a machine.

9. Competitiveness

The cloud grants SMEs access to enterprise-class technology. It also allows smaller businesses to act faster than big, established competitors. A study on disaster recovery eventually concluded that companies that didn't use the cloud had to rely on tape backup methods and complicated procedures to recover – slow, laborious things which cloud users simply don't use, allowing David to once again out-manoeuvre Goliath.

10. Environmentally Friendly

Businesses using cloud computing only use the server space they need, which decreases their carbon footprint. Using the cloud results in at least 30% less energy consumption and carbon emissions than using on-site servers. And again, SMEs get the most benefit: for small companies, the cut in energy use and carbon emissions is likely to be 90%.

Other Benefits Are

- Access the files from anywhere
- Create a backup of your data
- Stop worrying about additional software licenses
- Share content more easily
- Get things done without software hassles
- Access to applications from anywhere
- Support for teaching and learning
- Software free or PAYGO
- 24 X 7 access to infrastructure and content
- Opening to various universities and advanced researches
- Protection of environment by using green technologies
- Increased exposure of new IT technologies to students
- Increased functional capabilities
- Offline usage with further synchronization opportunities

Limitations

Cloud computing has the potential for improving the efficiency, cost and convenience for the universities and educational sectors, but it has **few limitations** such as;

1. Not all application run on cloud
2. Risk related to data protection and security and its integrity
3. Organizational support
4. Dissemination politics, intellectual property
5. Security and protection of sensitive data
6. Maturity of solutions
7. Lack of confidence
8. Standard adherence & Speed and lack of Internet can affect work methods

Conclusion

Cloud computing is an emerging computing paradigm and next generation platform that can provide tremendous value of information of any size. The shift towards cloud computing would enable the universities and educational institutions to save money and take benefit of the developing technology. Both private and educational cloud can provide the necessary computational facility on demand of the user without any expense and can create a common platform for sharing the various resources from the various institutions. In spite, of limitations of cloud computing and keeping in mind the present scenario of economic crisis many universities, educational intuitions, organizations etc are trying to adopt cloud computing as a solution to the developing technologies and try to reduce their expenses. The main objective of the paper was to identify the essentials of cloud computing which can be considered as a new dawn to the higher education and has the full potential to make a 'revolution' in the field of education.

Reference

1. J. L. Nicholson. Cloud Computing: Top Issues for Higher Education.
2. A. S. Dutta, Use of Cloud Computing in Education.
3. B. R. Kandukuri, V. R. Paturi, and A. Rakshit, "Cloud Security," in proceedings of the 2009 IEEE International Conference on Services. Computing, Washington, DC, USA, 2009, IEEE Computer Society, pp. 517-520.
4. R. N. Katz, The Tower and the Cloud: Higher Education in the age of cloud computing, 2008.
5. T. Ercan, "Effective Use of Cloud Computing in Educational Institutions,"

   Procedia Social and Behavioral Science, vol. 2, pp 938-942, 2010.

25

New Ways of Tomorrow Learning and Teaching Environment

Introduction

Traditionally, behaviouristic models have been used for the design of many interactive learning environments. In contrast, we propose a pedagogical model based on social constructivism and Phenomenography, which we believe is more adequate when, for instance, information seeking and the use of the WWW are natural components in the learning situation. To see learners as persons who continuously alter their conceptions and ideas by working with data, information and knowledge, i.e. to see learners as knowledge workers, corresponds well with social constructivism and Phenomenography. Frequently, the design of interactive learning systems focuses exclusively on computers and the virtual environments they provide, excluding the physical environment. We believe that the design of learning environments based on a combination of physical and virtual artifacts will enhance the learning experience. In this paper we present our efforts in exploring the implication of two learning theories, Phenomenography and social constructivism, for the design of learning environments that combine physical and virtual (computer-based) media.

There is general agreement as we approach the next century and next millennium that our society is changing into a knowledge and information society. The world is constantly evolving now at a faster pace than ever before, creating the challenge for individuals and organizations to deal with changes and for schools and universities to prepare people for changes. There is trend indicating that the amount of people working with knowledge and refinement of data and information is increasing. More and more of the laborers can be categorized as knowledge workers, hence knowledge workers is a group of workers who is growing in size and importance. Scientists, stockbrokers and journalists are examples of knowledge workers of today. The fact is that many tasks traditionally performed in physical environments are now done in virtual (electronic) environments, or they have been altered to fit to the new premises of emerging physical-virtual environments.

Knowledge Work

"The manual worker is yesterday. The basic capital resource, the fundamental investment, but also the cost centre for a developed economy is knowledge worker who puts to work what he has learned in systematic education, that is, concepts, ideas and theories, rather than the man who puts to work manual skill or muscle. History also indicates the existence of such metaphors, where the users have more control over the working situation, as in the case with craftsmanship a knowledge worker metaphor.

Pedagogical Issues

What kind of pedagogical framework has the ability to cope with the educational requirements that arise from this increasingly important group of laborers? A point of departure for this paper is a view on learning based on the following definition: "Learning is an active, constructive, cognitive and social process where the learner strategically manages available cognitive, physical, and social resources to create new knowledge by interacting with information in the environment and integrating it with information already stored in memory".

Furthermore, we assume that learning can be characterized by the following features:

Learning is embedded

Learning will take place in a situation we learn out in the real world where the knowledge and skills are needed to solve problems. "We must, therefore, attempt to use the intelligence in the learning environments to reflect and support the learner's or user's active creation or co-production, in situ, of idiosyncratic, hidden models and concepts, whose textures are developed between the learner/ user and the situating activity in which the technology is embedded."

Learning is a constructive process

As indicated by the fact that learning is embedded, we should view learning as a constructive process rather than a passive absorption of facts and rules. The view that the learner should acquire the expert's knowledge does not necessarily acknowledge this constructive perspective. Knowledge and skills are gained and regained over and over in an on-going process between the learner and situations in which the knowledge and skills are required. The central notion is that understanding and learning are active, constructive, generative processes such as assimilation, augmentation, and self-reorganization.

Knowledge is very much a question of understanding phenomena

The area of pedagogy traditionally takes a positivistic and quantitative view on knowledge. Phenomenography in contrast takes quite different view knowledge is understandings of phenomena, and learning is viewed as a process where these understandings are changed; this is a central principle. Other important characteristics are the analysis of the outcome of the learning process in qualitative terms, the move of focus from the "teacher-side" to the "learner-side" of the learning situation and the view on learning as a generative process, which is constantly going on.

The kind of motivation, and the kind of relevance of the topic, is two important factors that affect the level of processing. Internal motivation factors and internal relevance lead to a depth-directed level of processing which in turn implicates a better understanding or higher level of outcome. These relationships are almost functional, see Figure 1.

Active learning is good for the quality of the outcome

A deep-directed level of processing is characterized by an active way of processing the material active reading. Beside internal and external factors of relevance, the researchers have found the vicarious relevance important. Active reading has at least four components:

1. **Explore;** The ability to study the topic partly in the course material and partly by searching for material that is relevant in the learner's personal context.

2. **Form;** adding notes, making references to other relevant material, by changing the structure of the texts, change the text to fit the learner's understanding and previous knowledge, and more.

3. **Analyses;** The ability to analyze the topic and or the intended meaning of the text, ask oneself processing questions, working with the structure of the text, or by analyzing how one and other learners have worked or processed the material.

4. **Administrate;** The ability to keep track of the exploring, forming and analyzing activities by administrating references, recording how one have worked with the text, which questions one has asked oneself, etc.

New Ways of Learning and Teaching

In order to better prepare for lifelong learning activities, learners must be exposed to learning activities that require them to take on and develop many of the responsibilities normally afforded to educators. To achieve this requires moving away from a view of learning that is controlled outside the individual by a teacher, trainer, instructional designer, or subject matter expert to a view of learning that is internally controlled by the individual. As mentioned above,

IT plays an important role in the working situation for the knowledge worker of tomorrow. How and why should we use information technology in learning environments? These are two relevant questions to ask in this context. In this section we discuss these two questions putting our main focus on the "how question", although the "why question" is first briefly discussed. We believe it is important to give a historic perspective on the use of IT for the design learning environments in order to identify how and why to use modern IT in many educational settings.

Why

Traditionally there are three major motives behind the use of IT for learning: economical and efficiency motives have traditionally played a big role, and also the possibility to bridge distances in time and space. It is necessary to extend the concept of distances to also include distances between the ways of study or learning and distances between documents. We believe that an elimination of distances in learning environments, for instance, by forcing learners to study at the same location and time, and use the same material and study it in the same manner mainly have negative effects for learners' situation. Consequently IT plays a very important role for the learning situation of tomorrow, and must be viewed as a natural part of the learning environment.

How

Skinner, Pavlov, and Piaget all played important roles as founders of theories of learning. Skinner's and Pavlov's ideas about the way we learn things, based on the stimulus-response concept, were one source of inspiration for programmed learning or programmed instruction. Those theories have been used as the foundation for the design of the first generation of computer-based learning environments. Using this pedagogical model a huge industry of learning grew up during the early.

The First generation of ILE

Computer Assisted Instruction systems (CAI) are a kind of interactive learning environment based on programmed learning, which became common in the period from the mid of the 60s to the early 70s. Still, many projects are based on behaviouristic ideas. This seems strange since these ideas and all what they stand for have been almost completely rejected in traditional classroom learning environments. At the same time, there is a very simple explanation: two of the major advantages with programmed learning are the possibility of self-administration of a course and the simplicity of implementing a computer-based learning environment with a behaviouristic control mechanism, see Figure 2. Therefore, it is not hard to see the possibilities to make it serve as a basis for computer-based learning environments.

The Second Generation of ILE

Even if one can get positive results with regard to learning in these learning environments, there is much one can do to speed up the process of learning. One of the major drawbacks of these learning environments is the lack of individualization. The learning situation is one-to-one, but all learners are still running through the course in the same order. Below, we present three examples of ideas that have been exploited in attempts to improve performance:

1. multiple paths through the curriculum;
2. present the material in different ways;
3. analyze the errors that the learners do.

Knowledge of the domain the expert model

1. Knowledge of the learner (the student model)
2. Knowledge of teaching strategies (tutor)

The Third Generation of ILE

The ITS approach has many good results to show, although it has also been criticized for a long period. Much of the criticism has concerned the possibilities to trace learners' state of knowledge. Cognitive tools are artifacts that amplify, support, and unburden the user. They have the possibility to affect the task, and the user's state of knowledge. In some sense they amplify and unburden the user in the same manner that the winch amplifies our ability to lift things (heavy things), a backpack unburdens the carrier, and the hammer supports nailing. The cognitive tools approach has its pedagogic base constructivist ideas of knowledge and learning, where the learners consider as active knowledge constructors.

Learner centered design

Not many of the approaches used for the design of ILEs are able to meet the demands and requirements of tomorrow's learning situations. In these situations the integration of physical and virtual work as well as theoretical and practical work is very natural.

1. **Growth;** At the core of education is the growth of the learner; promoting the development of expertise must be the primary goal of educational software. Rather than just support "doing" tasks, software designed for learners must support "learning while doing."
2. **Diversity;** Developmental differences, cultural differences, and gender differences play a major role in the suitability of materials for learners. To be usable by all learners, a range of software tools that address these differences must be available.
3. **Motivation;** In contrast to software developed for professionals, the student's initial interest and continuing engagement cannot be taken for granted.

IT-augmented

In fact, we have to take future information technology into consideration because it will have a major influence on the conditions for future knowledge work and learning. Information access everywhere, through new 'physical' devices with computational power, will contribute to bridge the gap between the physical and virtual worlds. New tools will so close to our cognition and perception that they almost become part of our personalities. These new computerized environments will complement and eventually replace the desktop PC as provider of cognitive tools. All these aspects will cause a new knowledge reorganization that should not be ignored.

The Way We Use Computers

Using IT for learning has a long tradition but we need new ways of doing it Mainly because many of the traditional approaches of involving IT in learning situations do not meet the requirements of future more dynamic physical-virtual learning environments. A futuristic learning environment should include elements where learners can put the topic into a context and relate it to things, situations, and events that are relevant to them — promote active learning. One such element for instance, could be an open hypertext environment; open meaning that there are possibilities to search for information external to the course material, possibilities like those offered by the World-Wide-Web. It would also be open in a wider meaning, letting the learner view how other people (learners and teachers) have worked with the topic. Learning in such environment demands much support from the system, in order to help the learners to manage the new kind of learning situation. This support could be of the kind of: to establish goals, to manage goals, to manage the in-stream of information, searching for relevant information, etc.

Conclusion

To be able to meet the challenges for the design of tomorrow's learning environments we propose a pedagogical framework based on knowledge work approach to learning. This framework has its base in five cornerstones**:** Knowledge work tasks are those that most likely many people will be doing in the future. There is continuous knowledge reorganization in the society partly caused by the use of new technologies. People in the future will become more and more IT-augmented. The use of computers for learning purposes is still in its infancy. It reasonable to adopt Phenomenography and social constructivism, as a pedagogical base for the design interactive learning environments.

References

1. Broberg, A. (1997) Cognitive Tools for Learning. Licentiate thesis. Umeå University, report UMINF 97.18.
2. Cochinaux, P & de Woot P. (1995). Moving Towards a Learning Society. A CRE-ERT Report on European Education.
3. Drucker, P. F. (1973). Management: Tasks, Responsibility and Practices. New York: Harper & Row.

4. Drucker, P. (1993). The Post Capitalist Society, Editorial Sudamericana.

5. Gentner, D., & Nielsen, J. (1997). The Anti-Mac Interface. In Communications of the ACM, August 1997/Vol. 39, No 8, pp70-82.

6. Hoyles, C., & Noss, R. (Eds.). (1992). Learning Mathematics and logo. London: The MIT Press.

26

Tablet Computers in Education

Introduction

Tablet Computers are quickly emerging as a powerful Learning tool in higher education. The unique functionality of the Tablet Computer allows teachers to create lecture materials for their classes using digital format that can be distributed to students for later review. A tablet enhanced learning environment is an environment where single or multiple tablets are implemented to enhance student learning. Though a universally agreed-upon definition is currently lacking, there is some agreement that a tablet is a computer is a personal computer whose primary input device is a screen or a convertible notebook computer whose screen can be used as an input device.

The Tablet Computer is the next innovative device to hit the educational technology sector. Its design and handwriting functionality, challenges the way faculty and students integrate tablet computers into their teaching and learning process. Tablets are becoming increasingly common tools in schools. There's a wealth of options available, a range of web apps or apps designed for different operating systems and so many choices for teachers and students to make that it is sometimes useful to know the range of ways that they are making a difference across a range of different subject areas. Though this range can't be exhaustive or final, given the early stages of widespread adoption, it will provide a starting point for those aiming to use these tools to enhance learning through appropriate and effective use of the technologies available.

Tablet Computers in Education

Pedagogy is related to how teachers teach, and the strategies they use in their work. The impact of tablets on pedagogy has been a central focus of the Tablets for School. The success of tablets depends on the school's approach to learning, and the extent to which the tablets are integrated into this approach. Schools that link technology use to pedagogy, and set clear goals for use, are more likely to see positive effects.

Learning should never be technology led. Teachers teach, technology assists. This is an important statement, and one that is often forgotten. Focus should be placed on how the technology can be used to aid learning. There are a number of advantages to using this type of technology with students, one of which is the additional engagement that the touch interaction with the content brings. There is a clear educational advantage to be gained from better engagement, including increased stimulation, decreased 'time to learn' and enhanced knowledge retention. Additionally, tablet technology offers a change to the traditional use of ICT such as fixed computers or Laptops, allowing for additional usage scenarios and inclusion in learning activities not previously associated with ICT.

Tablet Computers in Teaching and Learning

Mobile learning involves the use of tablet computer technology, either alone or in combination with other information and communication technology (ICT), to enable learning anytime and anywhere. Learning can unfold in a variety of ways: people can use mobile devices to access educational resources, connect with others, and create content, both inside and outside classrooms. Mobile learning also encompasses efforts to support broad educational goals such as effective administration of school systems through the use of tablet computer devices.

Tablet computers provide a unique opportunity to create a truly portable learning experience. Lightweight with a long battery life, they offer possibilities not previously seen with other 'mobile' computing solutions. This lends itself to better use of technology within teaching. For example, quick access to reference material during a lesson, previously difficult to achieve with existing ICT, can bring key advantages and enhance learning. Using tablets in less typical scenarios, such as field trips, workshops or physical education lessons offers opportunities for research, evidence gathering and presentation. Brining devices such as these into the classroom and everyday life for students is in itself a learning experience. Couple this with the resources a tablet computer can deliver, such as text and reference books, audio and video resources, internet research, document preparation and review, and specific eLearning applications and activities and you have a truly versatile learning tool.

The increasing prevalence of digital technology in academia requires that teachers and students become more comfortable using technology to facilitate instruction and learning. This digital transformation has the potential to change the ways that teachers instruct, how students learn and how course material is delivered.

The Tablet PC is also quite handy for faculty use outside of the classroom. When preparing lecture material such as figures and diagrams, we were often able to draw and create these items more quickly. The Tablet PC has also been quite useful for note-taking at conferences, department meetings, research meetings, and committee meetings. Finally, the Tablet PC has promising potential for use as a distance education tool. All content can be managed through one tablet device: audio lecture, handwritten material, prepared electronic slides, and live software demonstrations. Several software programs allow such content to be streamed live for use with synchronous distance courses, or archived for asynchronous courses.

Face to Face Instruction

Tablets can effectively enhance instruction in a traditional classroom setting in various ways. Using a tablet, an instructor can construct and deconstruct notes and diagrams starting with a blank screen or using a skeleton outline of a topic. Given this ability, instructors can model how to solve problems and create materials through the course of a lesson. This allows the instructor to be better able to respond to feedback from students during a lesson so that he/she can 'change courses' or explain a topic in more detail should it be necessary. Tablets are advantageous when compared to black or whiteboards in that they allow the instructor to face the class. Furthermore, tablets are wireless devices and, providing that the connection to a projector is also wireless, the instructor is able to wander about the environment rather than stay at the front of the class. This affords instructors proximity to their students which, in turn, allows for better classroom management and interaction with students.

Digital ink annotations can be saved directly onto the original document and uploaded onto a webpage or Learning Management System to allow students access. In doing this, students can concentrate more on the instruction in class than on taking notes. Tablets are computers and, as such, allow instructors to incorporate and display a variety of multimedia and presentations. Again, the major advantage that tablets afford is that the instructor can write on these multimedia (including video, simulations and models) and presentations to enhance their effectiveness as learning objects.

Blended Environments

In a blended learning environment, students are able to not only access information from instructors but also actively participate in the construction of knowledge. When tablets are used by students in blended learning environments, new opportunities for collaboration and creative problem solving emerge. Teachers in this environment can switch from the role of instructor and distributor of information to facilitator. Interaction between instructors and students can increase because instructors spend less time teaching.

Students can use time to collaboratively solve problems and socially negotiate what they have learned. A tablet allows students to collaborate in new and meaningful ways. For example, students can access learning materials online and then co-create a concept map to represent their knowledge using software called Puzzle view.

Distance / Online Education

One of the primary benefits of using tablets in an online course environment is that students can receive more personalized notes and feedback from their instructors. Instructors can mark digital assignments using a tablet, and the ink annotations can be saved and sent back to the student on the original document. Because instructors can mark directly where they want to on the document, students ultimately get more specific and useful feedback on their assignments.

Another advantage that tablets afford is the ability to hold interactive virtual office hours. Using programs such as illuminate, instructors can conduct synchronous office hours and, in doing so, use their tablet to sketch or otherwise mark-up documents to support their explanations to students. The major use of the Tablet PC in this course was to replace the blackboard with the tablet. The machine was connected to a projector.

The use of the tablet, as an educational tool can have several benefits. These advantages include:

1. Being highly portable (easy to use in classroom, fieldtrips)
2. Consolidation of learning material into one device (textbooks, notes etc.)
3. No compatibility or technological issues since the same type of device is used
4. Quick access to the Internet
5. A convenient alternative to the laptop or desktop
6. Useful tool during group work and brainstorming activities (information stored in a drop box)

Conclusions

This paper has described how the Tablet PC can be used as an effective tool for grading, preparing lectures, and delivering classroom presentations. It provides a simple way to integrate live, handwritten material with slides and figures prepared in advance. Lectures can be easily captured for viewing at a later time. Rather than save the lecture as a static document, our work explored methods for capturing lectures into Flash movie files so that audio and gestures could be recorded. Students reported very positive feedback about the approach. In the future we intend to explore uses of the Tablet PC for distance delivery and collaborative applications where all students in a classroom are working on Tablet PC's.

References

1. Clark, C. (2004) Notre Dame Tablet PC Initiative. Retrieved from http://www.nd.edu/learning/tabletpc/
2. Lowe, P. (2004) Bentley College students evaluate Tablet PCs. Retrieved from http://www.hp.com/hpinfo/newsroom/feature_stories/2004/04bentley.html
3. Mock, K. (2003) The Development of a CS Course for Distance Delivery. The Journal of Computing Sciences in Colleges, 19 (2), p. 30-38.
4. Wachsmuth, B. (2003) SHU Tablet PC Project. Retrieved from http://www.cs.shu.edu/tabletpc/

27

The Process of Blended Learning

Introduction

Blended Learning is about effectively integrating ICTs into course design to enhance the teaching and learning experiences for student and teachers by enabling them to engage in ways that would not normally be available in their usual environment, whether it is primarily face-to-face. Blended Learning technologies are as follows;

1. Broaden the space and opportunities available for learning;
2. Support course management activities;
3. Support the provision of information and resource to students;
4. Engage and motivate students through interactivity and collaboration;

The learning and teaching activities need to be meaningful and relevant for the student learning. "Too often the opportunities and advantages of the use of technology in the learning process are poorly exploited".

Characteristics of Blended learning

H-learning means that learning requires students to meet for face to face classes while providing much of the learning content and interaction online via delivery software and instructional tools. The main characteristics of H-learning can be concluded as:

1. Mixed Mode: H-learning combines the socialization, group learning and hands-on opportunities of the classroom (face to face) with the learning possibilities of the online environment (U-learning).
2. Student Cantered: Learning shifts from lecture to student-cantered instruction.
3. Communications Important: The key element behind a hybrid learning environment is the scope and nature of the communication channels provided to support learners.
4. Access flexibility: Blending is used to provide a balance between flexible learning options and knowledge access.
5. Cost-effectiveness: Hybrid learning provides an opportunity for reaching a large, globally dispersed audience in a short period of time with consistent, semi-personal content delivery.

The process of Blended learning

Designing for Blended learning process requires a systematic approach:

Planning

Planning the first stage of the design process. At this point you should think about a number of critical considerations before jumping in to designing the blended learning components of your course.

Planning is developing a new course:

1. We suggest you first take a look at some general curriculum and course design guidelines.
2. It will be important to have course aims and learning objectives set before considering blended learning opportunities for your course.
3. Once you have a set of course aims and objectives you can then start to consider ways in which you might integrate blended learning in the design of the course.

Designing and Developing

First it is worthwhile briefly reviewing some general design principles which are presented below. You need to keep these principles in mind when either developing an entire course or developing a smaller component in blended learning mode.

1. Course learning objectives, teaching and learning activities and assessment tasks need to correspond with each other.

   Learning

   Objectives ⟺ Teaching and learning activities ⟺ Assessed outcomes

2. Activities should be purposeful and where appropriate and possible authentic.
3. Teaching and learning activities need to be clearly linked in time and content.
4. The work load for a blended learning course should not exceed that of a course in traditional mode

Implementing

Even a well designed blended learning element can fail, or at least suffer significant drawbacks, if time and consideration is not given to a range of issues associated with the implementation of blended learning in a course.

Course orientation

When student are required to study online, even for part of a course, creating an opportunity for students and staff to come together as a group is an important first step in building a successful learning and teaching experience.

So, consider designing formal course sense orientation program components that includes the following:

Purpose - Begin building a common sense of purpose for the blended learning components of the course.

Expectations-set clear expectations for students right from the beginning. Use consistent and transparent communication regarding these expectations to help students understand the blended learning process.

Guidelines-provide guidelines and tips on how to use the particular tools that you are integrating into the course well in advance.

Evaluating

As with any course, obtaining feedback about various aspects of the course experience is a crucial part of the course design process, as well as being important to your own ongoing professional development in curriculum design and teaching.

Evaluating in the blended learning environment entails the same basic elements of a course, however; because of "blend" and the use of technology, these will present an additional range of issues to gather data about. Herrington et al (2001) propose a model of evaluation for online learning and teaching which based is around the three main areas:

- Pedagogies-the learning activities which underpin the unit;
- Resources-the content and information which are provided for the learners;
- Delivery strategies-issues associated with the ways in which the course is delivered to the learners.

Improving

Blended learning can increase access and flexibility for learners, increase level of active learning, and achieve better student experiences and outcomes. For teaching staff, Blended learning can improve teaching and class management practices.

Benefits of Blended Learning

1. **Enhanced learning:** Students usually receive more feedback, and more frequent feedback, from their instructors. Students can acquire useful skills from using the Internet and computer technology. (Live instructor presence, technological enhancements) Students have more time to reflect and refer

to relevant course and other research materials when working and writing online than when responding in class.

2. **Support for student collaboration:** Real-time real-space interactivity and asynchronous online interactions, synchronous online interactions
3. **Course accessibility:** Students have access to unlimited up-to-date resources available via the Web. Live signing in live courses, transcription of audio and video, labeling of images with alt text online.
4. **Learner convenience:** Students have greater time flexibility, freedom, and convenience by working part of the time online. Time flexibility without full-term scheduling, a synchronicity (non-real-time learning), the repeatability of some automated learning, and the ease of accessing course materials
5. **Rich learner assessment:** Automated assessments, live instructor-led assessments, peer assessments live or via the online classroom.
6. **24/7 Accesses:** Students often develop or enhance skills in time management, critical thinking, and problem solving. Students typically have 24/7 access to online course materials.
7. **Multi-use / Dual use resources:** Course contents may often be used in both contexts (F2F and online)

Many students say that they learn more in a hybrid course, because they can use outside resources more easily than in a traditional course, but they still have face-to-face access to the instructor and the other students in the course. Almost all students who take hybrid courses appreciate the convenience and flexibility to adapt to individual work and family schedules.

Conclusion

Blended learning as the principle means of addressing the use of Information and Communication Technologies (ICT) to enhance its learning and teaching activities. Improving the blended learning experience for both staff and students. Designing for the teaching and learning activities need to be clearly linked in time and content. The blended learning is more efficient of teaching and styles of learning. Blended learning to provide opportunities for the use of technology in both staff and students.

Reference

1. Getting started with Blended learning (2007)- http:// www.griffith.edu.au
2. http://en.wikipeatia.org/wiki/Blended learning.
3. http://www.blendedlearning now.com/
4. http://coe.sdsu.edu/eet/Articals/blended learning/ index.htm.
5. http://www.e-learningguru.com/w papers/blended-bersin.doc.
6. http://www.knewton.com/blended learning/

28

Generating Employability Skills for Digital Age Students

Introduction

Many jobs now require a high level of IT competency and confidence. Digital literacy – IT and online communication skills – is necessary for living, learning and working. Colleges, universities and employers need to prioritize digital literacy. In our online and globally connected world individuals who are digitally literate are more likely to be economically secure. IT and online communication skills are especially important in higher education, as graduate jobs will almost certainly involve working via computers and portable devices. There is a clear need for education at all levels to help establish and develop the skills future employees will need. Universities and colleges have a responsibility to develop students into individuals who can thrive in an era of digital information and communication – those who are digitally literate are more likely to be economically secure and these skills are especially important in higher education given that graduate white collar jobs are almost entirely performed on computers and portable devices. But it's not just about *employability* – increasingly digital literacy is vital for learning itself. Digital tools such as virtual learning environments, e-portfolios and social networking software for peer mentoring are now common within further and higher education and students without the skills to navigate them risk suffering an inferior student experience at best, and being left completely behind at worst. It goes beyond IT skills; a complete culture change is required to live fully within the modern digital society, from understanding how to communicate ideas effectively in a range of media to managing digital reputation and history.

"We are living in a new economy—powered by technology, fueled by information, and driven by knowledge and the influence of technology will go beyond new equipment and faster communications, as work and skills will be redefined and reorganized". The key in engaging the digital generation is for educators to apply the right technology at the right time. Using technology advances, teachers can present lessons in ways best suited to the cognitive styles of their students. For example, the use of video, audio, and text can mutually reinforce concepts and enable students to engage the same ideas in multiple ways. However, accomplishing this means that educators must view technology not as "the enemy" but as a key tool to motivate and engage students. By addressing students at this level, schools can overcome problems with "emotional truancy," where students show up for class but essentially tune out the lesson.

Employability

A set of achievements, - skills, understandings and personal attributes – that make graduates more likely to gain employment and be successful in their chosen occupations, which benefits themselves, the workforce, the community and the economy is known as employability.

Employability Skills

A group of essential abilities that involve the development of a knowledge base, expertise level and mindset that is increasingly necessary for success in the modern workplace. Employability skills are typically considered essential qualifications for many job positions and hence have become necessary for an individual's employment success at just about any level within a business environment.

Digital Age

1. The digital age, also called the information age, is defined as the time period starting in the 1970s with the introduction of the personal computer with subsequent technology introduced providing the ability to transfer information freely and quickly.
2. The time period in which we live now where Internet and email are available is an example of the digital age.

21st Century Skills

Department of Commerce reports that "workers who use a computer at work can earn 17 to 22 percent more than other workers" (Economics and Statistics Administration, 2002, p. 49). These same analysts note that rapid change and increased competition require that workers use their "soft skills" (e.g., interpersonal, management, and problem-solving skills) to adapt quickly to changing technologies and organizational structures. The CEO Forum (2001) advises that "students require higher levels of education to succeed in the new knowledge-based economy".

Paths to Successful Education

Teachers are typically not digital natives; the key to success isn't to simply add technology to the classroom. Instead, the focus needs to be on enabling teachers to integrate the tools into their curricula, so they are comfortable letting their students use them. Both K-12 and higher education will evolve along four paths to help ensure that current and future generations are engaged in the classroom and have developed the proper skills to succeed in the global economy.

- **Customized**: Educational institutions will need to offer personalized instruction to accommodate different learning styles and tailor courses and services to meet the individual needs of students, faculty, and staff.

- **Collaborative**: The level of collaboration between students and faculty will continue to grow, and faculty will increasingly become facilitators who help co-create knowledge. Students and faculty will work in face-to-face and virtual teams worldwide to tackle complex and sophisticated projects, and bring together different perspectives and skills.
- **Creative**: By integrating the technology that students use, admire, and aspire to, education institutions will appeal to digital natives, driving innovation and enthusiasm and setting students on a path to success.
- **Distributed**: Students will increasingly be attending institutions virtually, making knowledge more accessible and available to a greater number of people.

Changing Behaviours and Emerging Benefits

While the pace of technological change appears to be rapid, it can take time to develop appropriate and effective responses. Technology offers flexible blended learning opportunities that work around employers' needs and can simulate real-life situations when financial, logistical or ethical reasons make these real-life experiences difficult to provide.

Developing and implementing the use of appropriate technologies and processes to Enable higher-education-level learning services to meet the needs of learners in the workplace, and of their employers.

Exploring Emerging Practice

1. Support openness and collaboration among colleges and universities by sharing effective practice.
2. Highlight opportunities to transform practice, uncovering some of the benefits and challenges as well as signposting information that is useful to know.
3. Stimulate debate that may help to propagate new ideas.
4. Working in partnership with students – how students are being engaged as agents of change and collaborators in their own learning.

5. Developing students' employability potential – how institutions are using technology to provide relevant and authentic learning experiences to enhance student employability and develop professional practice.
6. Preparing for the future – how colleges and universities are looking ahead and developing the skills, knowledge and cultural environment that will help to build the future.

Emerging Practice Technologies among Students

1. Improved preparation for practical laboratory work Video cameras
2. Enhanced relevance of module learning to overall course Laptop
3. Increased student enjoyment, engagement and motivation Web server
4. Vidiscript open source software
5. Reflective practice through peer review mechanisms embedded in social media Video conversion software
6. Range of student-developed materials to support revision
7. Integration of technology across Business School, leading to higher student engagement

Emerging Practice oOn the Part of Teachers

8. Enhanced interactivity in lectures
9. Improved lecture attendance
10. Support for students, particularly international students, during transition period
11. Collaborative development between students and staff, and between peers
12. Development of desirable employability skills (research, business and personal) for students
13. Student-owned mobile devices

14. Enhanced student engagement and motivation
15. Increased levels of attainment
16. Student advocacy leading to improved communication between staff and students
17. Support for staff in use of social media
18. Development of inclusive pedagogies
19. Developing professional practice
20. Augmentation to real-life working
21. Support for revision with detailed formative assessment feedback
22. Collaboration between academic specialists and learning technologists
23. Developing active and engaging problem-based learning experiences
24. Enhancing access to multimedia resources
25. External collaboration with other universities
26. Internal collaboration between academic staff and learning technologists

Conclusion

"The technology and the learning are developing together, and that co-evolution of learning and technology is really important for us to understand and to develop employability skills." In higher education we have to create a better learning environment for all learners, wherever and however they study. By enhancing the overall educational experience by improving flexibility and creativity and by encouraging comprehensive and diverse personal high quality learning, teaching and research will generate employability beyond digital age.

References

1. www.jisc.ac.uk/elearningprogramme Emerging Practice in a Digital Age

2. .http://www.heacademy.ac.uk/assets/documents/employability/pedagogy_for_employability _update_2012.pdf

3. http://www.businessdictionary.com/definition/employability- skills.html#ixzz305IECjAv

29

Learning Without Limits for Creating An Innovative Society

Introduction

The 11th Plan Guidelines (2007 – 2012) on Lifelong Learning and Extension speak of continuous up-gradation of skills to be a critical development issue. This, in turn, will ensure the production of man-power resources of the kind and number required by society. There have been innumerable lifelong learning programs implemented by governmental and non-governmental organizations, as also various universities right across the country for the past three decades. The massive number of non-literates (3.14 million) and neo-literates (110 million), has been estimated by the National Literacy Mission.[1]

The formulation of the 11th Plan brought in the Lifelong Education and Awareness Program (LEAP) by expanding the scope of its earlier avatar – the Continuing Education Program. The socio-economic changes that are taking place both within and outside the country, as also discussions at the global level, have been the cause of bringing in LEAP. The present scenario represents a knowledge based competitive economy which is technology driven and so the learning landscape is undergoing imminent changes in the country.

Growth Factor

The economic survey (2006 – 2007)[2] has recorded an average growth rate of 9.2% per annum. There has also been tremendous expansion in the Information Communication Technology (ICT) and taking into consideration the process of rapid globalization, there has come a need for changes in job skills and the work-force is expected to keep on learning and updating skills to survive global competition. The 61st Round of the National Sample Survey (2004 – 2005)[3] also stresses on the need for periodic skill up-gradation to compete in the globalised economy.

UGC Measures

In order to equip the labor force with relevant skills, it is imperative that a variety of learning and training opportunities are created. It is in this area that India's university system has a vital role to play. The University Grants Commission (UGC) have brought in a number of measures such as post-literacy programs, continuing education, population education, refresher courses and a variety of extension and field outreach activities. The UGC has also encouraged the universities with adequate funding to institutionalize these programs by setting up specific departments with core faculty, who in turn, would undertake teaching and research. The according of maximum priority to lifelong learning or in other words learning without limits is to help meet the demands of the emerging knowledge society and to help create a conducive atmosphere for creating an innovative society.

The Census Report (2011)[4] shows that half of India's population is within their quarter century of existence. While the enrolment ratio in higher education institutions is held to be 20% in advanced and certain developing countries, it is a sad reality that the gross enrolment in higher education institutions in India is only 10%. It is only the universities that can prepare the student to be a lifelong learner effectively. The youth of the country need to sustain their knowledge level skills at an international benchmark criterion.

Learning Avenues

The concept of lifelong learning or unlimited learning bespeaks the need for learning avenues that can be traversed even while one is engaged in fruitful employment. The years spent within the portals of a higher education institution will definitely have advantageous inputs on a person's psychic. But, when the economic status of an individual and family constraints impel the acceptance of employment, this sincere and hardworking citizen of the country should not be left in the lurch having academic doors slammed in their faces for want of regular study.

Distance Education

This is where the strength of flexibility of time, duration of learning as also choice of subjects comes into play. Self – learning, learning through the distance education mode, correspondence education, online education and also other modes of equipping oneself with knowledge have become a reality in the present day. There is no embargo on a student earning and learning simultaneously.

To Be Aware and Beware

A student in the present day whether pursuing studies in the regular formal stream or the distance education non-formal stream, needs to take into consideration the following:

- ***Purpose of Study***

  A student should be fully aware of the purpose for which he/ she is studying. If a student is working in a bank, studying courses that will aid him/her progress further on in the promotional avenue will be most helpful. Concentrating on subjects like banking services, CAIIB, chartered accountancy, financial management as also courses on technology would help further their promotional prospects. If such a person is going to concentrate on a course in philosophy, anthropology, classical languages etc., such a procedure maybe a soul satisfying action, i.e. acquiring knowledge for knowledge sake but will not help in improving the individual's quality of life or standard of living. The student should beware the lure of various courses which may help them pass time but would not be of intrinsic value in their careers.

- ***Affordability***

  A person wanting to pursue a particular course/subject should take into consideration his/her financial position. A student should also analyze the various financial avenues open to them such as scholarships, stipends, grants and loans. At every stage care should be taken to understand the ramifications of consequences in pursuing a particular course. There are many instances where students have committed themselves to serve the organization giving the scholarship/stipend etc. for a certain period of time and not being able to comply. When taking a loan scholarship one should scrutinize the rate of interest and the period of repayment in order to ensure that they are capable of proper and easy repayment. In this regard, care should also be taken to ensure that the course of study pursued will certainly pay dividends for rising the standard of one's living.

- ***Choice of Subject / Field of Study***

  Knowledge for knowledge sake is a commendable proposition. In the present day of whirlwind economy and super fast competition, one needs to surge forward both academically and economically. Selecting a subject/field of study therefore has to necessarily impinge on the fact of how fast such an endeavor will help the student ascend the economic ladder. Even when one is settled in a secure job one needs to update knowledge and come by certification to be authorized to practice their profession at any given level. A basic degree in medicine will ensure a job in a hospital with fixed timings and a regular pay cheque. If one wants to go beyond the basic level of medicine and become a specialist/expert one needs to update their knowledge by pursuing further degrees and courses. This is so for every profession in the organized, as well as, the unorganized sectors. Whyte (1989) has stressed that lifelong learners including persons with academic or professional credentials tend to find higher paying occupations leaving monetary, cultural and entrepreneurial impressions on communities.

- ***Metacognition***

  This is thinking about the process of knowing and refers to a higher order thinking which involves active control over the cognitive processes engaged in learning.[6] Knowledge is the awareness of one's own thought processes and learning styles and knowledge strategies involve using this awareness for different learning tasks. Exercising control and self regulating one's thought processes helps one not only to keep track of his/her thinking processes but also for evaluating them.

Conclusion

Lifelong learning that leads to the creation of an innovative society is not only a lifelong process but is flexible, diverse and available at all times and in different places. Crossing sectors of space and segments of society, lifelong learning promotes the acquirement of knowledge beyond traditional schooling and throughout one's adult life. In accordance with Delors' (1996)[7], Four Pillars of Education for the Teacher, one needs to know which is mastering learning tools rather than the mere acquisition of knowledge; one needs to do, which is equipping people for the types of work needed now and in the future, which includes innovation and adaptation; one needs to live together and with others peacefully resolving conflict, discovering other people's cultures, fostering community capability and individual competence and capacity with economic resilience and social inclusion and finally one needs to be with education contributing to a person's complete development of body, mind, intelligence, sensitivity, aesthetic appreciation and spirituality. These components can be underpinned by the label learning to learn lifelong to create an innovative society that will "strive, to seek, to find and not to yield".[8]

References

1. NLM – Literacy Facts At A Glance, 2007.
2. Economic Survey 2006 – 2007.
3. National Sample Survey, 61st Round, 2004 – 2005.

4. Census Report 2011.

5. Whyte, Cassandra B.; Student Affairs – The Future; Journal of College Student Personnel; Vol. 30, No.1, 1989.

6. Livingr, A.; Metacognition: An Overview; 1997.

7. Delors, J.; Learning: The Treasure Within; Report to UNESSCO of the International Commission on Education for the 21st Century; UNESSCO, 1996.

8. Tennyson, Alfred Lord; Ulysses; MacMillan & Co., 1963.

30

Fast Moving Age the Younger Generation

Introduction

In a world of continuous change, few are confident enough to predict the future, yet the need to look ahead and prepare is vital. The objective of the paper is making the Gen Next as an employable generation through innovative educational methods like Blended Learning and thus preparing the generation ready for the Digital Age and era beyond the Digital Age. Though the conventional method of teaching process is useful and achieves its purpose, in the fast moving age the younger generation has to be more technical savvy. The new teaching learning process is the need of the hour and it will make the learners to gain confidence and make them employable to the core, anywhere in the world. Only when there is a rethinking in our approach in learning and education, we can enjoy the complete advantages of the new technologies.

The purpose of education is often considered as a "movement from dark to light", "ultimate change towards betterment "or" preparation for life", but, a content livelihood is the prime focus of education for any individual. Mere knowledge in the respective subject will seldom support one to get his dream job. An aspired livelihood can be achieved only when one is employed better. Employability skills will help one to be placed well. In the current Computer age, every profession, in one way or the other, is interlinked with digital technical knowledge. So, literacy in digital technology, employability skills, and a better livelihood are related to each other.

"Tamil Nadu Teachers Education University" in its web page has proudly stated that it is in "pursuit of excellence in Promoting human values for social harmony and to make colleges of education excels through innovative teaching, research and extension activities." Yes, TNTEU University has futuristically foreseen the need of innovative teaching methods and hence emerges this subject of discussion.

The unique word "Employability" should have been coined from two words, Employee's and Ability. Employability, according to Manchester Metropolitan University, is, "the development of skills, abilities and personal attributes that students' capability to secure rewarding and satisfying outcomes in their economic, social and community lives."

Learning Computer as a subject or gaining computer skills through co curricular or extracurricular learning activities will not help one to attain Digital Fluency. The core method of teaching through Digital technology will for sure help the learners to gain digital literacy. More over Digital technology is not confined to computer alone. It has a vast area to cover, start from children's toy to satellite. So, the very teaching method for the next generation student must be through Digital Technology. Such learning process will instill the digital fluency within the learners in a subtle way.

One among the innovative way of digital learning process is "Blended Learning". It is a very unique and innovative method of learning practice, combining teaching methods both from face to face and online learning. Sometimes learning through face to face method and digital class room, it may not be online, but offline is too, termed as "Blended Learning". It meets all the expectations of 21st century learners in respect to efficiency, digital fluency, self learning opportunities, optimism, flexibility and personalization of students' learning experience, which makes them employable to the core. It is not of acquiring digital knowledge but learning every subject using and supported by the digital tools. The learners must be able to apply digital tools. Learning can happen through any digital method, visual, audio or textual mode.

Building Innovations

When creativity is thinking up new things, innovation is doing new things. Innovation follows creativity. Innovation's last phase is making invoices, as termed by the trading community. Ideas in paper are turned to be currencies in trade. But in field like education, innovation means much different. The institutions and policy makers aspire to utilize innovative ideas for the uplifting of humanity in all aspects. Considering the growth of the digital technology as well the expectations of the employers the learners of coming generation have to get updated to meet the job market requirements. Today's learners are the tomorrows, executives, CEOs, labourers, teachers, entrepreneurs, policy makers and more. So, learning methods have to be innovative and creative to imbibe the required technical as well digital skills to the students.

Digital Literacy

In this digital age, our definition of literacy is changing completely. Now a day many jobs require a high level of IT competency and confidence. As such, the concept of Digital Literacy – those capabilities that equip an individual for living, learning and working in our IT-enabled society – is one that needs to be taken seriously by schools, colleges and universities, as well as by employers.

We live in an online and globally connected world. Society has a resulting need for citizens who can thrive in an era of digital information and communication. Those who are digitally literate are more likely to be economically secure, and these skills are especially important in higher education given that graduate jobs will almost invariably involve some level of contact with computers and portable devices. Against this backdrop, there is a clear need for education at all levels to play a part in establishing and developing the skills that the future employees will need.

At the same time, delivering digital literary goes beyond simply teaching the IT skills; a paradigm shift is required to live fully within the modern digital society, from understanding how to communicate ideas effectively in a range of media, to managing digital reputation and history, and understanding how to remain secure and protected throughout the process. Gone is the" Green Revolution" in agriculture which was an outcome of advances in Biotechnology and we are going to have a "Learning Revolution" in education, thanks to new Digital Technology.

Digital literacy gives young people the ability to take advantage of the wealth of new and emerging opportunities associated with digital technologies whilst also remaining alert to the various challenges technology can present.In fact, digital literacy is the 'savvyness' that allows young people to participate meaningfully and safely as digital technology becomes evermore pervasive in society.Schools are to be encouraged to embed the use of ICT in all subject areas of the primary and secondary curricula. Considering how digital literacy supports subject knowledge can help to ensure that technology-use enhances teaching and learning rather than simply becoming an add-on. Indeed, formal education must seek to prepare young people to make sense of the world and to thrive socially, intellectually and economically.

It can be said that digital media is now a central aspect of most people's lives, whatever their age.The skills, knowledge and understanding of digital literacy are therefore becoming indispensible as young people grow up in a society in which digital technology and media play an ever more important role. Digital technology makes the young people creative, and in return, the soceity becomes creative soceity.

Why learning through Digital mode in School Level?

Every third person in an Indian city today is a youth. By 2020, India is set to become the world's youngest country with 64 per cent of its population in the working age group. Quoting a report "The Hindu" newspaper says that the southern and western States will be the first to experience a growth dividend as they account for 63 per cent of all formally trained people. The largest share of youth with formal skills is found in Kerala, followed by Maharashtra, Tamil Nadu, Himachal Pradesh and Gujarat. The report finds that a person in an urban area has a 93 per cent greater chance of acquiring training than someone in a rural area. When the teaching pattern does consist uniform technology like Blended Learning, irrespective of territorial bindings and curriculum methods, the future generation will be more employable and well equipped to take up a career anywhere in the world.

The student population from rural India is in many fold in number than students from urban. They are the people, mostly first generation graduates of the family, who focus on IT and ITES careers. Thanks to MNCs which offer job scope for those students.In county like India, where majority of population live in villages, access to digital gadgets and opportunity to attain digital literacy is denied to every citizen.They dependent on schools and colleges for even to learn basic knowledge in computer. With the very basic skills in technology, they seldom get well paid career. But when the method of teaching itself is based on digital technology with Digital classrooms from the school level, it is easy for the rural students too to become fluent in digital technology. Normally children arrive schools with basic knowledge of digital technology. It is not exaggerating if it is said that they come with their mobile phone or any other digital gadgets in hand to schools in urban India. When they are taught with black board or any other conventional method of teaching, it is not fair in the part of our educational system. They must be encouraged to enhance the skills they posses when they join the school. We say teacher is one who “Knows the way”, “shows the way” and “goes the way”. So, teaching all subjects through digital technology, like method of Blended Learning, will be interesting, easy to learn, as well they can attain digital fluency, in a professional manner. The level of motivation will be increased when they are taught through the mode they are familiar with.

Employability and Employable Generation

The term “Employability “can be defined in multiple ways according to the need of the industry, expectations of individuals and society. Employability in the words of Professor Mantz Yorke," is a set of achievements – skills, understandings and personal attributes – that make graduates more likely to gain employment and be successful in their chosen occupations, which benefits themselves, the workforce, the community and the economy".

It is estimated that around 90% of all new graduate jobs in United Kingdom require a high level of digital skills. Though it is the status in UK, it is the global demand. It will not take years for India to get the same scenario. So, the policy makers and educational institutions must focus on creating an Employable Generation rather than focusing on instilling employability skills in the learners.

Current status of the Job Seekers

Surveys on the employability skills of Indian graduates, graduated in any field of study, say, most of the job seekers are not employable in medium and high profile careers. They are not good in communication skills, don't have sufficient digital literacy and other core requirements for a good profile jobs. Neither Indian companies nor MNCs will employ them without a basic training. It is understood more number of trainees are rejected during the training period itself. Such happenings make the rejected hands feel dejected and they think their future is dark. It is the status in all the field of study, like, management, technical and even in teaching profession.

The learners are not the only reason for such adverse scenario but the system we follow too plays major and vital role in this. So, to make our future generation employable we need a system which makes the learner master in all the fields required by the employers.

Blended Learning

"Teaching in the Internet age means we must teach tomorrow's skills today." Jennifer Fleming. "Preparing for future" can be termed as *motto* of Blended Learning. Though there are other new age teaching concepts like Flipped class rooms, Learning without Limits, Cloud Computing , Blended Leaning seems to be more innovative since it not only a blend of technologies but also a perfect blend of Traditional method of class room as well a New Age class room.

Blended learning, where multiple learning environments and activities are combined is a decades' old innovative concept of teaching. But contemporary definitions of blended learning take into account that technology can play more. Current as well futuristic concept of blended learning represents a combination of online and face to face experiences. It is the best of both worlds. Blended learning is a student-centered approach to creating a learning experience whereby the learner interacts with other students, with the instructor, and with content through thoughtful integration of online and face-to-face environments. Some time Blended Learning consists of face to face instruction and usage of off line Digital tools instead of on line lessons.

In contrast to teacher-centered, rote-learning approaches, blended learning environments provide multiple ways to access content and to demonstrate mastery. As a result, they lend themselves more readily to differentiation of content and process. A blended approach also gives the learner the opportunity to be more responsible for his or her learning, which creates a learning situation that may be more meaningful on an individual level. Because the learner comes to construct knowledge through personal effort, she or he is more likely to demonstrate understanding beyond rote memorization, and to transfer what she or he has learned to new settings.

Blended Learning – An inevitable Teaching Method

India is a country which had more effective and traditional teaching methods like *Gurukula* method. Though it was age old, it has its own value and we respect such methods as they were man making way of teaching. Having such great methods of teaching we need not have to switch over entirely too complete online method of teaching process. Our culture respects *Guru* as father, mother, guide and God. Our *Vedas, Upanishads, Epics* like *Mahabharata and Ramayana*, master pieces like *Thirukural* always speak high and great of Gurus. None other country gives this much respect and high regard to *Guru*, the teacher. Still our education system mostly depends on teachers. We, Indians give more importance to moral and man making education than attaining mass production of graduates. In this back drop, it is difficult to imagine teaching without a teacher or learning without a Guru.

In this digital era, traditional classroom teaching methods are not much effective to achieve current learning standards. Technological approaches alone can't provide students with deep and meaningful learning experience. But the combination of both, say, Blended Learning and face to face teaching can help an individual to attain moral values, command over the subject as well digital fluency. Such an employee with a multiple skills, moral values, digital literacy and adaptability is most wanted by the employers and in coming years, they are the only preferred hands by employers in any field and anywhere in the world. So, for country like ours, Blended Learning could be the most apt mode of teaching, where we have face to face instruction and technology based learning. In this method of learning, the learners will have a personal touch with the teachers as well they are independent in learning. It could be a perfect blend of modern and traditional ways of learning.

Getting blended is vital at this moment. Blended learning is more than electronic textbooks and productivity tools. It means inventing or adopting new learning environments that work better for students as well teachers. It increases opportunities for students to engage with technology such as teacher using digital class rooms, a school computer lab, and computers using digital curriculum in the class rooms are more supportive for the learners to attain digital literacy and to get the dream jobs in future. Clearly there are more opportunities for exploration and growth in the use of blended learning from the school level. Some of this growth may be driven by increasing student demands for more learning process.

Implementation of Blended Learning

The curriculum of the century is activity based. Any digital method of teaching involves visual, audio or textual, is sheer activity oriented only. Introducing the Blended Learning is not going to be tough t asked and it can be executed to the learners in a subtle way. Following stages may be considered important for the learners while implementing the system in the class room.

Being Motivated

Understanding the significance of the learning method

Getting accustomed in handling digital tools

Creating awareness of technicalities of the digital tools

Using the digital tools for communication and learning purpose

Acting independently with the digital technology

Being motivated

Motivation is the driving force for success. The learners have to have a change in their attitude to be taught through a different mode of teaching method, an innovative method. They may feel fish out of water in digital class room and it may be very difficult for them to come out of comfort zone, an accustomed zone of conventional mortar class room learning. When they are motivated they will readily open their mind for new learning. Yes, mind is like a parachute, it works only when it is open.

Understanding the significance of the learning method

It is in the hands of the teachers to make them to understand the dire need of the change of learning which is going to make them employable. Lot of comparisons can be sited from other countries and cultures to make them to realize the value of the Blended Learning. Even they can be asked to prepare papers supporting the idea. Discussions can be arranged to speak for and against the concept where their eyes can be opened.

Getting accustomed in handling digital tools

It is very vital stage of learning process. Students from rural areas usually will have a pessimistic attitude towards digital tools. It must be taken care that they must not keep aloof in the class rooms and it can be monitored no inferiority complex comes in learners from rural areas. Slowly the digital tools can be introduced to the learners and till they feel free in handling the tools they must be free from core teaching.

Creating awareness of technicalities of the digital tools

Simply using the digital tools will not help the learners to attain expertise in the field. Apart from software knowledge they must have the basic hardware skills too. It will help them to become an all rounder in his field. So, basic technicalities of the digital tools can be taught to the learners. It is like car drivers knowing the mechanism of the car, which will help them to attend the faults in the machine, complete his journey successfully even after break downs.

Using the digital tools for communication and learning purpose

Once they are motivated and aware of the importance and necessity of the blended learning, accustomed in handling the digital tools and acquire hardware skills, it is right time for them to be introduced to proper and fully fledged learning. The regular subjects will be taught through the blended learning method. Face to face as well online and off line classes will be given. They will gain confident towards the teachers and the new method of learning. Apart from regular subjects they must use the digital tools for communication purpose too.

Acting independently with the digital tools

This is the last phase in Blended Learning. It is an assessment of their learning. Seminars, symposiums, conferences can be conducted in this phase. The learner becomes a teacher now. They can be asked to handle classes for their peer group using the digital tools. Question answer sessions, group discussions on their respective subjects can be arranged in which the Blended Learning pattern can be followed. When they act independently they get confidence in their related subjects as well they feel good and positive in using the digital tools for all purpose.

Conclusion

To conclude, a survey conducted in America can be sited which has found that college students prefer blended learning course over those that are solely face to face or solely online. This is the scenario everywhere in the world. “We need to give people a new set of skills in an explicit way that will make them more marketable for the job market”, foresees Cristina Costa. Yes, by providing relevant and authentic learning experiences that offer opportunities to develop and evidence professional practice not only enhances student employability but also more importantly makes good business sense for colleges and universities, for employers and for the economy as a whole.

Normally computers are used as source centre of information and the learners are taught how to browse, send E-mails, know to work in word or excel. But the learners must become fluent with computer so that they can create and express instead passing information. To help the learners to attain Digital Fluency, the mode of teaching must be an innovative one. Among all other technology based teaching methods Blended Learning will be an opt one for our country. When the forth coming age is going to be a Digital Age, the job aspirants must be a computer literate. Any knowledge the learners get learning computer through extracurricular or co curricular activities will make them aware of computers not expert in it. They can access computer, but they cannot express. They can play for lifelong but cannot make it as bread winner. Shortly, it can be said Blended Learning which is a holistic approach to technology enhanced learning will make the new generation learners employable and we can have an employable generation on the other hand.

References

1. Careers & Employability Service, www.mmu.ac.uk/careers/guides , Manchester Metropolitan University
2. Learning & Employability – Series One – Employability in higher education: what it is - what it is not – By Mantz Yorke, published by The Higher Education Academy, Innovation Way, York Science Park, Heslington, York, UK.
3. Race Online 2012:www.raceonline2012.org/stories/jobcentre-plus
4. Cristina Costa, Research Technologies Development Officer, Research and Graduate College, University of Salford
5. Echo360 2012 student survey, "Blended Learning Technology: Connecting with the Online-All-the-Time Student," www.echo360.com/studentsurveys Ibid